The Art of Camping

The Art of Camping

The History and Practice of Sleeping Under the Stars

MATTHEW DE ABAITUA

HAMISH HAMILTON
an imprint of
PENGUIN BOOKS

HAMISH HAMILTON

Published by the Penguin Group
Penguin Books Ltd, 80 Strand, London WC2R ORL, England
Penguin Group (USA) Inc., 375 Hudson Street, New York, New York 10014, USA
Penguin Group (Australia), 250 Camberwell Road,
Camberwell, Victoria 3124, Australia (a division of Pearson Australia Group Pty Ltd)
Penguin Group (Canada), 90 Eglinton Avenue East, Suite 700, Toronto, Ontario, Canada M4P 2Y3
(a division of Pearson Penguin Canada Inc.)
Penguin Ireland, 25 St Stephen's Green, Dublin 2, Ireland (a division of Penguin Books Ltd)
Penguin Books India Pvt Ltd, 11 Community Centre, Panchsheel Park, New Delhi – 110 017, India
Penguin Group (NZ), 67 Apollo Drive, Rosedale, Auckland 0632, New Zealand
(a division of Pearson New Zealand Ltd)
Penguin Books (South Africa) (Pty) Ltd, 24 Sturdee Avenue, Rosebank, Johannesburg 2196, South Africa

Penguin Books Ltd, Registered Offices: 80 Strand, London WC2R ORL, England

www.penguin.com

First published 2011
1

Copyright © Matthew De Abaitua, 2011
Illustrations copyright © Paul Blow, 2011

The moral right of the author has been asserted

Set in 11/13 pt Dante MT Std
Typeset by Palimpsest Book Production Limited, Falkirk, Stirlingshire
Printed in Great Britain by CPI Mackays, Chatham ME5 8TD

A CIP catalogue record for this book is available from the British Library

ISBN: 978-0-241-14513-5

www.greenpenguin.co.uk

MIX
Paper from
responsible sources
FSC
www.fsc.org   **FSC™ C018179**

Penguin Books is committed to a sustainable
future for our business, our readers and our
planet. This book is made from paper certified
by the Forest Stewardship Council.

For Cathy

'Discomfort, after all, is what the camper-out is unconsciously seeking. We grow weary of our luxuries and conveniences. We react against our complex civilization and long to get back for a time to first principles. We cheerfully endure wet, cold, smoke, mosquitoes, black flies, and sleepless nights, just to touch naked reality once more.'

John Burroughs, *Under the Maples*

'We flee away from cities, but we bring
The best of cities with us'

Ralph Waldo Emerson, 'The Adirondacs'

Contents

I

Packing and Pitching

The other passengers stared at us with appalled fascination and, in one case, contempt. I bowed my head with shame. What a sight we made, a broad-shouldered, big-bellied, six-foot-two man, face reddening under the strain of an eighty-litre rucksack, and his wife, petite and five foot nothing, whose rucksack made her look like a woman backing into a wardrobe. And we had a child too, a blonde toddler kicking away in a large three-wheel buggy. London transport etiquette, slim volume that it is, was breached. The passengers hadn't witnessed a bus etiquette calamity like this since a Vietnamese man transported polystyrene crates of tilapia on the 277, spilling icy fish water over the trouser suits of commuters at eight in the morning, an etiquette breach of such severity it required a new warning sign to be pinned up next to the driver: 'Please do not bring your fish on to this bus.'

Cath's rucksack contained two weeks' worth of clothes, enough footwear to cover every eventuality of weather and fashion, three sections of plastic origami that unfolded into seats, a bag of tea lights and flame-retardant paper lanterns, various soft toys, thin and flat works of children's literature, warm jumpers, waterproofs, sunglasses and a Tupperware box of ground spices. Balanced on top of the buggy, there was a blue cool bag containing frozen litres of milk, baby bottles, fruit, snacks and sausages. The bus juddered to a halt and as one overladen four-legged, three-wheeled beast we stumbled back and forth.

The Camper's Handbook of 1908, written by Thomas Hiram Holding, the father of modern camping, has this to say on the matter of packing: 'In camping, DETAIL is everything. I carefully consider the question of clothes, strains, weights, sizes, the bulk, and the packing to an almost extreme point.' Holding was a pioneer of cycle camping and devised lightweight, easy-to-transport kit for a weekend in the country. Prior to his advocacy of packing light, the British embarked upon a camping trip as if colonizing another part of Africa: on a trip to the Lakes, one nineteenth-century camping party took two tons of kit packed upon horse-drawn carts, including a harmonium, a separate pantry tent, a crate of biscuits and a telescope. (To be fair, some of their really heavy items, such as the cast-iron fireplace, were then buried in the earth with the intention of digging them up the following year.)

My system of packing followed the spirit of Thomas Hiram Holding, being so detailed and so highly strung that an item as small as a spatula could throw it off whack. It surprised me how much pride and enjoyment I took in packing. During the long period of stupefied indolence otherwise known as our twenties, Cath and I never took a single significant holiday. We neither planned nor prepared for anything. Preparation is the opposite of cool. It smacks of the military, and Scouts. Making it up as you go along, improvisation, youthful spontaneity, these are the values of the hip. Nature demands preparation. The city hates it. The city rewards improvisation. Plans made and dropped. If you are bored, hail a cab and move on. You can't hail a cab in a field, you can't pull that ripcord and wake up in your own bed, although Lord knows enough angry people have thrown a sodden, torn tent into the boot of a car at three in the morning and then driven home.

The camping gear was laid out in my bedroom, the converted coal cellar of a Victorian terraced house on the A1207, otherwise known as Graham Road. The sound of urban surf echoed in the light well: the backwash of buses sluicing through rainy gutters, strangers arguing, walls vibrating with the rhythmic compressions dropped from the bass bins of a passing BMW. I pulled out some Ordnance Survey maps of the west coast of Ireland. A map of the countryside is a promise of exotic territory to a man who sleeps under a busy street in Hackney.

There is pleasure in packing for a camping trip. Horace Kephart, an American woodsman of the early twentieth century and author of a large volume on camping and woodcraft, wrote a fond account of the camper's fossicking around with his gear: 'It is great fun, in the long winter evenings, to sort over your beloved duffel, to make and fit up the little boxes and hold-alls in which everything has its proper place, to contrive new wrinkles that nobody but yourself has the gigantic brain to conceive.' Kephart, a librarian by trade, turned his back on domestic life. 'To many a city man there comes a time when the great town wearies him. He hates its sights and smells and clangour. Every duty is a task and every caller is a bore. There come visions of green fields and far-rolling hills, of tall forests and cool, swift-flowing streams.' Living in the city is exhausting, especially the narrow, high-sided streets of East London. We worked in the half-a-yard of space between nose and computer screen, then came home to Hackney, a labyrinth without a roof. We were sick for want of a horizon.

It took two hours to pack. Cath counted out underwear for each day of the trip and thermal vests for the cold nights, then came the multicoloured bundles of children's clothes, and everything had to be wrapped in polythene compressor bags if we were to fit it all in. At the base of my rucksack went a sheaf of nappies, wipes and nappy sacks, and the largest of the compressor bags containing clothes. Then came the Trangia, our portable kitchen, a meths burner with pots and pans all packed inside one another like Russian dolls. It smelt of strong tainted alcohol, and the base was coated in a black film. It required a bag of its own. Then more bags of clothes, none of which were mine, the overflow from Cath's packing. I resisted the urge to complain about the four hats packed for our child, Alice: one waterproof hat, one extra-warm woolly hat, one sun hat, and – because she cast all of these hats off her head the moment they were placed upon it – a fourth hat, the only hat Alice would deign to wear, a flimsy cap that served no purpose other than to fill up space.

Next came the knives. A Swiss army knife, of course, but only for its nifty pair of tweezers, necessary for extracting nature's slings and arrows – the ticks, stings, thorns and splinters that are a part of any camping trip. As a knife, it is useless. Horace Kephart counselled against it: 'Beware of combination knives; they may be passable corkscrews and can openers, but that is about all.' I disagree with Kephart – they are also useless as corkscrews. Kephart packed a small sheath knife with a four-and-a-half-inch blade. Because I had no intention of gutting animals on our trip, I packed a French Opinel knife with a beech handle and three-inch stainless-steel blade.

Then the beds, each about the size of a toilet roll, in a drawstring bag of their own. Not for us the comfortable air bed, these 'Therm-a-Rests' only required four long exhalations to inflate. Big comfy air beds were too heavy for our frugal packs. Also, on a chill night, all that air can form a solid block of cold that sucks out body heat; or, as Horace Kephart puts it, 'An air bed is luxurious in

moderate weather, but too cold to use late in the season unless
well insulated with blankets or a felt pad. The thinner the bed the
less objectionable it is in this respect, as it does not then steal so
much of your animal heat.'

With my large hands, I kneaded the gear together into the bag,
pushing down firmly as if the rucksack were a well in which I was
drowning a legion of cats. Packing requires compression, which
requires anger. Over time, I have come to regard this as Dad-
anger, the red energy required to haul a complaining family
through the crowded British transport system: traffic jams, caravans yanked along the hard shoulder by the wrist, the motorway
services at feeding hour, buckets of chicken served to families
dressed in their pyjamas, the first bank holiday of the year.

The neck of the rucksack swelled with last-minute towels and
jumpers. I garrotted it, then covered it with a hood, under which
sleeping bags were crammed. Into the pockets of netting either
side of the rucksack I slipped bin bags and water bottles. A sheepskin rolled around a Therm-a-Rest was the child's bed. I strapped
this on to the rucksack and then I was done.

Cath popped her head around the bedroom door. 'Don't forget the tent.'

I had forgotten the tent.

The tent was a four-man tunnel tent with three poles, weighing about nine kilograms, which made it slightly too heavy to
strap to the rucksack. Instead, the tent was wheeled around on its
own little shopping trolley, secured in place with elasticated
straps. 'Don't forget the tent' was our mantra because it was the
only item of luggage not attached to us, and so liable to get left
behind in the numerous changes en route, from bus to Underground train to mainline train to coach to aeroplane to bus again.

Margaret Thatcher is attributed as saying, 'If a man finds
himself a passenger on a bus having attained the age of twenty-
six, he can account himself a failure in life.' So how should I
account myself, as a man past the age of thirty who had turned his

beautiful young wife into a pack horse and commandeered his toddler's buggy to transport supplies? On the bus, the other passengers did the accounting for me. Under their gaze, I felt a keen sense of shame, so keen that I could take it no longer and tromped up to the top deck. Unfortunately the top deck was shallower than I expected, and my rucksack became wedged between the floor and ceiling. If the lower deck had scrutinized me with appalled fascination, the top deck, populated by hipsters commuting to unpaid internships in Shoreditch, merely sighed with contempt. I couldn't take the rucksack off. The aisle was too narrow. Nor could I move forward wearing it. The only way I could progress was to crouch. But the rucksack was really heavy. The bus lunged through the traffic lights. I staggered and fell on to my hands and knees, and, thusly humiliated, I crawled past the indifferent passengers to the single spare seat at the back of the bus.

Downstairs the passengers were mainly elderly citizens, and Cath fielded their concerned enquiries.

'What are you doing?'

'Going camping.'

That was insufficient explanation. Cath did her best to clarify to the doubting passengers the method in our seeming madness. Cath is always quick to shoot me down if I make it sound as if these camping trips are all my idea, some deranged man project to which the family is in thrall. No, she is an equal partner.

There are very good reasons for going camping, especially if you've got small children. Camping and parenting are two activities that, from the outside, appear to be a perverse and wilful abandonment of an easy life. The decision to have children, to embark upon such a messy and demanding adventure as parenthood, is analogous to the decision to go camping, heedless of the weather forecast, with limited resources to hand, a hazy idea of the destination and no certainty of what the future will bring. Camping is unpredictable, and that is why it is superior to two weeks in a Spanish resort, or a month in a Tuscan villa. The same desire for unpredictability lay behind my advocacy of having children. As ridiculous as it seems in retrospect, I grew bored with the twenty-something life of parties and drunken, angsty conversations and dithering around with commitment, and saw parenting as an adventure with an uncertain outcome. Camping is one of the defining decisions Cath and I have taken as parents; even if we have no idea how that decision will turn out, at least it has been made and life moves on.

These are different arguments from the ones Cath essayed on the bus that rainy Friday morning. She let the facts speak for themselves.

'We like camping.'

'But what about the child?' asked the passenger.

'She likes it too.'

'You must get very cold.'

'We take jumpers.'

'Why don't you have a car?'

Now that was a good question. The fact is that Hackney has the lowest ratio of car owners per head in the UK. For the decade we lived in Hackney, a car was unnecessary. Where would you park it? How could you leave anything of any value out on these streets? We didn't need a car for shopping. Tesco was a five-minute walk from our house. My dad tried to drive there once, tried to cover those 200 yards through Saturday's traffic; it took him an hour, and he was a wreck by the end of it. Cath and I were proud of our walking, our bus-bothering and our dashes to the station. The money we would have blown on car insurance and petrol went on taxis, buses and train tickets. All very reasonable until you start camping.

At Liverpool Street, in the heart of the financial centre, we got off the bus. And then, in a second breach of London etiquette, boarded a Tube train with all our stuff. People on the bus had made eye contact, whereas on the London Underground there was a faint aural bullying, harrumphs and coughs of disapproval. This particular trip was taken before the terrorist attacks of 7 July 2005, after which rucksacks on the Tube became so problematic we preferred to traverse the city by minicab, a deluded plan that would end with an Eastern European cab driver shouting, on his fourth revolution of the Old Street roundabout, 'What is this? Where am I?'

Onward to Stansted airport, where, in the face of Ryanair baggage restrictions, I was forced to include the tent as hand luggage. This ensured a difficult journey through customs. All morning we had wantonly disregarded the conventions of public transport, but it was only at the airport that the authorities could punish us for our transgression. The customs officer unfurled the tent as if he had never seen such a thing. He gazed down at the flysheet and groundsheet with contempt, and then he found in the tent bag some things he really didn't like, a rubberized mallet and a bag of metal pegs.

'What are you intending to do with these?'

I squinted with the effort of resisting sarcasm. 'Put up my tent.'

'On the plane?'

'No, afterwards.'

'What are these for?' He was holding the poles, delicate sections of fibreglass strung together with elastic.

'They are the poles that hold the tent up.' I pointed to the flysheet flat on the ground. 'We can't sleep in it when it is like that.'

I wanted to say, Don't worry, I won't attempt to hijack the plane to Cork by assembling a four-man tunnel tent in the aisle. Nor will I attempt to peg out the crew.

The customs officer looked deeper into the tent bag and found something very suspicious. Dust.

'This is very dusty,' he said, turning the bag inside out, showing me all the dust.

'It's soil,' I said. 'It's very soily.'

He took a sample and went off to test it. Fortunately the results showed that the soil all over my tent was soil, and not the residue from camping on a field of brown heroin.

The shame of the bus was replaced with indignation. I hate flying. I hate the way sounds become flat and reedy in the changed air pressure. I hate the uncertain feeling in my coccyx once the earth is removed from beneath the wheels. I hate the staged normality of the food service. I hate the threat of the oxygen masks, what it would feel like should the cabin decompress and a mask fall jerkily down before me like a thief from a gibbet. I hate feeling helpless inside modernism; I hate the fact that I have an anxiety attack for the entire flight and so time crawls by on its belly. Flying relies on a stupefied consensus – the in-flight movie, the terrible food, the little eyewash container of red wine – so that you can avoid thinking about the terrifying reality of your situation, with 100,000 pounds of thrust up your jacksie and only one stray Canadian goose away from bird-strike. That dumb consensus begins in the airport, with increasingly arbitrary rules concerning baggage allowance and liquid soap and suspicious shoes. Surely it would be safer and more convenient to simply drug the passengers at passport control and stack them in the hold? The deliberate mundanity of flying helps us to ignore what is actually happening. Camping is the opposite. It demands your attention. It strips away deadening domestic routine for a more realistic vision of who we are and what we are doing. Spend a weekend in nature and, on Monday morning, civilization seems more arbitrary, more of a decision that someone once arrived at, and not an inevitability. As I stood alone at the departure gate with my tent sprawled all over the floor, I thought, I shouldn't be ashamed of this, I should glorify it.

It is a bright, fresh spring morning. The ground is soft after days of rain. The field is boggy at the edges and then falls away into one of the many gullies that criss-cross Wapsbourne Manor

9

Farm. Glimpsed through coppiced trunks, a tyre on a rope twists idly over a ditch like a rustic Foucault's pendulum. Five years after my attempt to board a Ryanair flight with my tent as hand luggage, we are still camping, we will always be camping. We have acquired two more children and a bigger tent. We can no longer carry everything we need on our backs. We are ordinary car campers.

Cath and I pitch the tent. We discuss in muttered married tones exactly which spot to choose. A bed of wood chips has been laid over the mud. The field is drier towards the centre, but I want to pitch on the perimeter. We debate which sodden, scorched fire pit to make our own, a faint echo of those stifled discussions married couples have in earshot of salespeople. In choosing a pitch, I consider distance from facilities, prospect of shade, firmness of ground, the proximity of water and the position of other campers: there is a fine difference between joining a group and infringing upon it. Cath directs me to rotate the tent until the entrance faces the centre of the campsite, a sign that we will be part of the community. Our tent is large and comfortable and shelters the tame adventures of the family. We build it together, click out and slide the poles into their sheaths, fit the little hat that the tent uses for ventilation, wrestle the structure tense and upright and then rush to peg out the wings before they attract the attention of the wind – how intimate it is, the act of pitching, a waltz with equipment, our marriage in action. Other campers avert their eyes as we work.

There is no conversation during tent pitching; experience has taught us that this is a job best undertaken with the minimum of dialogue. Assertions remember their manners and mutate into suggestions. Our two toddlers Alfred and Florence, born a year apart, mill at our feet. The toddlers become entangled in the tent's delicate parts, then flee laughing to the briar patch, then to the gully. I hear a fellow camper complain that the toddlers are twanging his guy ropes. I call them back to me sternly.

The toddlers demand to be fed, and need to be changed, and exit pursued by me clutching a nappy, then return with questions concerning the sun and aeroplanes, questions that won't wait. 'Talk!' demands the boy. But I refuse. The sun is high. We need shade. The tent must go up. And water must be fetched. Overhead, tasks circle in their flight plans. The tasks are relentless. This is true of parenting even without the complication of camping. All camping families are alike because the tasks make us so. We are up to our eyes in it.

The tent is raised, and what an awesome structure it is, an exemplary fusing of modern technology with a nomad aesthetic. Our tent is a pyramid with a hexagonal base rising up to a high vent; three bedrooms slope off to the north, west and east, with the southern point used as an entrance. The airy, high-ceilinged central section keeps us cool during the day, and the low, snug bedrooms insulate us at night. When I see it from a distance in the dark, lit up by glow sticks and lanterns so that it looks like an Egyptian UFO, I am reminded that some scholars liken the Hebrew word for tent, *ohel*, to the Arabic *ahl*, one of many words for family or tribe. We are a camping family.

On both nights at Wapsbourne Manor Farm, the children wake crying and I crawl into the cold heart of the tent and curse the hour we decided to be a camping family, muttering and shivering into my jeans, wondering why, why do we do it? Sockless on the cold groundsheet, I realize it is all my fault: I pitched the tent on wet mud. With a groundsheet over it, the soaked earth does not dry out. As a result, the tent is colder than it should be, and that is why the children are crying.

I chose the muddy pitch because the dry patch was too close to a neighbouring tent. By keeping my distance, I was obeying the Bedouin proverb 'We pitch our tents far apart so that our hearts stay closer together.' Far apart so that the sound of snoring will not disturb. Far apart so that the first thing you see in the morning is not a camper's battered, hungover face as it emerges from the tent to verify suspicions about the weather. And, most crucially, far apart so that we are spared the hell of one another's domestic routines. No one should have to listen to me harrying the children into line. No one should have to listen to Cath and I debate breakfast, the constant exchange of banal information required to keep the family on target. I cite this Bedouin proverb whenever friends suggest renting a cottage together. Regardless of everyone's good intentions, cottage holidays have an undertone of passive-aggressive negotiation. Families can't share kitchens. Let us come together around the ancient brotherhood of a campfire, rather than around a dining table with the performance anxiety of bourgeois cookery and overfamiliar topics of conversation.

If you pitch the tent in the wrong place, you have all night to brood on your mistake. Since acquiring a car, I have the nuclear option of loading the children into the back seat in the middle of the night and driving home. I have never pushed this button, but I have been tempted. At small, barely organized festivals, we have been forced to camp within earshot of the stage, listening to drug monkeys fight over the soundsystem at three in the morning with no crowd left to soak up the bass (I must remember to pack earplugs more often). On a couple of occasions, the whole camp has been a disaster and it has seemed almost preferable to drive home in the dark than to remain.

The first camp of the year is invariably disorganized and fretful, as you try to remember your gear and the routine of camp life. Pitching at Wapsbourne Farm was to make up for a disastrous trip there earlier in the year, when we were the sole campers. In March, the ground was hard with frost and the trees were bare. Night fell quickly and the land grew cold. I lit a fire and the barbecue but was unprepared for the overwhelming blackness of the night. The fire made no inroads into the dark. The barbecue had a lid and so was effectively invisible to the small children swarming around me. For safety's sake, I emptied the barbecue coals into the campfire, burning my fingertips in the process. Agony! I ran around in the blackness bewailing my lot, cursing my condition, chased by hungry, screaming children. A handful of sausages survived the crisis. The two toddlers wolfed them down. Neither Cath nor I felt like eating, and our eldest child was swaying and sickening.

Surely I would drive us home.

In retrospect, I was far too mad at this point to drive. Mad with the night, and the sickness. We attempted bedtime. A fitful hour of sleep was had, and then the vomiting began. We had swine flu, and one unexpected consequence of the mass inoculation of the toddlers against it was that they were bursting with energy and wanting attention and activity at the same time as Cath, our eldest daughter, Alice, and I were crawling around the groundsheet in a hallucinatory condition of perpetual evacuation.

Four in the morning is the hour when, statistically, people are most likely to die. Tom Wolfe calls it the drinker's hour, the time when you wake up startled after an evening's binge, every cell poisoned, and your mind a washing machine spinning the dirty laundry of the soul. I reckon that four in the morning was a shift-change for our primitive ancestors; sleeping in groups and on the plains, they had a rotation system to determine who kept watch. The only one of our party still awake, I lay in the tent feverish and listening out for predators. I felt like I was about to die, that all the hype about swine flu might turn out to be true. Could I drive home now? I wondered. Waking the children and loading them into the car would be easy. Driving across a dark field and the night lanes less so. And there was the risk, what with my impending death, that driving might be beyond me. Ever considerate, I did not wake Cath to inform her that I was about to die, reasoning that she would prefer to sleep through my death and then clear up after me in the morning.

The first time Cath and I pitched a tent, a minuscule one-man tent in a small field in Dover, we pitched it inside out. We were nineteen years old. The equipment was borrowed; Cath took her brother's large blue rucksack, I carried my cousin's newfangled red one. The tent belonged to my sister and was so low I had to shuffle into it on my elbows. Because I pitched it inside out, come the morning dew the tent had sunk against my face. In the grainy blue light just before dawn, I dressed, packed the rucksack and chivvied Cath out of her sleeping bag. I was pleased to be up early in good time for the ferry. The responsibility of navigating Europe weighed heavy on my shoulders, my thoughts were criss-crossed by railway timetables. Punctuality was more important than sleep, to me. Not to Cath. If the tent had not been pitched inside out, and collapsing all around her, then it was likely that we would have had our first camping argument that morning, with her dallying in bed and me keen to strike camp and get going. It turned out that we were so early for the Dover ferry that the boat was still in France.

Our tour of Europe was lonely and uneventful. We met no one. We pitched our tents too far apart from the other young adventurers, the lean, tanned continental backpackers who seemed so much more sophisticated and at ease with themselves than us, two pallid northerners stomping around the cobbled streets in Doc Marten boots. In the same way that the Bedouin men sit in the porch of their tent to socialize, we should have signalled to our fellow campers that we were open to conversation.

The poet Alphonse de Lamartine recorded his journey with the Bedouin people in *Travels in the East*, published in 1850. He describes how the Bedouins pitched their tents:

. . . the Bedouin [men] dispersed into a fine plain, jumped to the ground, struck their lances in it, and fastened their horses to them. The women ran on all sides and pitched the tents near their hus-bands' horses. Then, as if by enchantment, we found ourselves in a sort of town . . . The women alone had the office of fixing and

taking down the tents, and they performed the matter with a surprising address and rapidity. They, in general, execute all the
labours of the encampment.

Not only did the Bedouin women pitch and strike camp, they also
wove the distinctive black tents from goat hair and sheep's wool,
hence the tent's name of *bait sha'r*, the house of hair.

The Victorian writers who travelled with the Bedouin were
convinced they were observing the society of the patriarchs of
the Old Testament: the Bedouin men, following the custom of
Abraham, sat in the tent door in the heat of the day; the tents
matched those described in the Bible, with a rough hanging sep-
arating the public area of the tent from the private – out front,
social life; out back, the private chamber of the family. The Book
of Judges describes how, in this bedroom, Jael, the wife of Heber,
hammered a tent peg through the skull of a rival captain, Sisera.
In Isaiah, God is described as spreading the heavens like a tent, a
metaphor that reappears whenever we gaze up at a canopy of
stars. He pitched the heavens by himself, demonstrating his
power and his dominion, then instructed the Israelites to expand
their domain with another camping metaphor: 'Enlarge the place
of thy tent, and let them stretch forth the curtains of thine habi-
tations: spare not, lengthen they cords, and strengthen thy stakes.'
And Exodus concludes with the detailed instructions given to
Moses on Mount Sinai for the lavish construction of the tabernacle, the tent of meeting, a place for God to dwell within the
encampments of the Israelites.

Mankind has slept in tents and congregated around campfires
from the very beginning. Archaeologist Frank Hole led numerous digs around Iran and Iraq, investigating the domestication of
animals, from about 8,000 years ago. The Neolithic campsite of
Tepe Tûlâ'i, near Andimeshk in the region of Khuzistan, Iran,
appeared to be little more than a mound about sixty metres in
diameter and a metre and half high. It was occupied for perhaps

200 years somewhere between 6200 and 5900 BC. In 1973, Hole excavated the site with the help of local workers. From ash deposits, the remnants of ancient campfires and shards of prehistoric pottery, the purpose and age of the site was determined: Tepe Tûlâ'i was the camp ground of pastoralists used seasonally by people who may have practised limited agriculture elsewhere. Shards of flints and ashy areas were uncovered up to 100 metres away from the mound, indicating an extensive settlement. Bones of goat and gazelle were found, the goats most likely herded, the gazelles hunted on the Khuzistan plain. The discovery of forty-four canid bones suggested the tribe kept dogs. The local workmen confirmed that the layout of this Neolithic camp was identical to modern nomad camps. The dig exposed distinctive rounded boulders identified by the local workmen as coming from the Karkheh river, about three miles away. They recognized the arrangement of the stones, in three rows, as the *chul* or platform on which bedding is placed in a tent. Frank Hole writes:

> The men we employed had camped in this very area themselves in years past, using structures identical to the ones we were digging. During winter they used the typical Luri tents with black woven goat hair tops, whereas in the summer they made koolas, open sided structures of poles and thatch or reeds.

Our physicality is largely unchanged since the Neolithic era. Our bodies evolved to camp. In the late nineteenth and early part of the twentieth century, a time of great concern over the degenerating physical condition of civilized man, going camping was seen as a way of compensating for the enervations of urban life. Tormented by the lack of individual power that comes with mass industrialized society, campers clothed themselves in myths of ancestors or nomadic others; this appropriation of authenticity, using camping to make ourselves feel more real, continues today in the glades of Wapsbourne Farm, where there are tipis and yurts for rent. The lives of the nomadic people such as the Qashqai, the Bedouin or the Sioux provide romantic myths for the campers of Western society; the more advanced and complex our lives become, the more we need a temporary vacation in the simple life.

In 1913, a 44-year-old Boston artist, Joseph Knowles, went into the woods naked, without matches or knife, clothing or food, to prove that he could survive just as well as primitive man. He endured a full two months and then was discovered stumbling along a railroad track in a bearskin. The survivalist experiment was accused of fakery, with witnesses reporting they had seen Joseph call into the lodge of a journalist for a hot meal now and again. Regardless of such accusations, Joseph Knowles's heroic trip was celebrated because it reassured society that a soft underbelly could quickly be toughened by a spot of camping. 'The best vacation the over-civilized man can have,' writes Horace Kephart, 'is to go where he can hunt, capture, and cook his own meat, erect his own shelter, do his own chores, and so, in some measure, pick up again those lost arts of wildcraft that were our heritage through ages past, but of which not one modern man in a hundred knows anything at all.'

Contemporary campers may not get to kill their own food, but camping remains a school in self-reliance. The educational role of camping goes all the way back to the Campus Martius of Rome, the martial field where soldiers trained and games were held, and continues today in the 'campus' grounds of universities. We camp to improve ourselves: I take my children camping because I want them to learn about weather and fire and acquire the physical courage that comes from unsupervised exploration of the countryside. The digital realm is a poor playground because it is without risk: video games put players in the hunter's zone of total concentration but disconnect that mind state from physical reality. Actions with consequences that can be erased by pressing the restart button teach us nothing. Camping unplugs us and our children from the ceaseless distraction of the digital realm, if only for a weekend. Adversity and limitation, and the freedom from the neediness of modern media, are character forming.

The use of camping as an educational experience crops up in the Forest School of the 1930s. Modern, ever-hovering helicopter parents are advised to look away from the section in Chapter 5 where important figures in the Forest School let their three young children (aged seven, nine, and ten and a half) camp in a wood beside a river without any adult supervision whatsoever for six days.

For adults, camping offers not a break from work but a different type of work. Simple minor tasks, such as pitching a tent or setting the campfire, which have instant and tangible rewards, take precedence over the complex, abstract or deskilled work of the town and city. Beneath this seemingly innocuous recreational pursuit lies a drawing apart from the mediated, passive, mortgaged, stressed lot of contemporary life. To its believers, camping is freedom; to its detractors, it represents a perverse nostalgia for the prison of nature that mankind spent millennia trying to escape. For every person who comes away from a camping trip convinced of its virtues, there is another vowing 'never again'. In this account, I have included some of my more challenging experiences because the unpredictable nature of camping is what makes it superior to simple consumer leisure activity. The times when Cath and I camped and had the time of our lives, I have largely omitted. Happiness writes white.

In writing this book, I have chosen a left-hand trail through the history of camping. It begins with the late nineteenth-century love of the primitive and the yearning for a lost affinity with the land. Along the path we will meet Ernest Thompson Seton and his Indian-inspired Woodcraft Way. Further along, this Woodcraft Way leads to radical camping groups such as the Kindred of the Kibbo Kift, and the progressive experiments in camping and education that took place at Sandy Balls in the New Forest under the guidance of the Order of Woodcraft Chivalry. The trail forks. We will pass the disturbing wood of the German youth movements the Wandervogel and the Bünde, but not venture too deeply into that particular heart of darkness. This left-hand trail is a countercultural route. The right-hand trail takes in mass mainstream movements like the Scouts and the Guides, the educational summer camps of America, the Alan Rogers camping guides, stories that I will leave to others to tell. The scope of this tale is also necessarily limited, mainly to Britain and America, which means omissions of camping history from the rest of the world, from Australian bushcraft to the revolutionary role of Czech woodcraft movements.

Along the way, we will be accompanied by camping mavericks such as Nessmuk and Horace Kephart, who taught America how to camp in the wilderness even as that wilderness was imperilled by industrialization. Our American story begins with the Philosophers' Camp in the Adirondacks in 1858, attended by the transcendentalist poet Ralph Waldo Emerson, whose writing changed the relationship between the American soul and the wild. After the Civil War, Americans head off into the wilderness in droves, inspired by the camping zeal of William H. H. Murray, only for their enthusiasm to meet with blackfly and relentless rain. In the early years of the twentieth century, we will hover around the campfire with Theodore Roosevelt and John Muir as they negotiate the safeguarding of the wild for future generations of campers. The arrival of the car both imperils and opens up the wilderness. We will join Henry Ford and Thomas Edison as they camp together and inaugurate an era of autocamping. Technology, in the form of modern tents and gear, is deployed to bring us closer to nature, with mixed results. In the counterculture of the 1960s, we will meet the people responsible for inventing the dome tent and leading the innovation in lightweight camping gear that creates a back-packing revolution.

The fashion for camping comes and goes. At the time of writing, at the beginning of the second decade of the twenty-first century, camping in Britain is enjoying a renaissance. One in five adults has been on a camping or caravanning holiday in the last three years, and a further 7 per cent would like to in the future; right now, 4.2 million Britons are considering sleeping under the stars. In 2010, Mintel found 40 per cent of Britons were not intending to holiday abroad, and UK campsite bookings increased by 16 per cent, with a doubling of tent sales. The Camping and Caravanning Club reported that its membership had grown by 52,000 in 2009, with increases particularly high in the thirty to forty-nine age bracket. It is telling that the average age of the club has dropped from fifty-five to forty-nine, due to the uptake of camping among younger families who want to give their children a back-to-basics experience. The Camping and Caravanning Club estimates that one in a hundred adults in Britain are members.

There are economic reasons for this: Britain's currency is weak, its airports are dysfunctional, people are markedly poorer than they were, and anticipate becoming poorer still. There are also cultural reasons: certainties concerning our way of life are under pressure, the environmental movement suggests that the current direction of civilization is unsustainable, and the method of paying for it, capitalism itself, is undergoing an enema. At this moment in time, people want to know, could there be another way of life? Can I survive with less stuff? Should I run for the hills? All good questions that people have asked before, throughout history, and which have inspired people to go camping. We know that travel gives us a different perspective on home; camping gives us that and something more, its nomadic roots questioning the need for home itself.

In modern times, we camp to be part of something larger than ourselves: the wilderness, the Glastonbury crowd, a political group, a church, the Boy Scouts, nature, history. Camping replaces the limitations of four walls and the glowing screen with the otherness of the outdoors. The windows to the soul are thrown open. A landscape is a state of mind. Because I am ignorant of fauna and flora, and spend the majority of my time in a room staring at a screen, I experience nature as an otherness rather than as a familiar domain. I hunger for the horizon and the pagan church of the woods. I lie in my sleeping bag and listen to the catechism of the dawn chorus and the babbling brook. For me, the art of camping is enjoying the otherness of nature while mitigating its hardships: take too much gear and the mystical quality of the land will prove elusive; take too little, and any higher thoughts will be obliterated by physical discomfort. So find a spot of level ground, ideally one that takes the sun in the morning, is elevated above its surroundings but with some natural shelter, a patch of ground that is not under a tree or within the overflow of a nearby stream, with access to firewood and water and a friendly distance from fellow campers, and clear the ground of twigs and stones in preparation of lying cheek to cheek with the earth. Pitching a tent is an act of hope: hope that you might experience something truthful, hope that you and yours will be improved by the experience, but, most of all, hope that it will not rain.

2

The Captain of the Camp

My plan was to tour the Ring of Kerry by bus, pitching our tent at various beauty spots along the way. In a small notebook, I recorded bus timetables and the phone numbers and addresses of likely campsites. Although I spent many evenings devising this schedule, I was resolved not to suffocate the camping trip with planning. I would strike a fine balance between organization and freedom. I would be a steady hand upon the tiller, not an overbearing one. I would be a swan, serene on the surface, briskly paddling underneath.

The Ring of Kerry is on the south-western side of Ireland, a spectacular area of mountains and lakes girdled by a circular road. Our first stop is the campsite of Mannix Point in Cahersiveen. According to my notebook, the bus ride is thirty-eight miles. We arrive on schedule and are met by the owner, Mortimer Moriarty, a lean, pipe-smoking man who, in the manner of many campsite owners, keeps a very scruffy car. Mannix Point has braziers for peat fires, and a battered piano in a parlour for the campers to play. We pitch our tent beneath palm trees on a spit of land from which I can observe the feud of three different weathers – lagoons of blue sky to the north, grey gothic shadows to the east and a single furious rain cloud kicking off in the west. I close my notebook, make a cup of tea and sit upon a large flat stone overlooking the bay. I am astonished to be camping next to the Atlantic Ocean. The view includes Valentia Island, from where early transatlantic cables carried dots and dashes to the New World. The distant hurricanes of the Caribbean send back transmissions of their own in choppy swells.

At rest, I become keenly aware of my inner voice. In the silence of the bay, this voice is almost audible. Most of my thoughts are lines of dialogue between myself and a hectoring imaginary interlocutor. He has elected himself captain of the camp. He knows the exact time that cooking should begin, what provisions need to be obtained and how they must be rationed. He has studied the maps and is always keen to push on to our next destination. I wonder if it would be possible for me to train a different inner voice? Instead of an inner captain with his punishing and unnecessary itinerary, I would like a free spirit to act as my imaginary counsel, a savage poet who has filled the notebook with something other than timetables.

The next morning, we rent bikes and ride up to the peak of Valentia Island. I haven't ridden a bike for a year or two. It feels fantastic to travel at my own volition and at faster than walking pace. Freewheeling back down again, with the sun glittering upon the waters of the bay, my daughter's sleeping, helmeted head knocking against my back, I am truly happy. I am in my early thirties, a sweet spot of young parenthood; I am pompously sloughing off a decade of meaningless hedonism for something more substantial, something I can hammer pegs into. I experiment with furrowing my brow and wearing a flat cap. Camping is a rite of passage. I am freewheeling into a new phase of adulthood.

Over the next few days, we fall into a healthy routine, breakfasting on eggs and smoked salmon from the local smokery then riding out to a beach or castle ruin. Cath and Alice are content but my inner captain grows restless at such idleness; he wants to move on. My notebook indicates all the goals we have yet to attain. Who knows how long this good weather will last?

We strike camp at Mannix Point and catch the bus to Caherdaniel. I am concerned that I won't recognize the bus stop for the campsite until we have passed it by, then it will be too late; in rural Ireland, the bus stops are miles apart. According to my notebook, the campsite is only a few miles out of town. I make a guess at the speed of the bus and calculate that we should stop after a drive of about ten minutes. After passing through the village of Caherdaniel, I silently count 600 seconds then ask the bus driver to let us out.

'We'll see you again in a couple of days,' I say, as I remove our camping gear from the hold. 'We're touring the Ring of Kerry by bus.'

'This is the last bus,' he says as he settles in his seat.

'The last bus of today.'

'Last bus of the season. Last bus till' – he looks at his watch – 'till March.' And then he drives off.

I stare at my notebook. There is nothing in it about seasonal timetables. Then I realize that we are not where I thought we were. Whatever calculation I was making on the back of the bus did not tally with reality. Madness is a form of perverted logic.

'Why did the bus driver let us off here?' asks Cath, looking at the desolate patch of road.

'I asked him to.'

'Is this the campsite?'

'No.'

'Why didn't you ask the bus driver to let us off at the camp-site?'

Because the captain doesn't ask for help! The captain is decisive. He leads; others follow. Only the ignorant ask questions! I lead the family along the roadside. There is no path. I am keenly aware of how vulnerable we are. This is where all my planning gets us, wearing rucksacks and wheeling a baby buggy along a road at dusk in the middle of nowhere. We don't get very far before, mercifully, a car stops and a concerned Swiss woman emerges. She insists upon driving us to our destination, and as I load the buggy into the boot of her car, she points to my family standing in the road and asks, 'Don't you think this is a little dangerous?'

I am a swan. An upside-down swan. On the surface, furious peddling, and underneath, gracefully drowning.

Four men undertook a cycling tour around Connemara in Galway, Ireland, in 1897. The men travelled from Sligo, in the north-west, through Swinford and Castlebar. The leader of the tour and self-appointed 'skipper' was Thomas Hiram Holding, a 53-year-old tailor. Holding averaged a month of camping every year, estimating that he had covered 4,000 miles on river, lake and estuary in the United Kingdom. Eleven years previously, in 1886, Holding and three others had undertaken a camping tour of Scotland's western lochs by canoe. He was skipper, and the other three men, who were not previously acquainted, were allocated the roles of purser, mate and cabin boy. The men had white-collar jobs, and this camping tour, taking in the islands of Bute and Arran, promised them a physical hardihood denied to them by their urban work and life. The tour was also a rite of passage, much along the same lines as I underwent in Kerry; two of Holding's party were 'fairly much married' and two were anxious to be, and so the trip allowed the unmarried men to 'study the characters of the settled and sensible men who had become sobered and broken to the most earnest duties of life'.

With so much camping experience, it was natural that Holding would assume the role of captain or skipper. His fellow travellers subordinated themselves to him readily in a way that will be familiar to anyone who has attended a stag party, when strangers thrown together fall into line behind a putative leader, the best man. As captain, Holding was responsible for the assembly of the tent and gear, which at the time was either commissioned or made by the campers themselves; when a married couple of Holding's acquaintance revealed that they intended to cycle-camp around Scotland on a tandem, he commissioned two collections of tent and gear, each weighing fourteen pounds, made by seven people in four towns. The camping trip around Connemara had been Holding's dream for fifteen years, though it was only with the invention of the safety bicycle with its rubberized tyres that such a camping tour by bike became feasible.

The role of captain of the camp appears throughout the early camping and outdoors manuals. According to Holding, the captain is a role assumed by 'one who invites a friend and who has taken part in a previous expedition', and the position entails the delegation and division of labour:

> The shrewd camper will endeavour to divest himself of as much responsibility as possible . . . placing at least a fair half of the work on the other fellow. This is not easy, for three reasons. First, the chum may be one of those men who hate responsibility. Secondly, he may be filled with the notion that he is on holiday. Thirdly, he may want everything to be very easy.

It was the captain's responsibility to ask farmers for permission to camp on their land, and to negotiate a suitable rent and the purchase of milk and eggs. Holding was also self-appointed chef, and saw to it that rations were fairly doled out to his fellow campers. The captain ensured the campers did not stay up too late and that they rose early to enjoy the day. He embodied the aspirations of the tour; he was the campers' better self.

For their trip around Ireland, the four men slept three abreast in a small tent with Holding sleeping crosswise at their feet. 'Of course, the whole thing was an impossibility taken seriously,' he writes, 'to stow four full-grown men into a little tent, weighing two pounds, with a floor space of five foot nine inches by six foot. But, really, in making the best of it, it is surprising how snug we were.' On a typical morning, the men would wake and take turns to bathe in the river, with the captain taking a dip first while his juniors washed up from the previous evening's meal. If it was raining, all four men would have to dress at the same time in the little tent. Breakfast would be cooked on a methylated spirit stove called the Mersey, developed, as the name indicates, by a Liverpool architect who shared Holding's passion for canoeing; the Mersey was a forerunner to the nestled pans and meths burner of the Trangia, with the stove fitting inside a nest of pots and the frying pan employed as a lid. A pot of porridge would be followed by thick slices of bacon and fried potatoes. After the morning's exertions, the campers lay back to smoke a pipe and watch the clouds drift by.

To excel at camping, Holding felt that 'All the savage must not have been refined out of a person – just a fragment must remain for the thing to be successful.' By 'savage' he meant the American Indian or the Romany Gypsy, two peoples who are co-opted into acting as symbols of camping freedom, 'the utter self-willedness, the abandon, the go-as-you-pleaseness, the freedom of the life'. That freedom requires the forethought and discipline of the captain to attain. The art of camping arises out of this paradox between planning and freedom, soldiering and romanticism, the captain and the Indian.

Thomas Hiram Holding's reputation as the father of modern camping rests upon *The Camper's Handbook*, published in 1908, which established him as a figurehead of a camping craze. It was described by the *Daily News* as the 'Camper's Koran'. Photographs of Holding at this middle stage of his life show a hearty, kindly gentleman in a straw boater, grey at the temples with an amenable moustache, the sleeves rolled up on his collarless white shirt and a pipe tucked in his left hand. And here he is again, wearing the rough and slovenly look of a man who has spent three days or more at camp. He is aft of a sailboat, sporting a battered straw boater and the beginnings of a salty beard, a comfy jumper and bare calves and feet. On weekdays he was a London tailor and editor of a tailoring magazine, and on weekends he was the Old Skipper.

Thomas Hiram Holding was born in Prees, Shropshire, in 1844 to Mormon parents. The family emigrated to Salt Lake City in 1853. On the long trek across America, two of the four Holding children died. Thomas Holding first experienced camping as a nine-year-old boy pitched on a plateau overlooking the Mississippi. The camp numbered 300 people in tents and wagons and lasted for over a month, on land that thundered with a multitude of wild game, antelope and buffalo. After the tragic death of their children, the family did not settle in America and returned to England.

In American camping manuals, the captain of the camp is like the leader of a mountaineering expedition or a colonial exploration. Alpheus Hyatt Verrill, an American archaeologist, explorer and hack, wrote that the man with the most experience in woodcraft should be camp captain, and if that criteria was shared by all members of the party, then a good-natured man who was practical and calm and possessed sound judgement should be selected. For the American woodsman, the captain was not a martinet – when disagreements arose, Verrill suggested holding a council and if the majority of the party did not agree with the leader, he should waive his authority. The captain enacts the sound judgement of the group, a necessary task when camping far from civilization in the remote lakes and mountains of the Adirondacks.

In April 1906, Thomas Hiram Holding founded the National Camping Club. One hundred and fifty members, men and women alike, enrolled within four months. By the time of the publication of *The Camper's Handbook*, two years later, membership of the National Camping Club had grown to over 800. Camping fever spread across the classes and professions: 'Almost every division into which society in England is split has contributed to the ranks of the Camping fraternity of today,' he wrote. The local press noted with surprise the mixing of the classes that took place in Cunningham Camp, one of the first known British campsites. It was not only working-class youth who travelled from Liverpool to the campsite at Howstrake on the Isle of Man; the middle classes went to the seaside too, spending their holidays alongside their social inferiors in a proto-holiday camp that, by 1904, consisted of 1,500 tents in serried ranks over five acres.

The growing authority of the Camping and Caravanning Club replaced the role of the camp captain. The club became the repository of camp wisdom and rules. The role of captain or skipper was demoted to mere 'camp steward'. The camp steward was required due to the absence of paid help, and their authority was limited: 'they may call upon members to fetch water, remove rubbish, and perform other acts for the well-being of the camp.'

The position of camp captain may appear to be an amusing relic. However, on large group camps, a lot of simmering resentment could be avoided through the election of a captain, someone to allocate jobs so that one diligent sod does not get landed with all the work. The sheer amount of stuff the group camp entails, with needless duplication of equipment, could be reduced by stout organization beforehand. Every year, we organize a group camp on a site in the woods of Dernwood Forest in East Sussex, and my fingers itch for a captain to be elected, an agreed authority figure who could resolve the awkward negotiations about what needed to be done about the rubbish, or the firewood. Instead of a camp captain, we fall into the role of hosts, as if the camp were one long dinner party; as host, I am the one who must wheelbarrow the rubbish to the recycling, cook the meals, clean up the camp of a morning and deal with whatever outstanding bills the others have neglected to settle. During such self-pitying moments, I echo Holding: Ah, if only some of the party weren't so foolish as to envisage a camping trip as a period of unbroken leisure!

Contemporary campers will not be ordered around, especially when they feel that they are on holiday. Instead we must inspire by example. Or, more accurately, guilt. The majority of people, upon seeing my labours at camp, will set to some task for the good of the group, such as washing-up or gathering firewood; trusting to the innate goodwill of the camp is, for the course of a weekend, preferable to a prolonged period of organization. If we spare ourselves the officiousness of the camp captain and steward, can I instead recommend one simple rule for a group camp: that every camper should bring along one item for the benefit of the group. It could be an axe, a campfire tripod, a tarp or, in the case of one fellow camper, a cask of seventy-two pints of local ale. Pack one item to delight and surprise the camp that will improve the lot of us all.

Thomas Hiram Holding's *The Camper's Handbook* includes assertions on the advantages of camping, and useful sections on beds, tents, clothing and cooking. He is full of sound advice: the ideal number of people in a camp is three; if a man keeps you awake, you have a right to stop his SNORING. He asserts that a camp needs an activity, a common purpose. 'A fixed camp,' writes Holding, 'to be a success, should have a programme and interest of some kind sustained without pressure or fag.' The captain would ensure the following of this programme and prevent the group from becoming diffuse and aimless. In this tradition, camping was a sport, not a holiday, something that required 'a little intrepidity, some courage, and even determination'.

The sport is not confined to men. Women are more than welcome:

> Perhaps I may be permitted to say here that I have seen them excel men, too, in smartness and cleverness. How quickly they pick up the making and mounting of a tent and its appliances, the cooking and the tidying up, and how they take to the bathing. How the beautiful spirit of brightness and the merry ring of their laughter within hearing of the men is an added pleasure to all.

And because there is nothing women enjoy more than having a man advise them upon each and every aspect of their lives, including their clothing, Holding takes the liberty of discoursing on a lady's correct dress for camp, including her corsets ('A very narrow, soft and pliable waist girth in place of a corset should be worn'), skirts ('The best kind of skirt for camping is one that finishes three inches off the ground. It should not be less nor need it be more') and even knickerbockers ('Soft angora, not cashmere').

The first lady to camp with Holding's association of cycle campers was Mrs F. Horsfield. She contributes an essay towards the end of *The Camper's Handbook*, entitled 'Ladies and Cycle Camping', to address the concerns of women directly. Mrs Horsfield describes the appeal of camping for the Edwardian housewife. Camping is a break from domestic chores. Compared to dusting and tidying the various large rooms of a family home, the task of setting a tent straight for a day is minor, and the cooking involved at camp far less formal than at home. She is proud of her involvement with the practical side of the sport. Holding and his campers were making their own tents and often their own gear, and Mrs Horsfield considered women invaluable both for the running repairs they made to the tents and for their manufacture during the winter. On her cycle, with panniers and Japanese baskets, she carried a similar load to her husband, twenty pounds'

worth of kit compared to his twenty-eight (and here the description of his camping gear makes me shiver as I notice he is lugging
around an Edwardian camera and numerous 'photographic
plates'). A separate site was set apart for ladies and married couples at camp, and married ladies would chaperone the single
women among them; nonetheless, the freedom of the open air
and the informality of camp was thrilling for the Edwardian
woman.

To women concerned about taking their children camping,
Mrs Horsfield reassures them that she recently returned from a
camp to which she took a twelve-year-old boy and a twelve-
month-old baby. 'It requires a certain amount of determination
to take a baby Camping, but those who live in large towns will be
well repaid by the greatly improved health of their children after
a week or two under canvas.'

Both Holding and Mrs Horsfield address the matter of food,
although his recipes are more exhaustive, and far less appealing,
than hers. His review of seemingly every tinned food available
defeats any reader, and Lord knows what he thought he was
doing making blancmange in the woods.

To the Edwardian gentleman camper, the composition of the
camping group warranted careful consideration. Thomas Holding and Alpheus Hyatt Verrill considered their choice of mates as
if casting for a reality TV show. Holding compiled a catalogue of
comic stereotypes of the camper, from the Fine Weather Camper
to the Ideal Failure, always grumbling at the method and the
hurry of the captain. Desirable types included the Energetic
Camper, the Self-Reliant Camper and, best of all, the Ideal
Camper, in possession of the cardinal virtue of extreme patience
and mindful of the principle that 'An unpleasant word said
between two men in camp sticks for ever. Moral: then don't say
that word.'

Holding's good humour is contrasted by Alpheus Hyatt Verrill's rant against unsuitable camping mates: 'Avoid going camping

with irritable, impatient, lazy, super-sensitive, nervous, peevish, superstitious, or over-fastidious individuals. Don't expect a man who drinks to excess, or one who is lost without his club, his evening clothes or his daily papers, to make a good campmate.' All the manuals agree that camp should be temperate, one custom that does not deserve to be revived (although I could be persuaded to withdraw my recommendation of whisky as a camping tipple; at the group camp, a bottle of single malt opened at midnight around the campfire caused mayhem, with one lady seeking our assistance with her toilet, and then promptly disappearing into a ditch). Verrill reasserts that patience is the prime necessity, and he highlights another quality pertinent to the contemporary camper: 'One must take things as they are, not as one would wish.'

The Edwardians thought the open air was restorative, which was understandable in a society where rapid industrial growth overwhelmed its cities with polluted fog. Civilization made the Englishman sick. 'Has there ever been an age as sick as ours?' asked back-to-the-lander Edward Carpenter. Sleeping under the stars was the cure, and houses were designed with special open-air balconies for this purpose.

Country air was purifying. The outdoors was a virtuous contrast to the moral and physical squalor of the cities. Holding preached the gospel of 'muscular Christianity'. This term first appeared in the 1850s to describe the novels of Charles Kingsley and Thomas Hughes, two sportsmen and advocates of the strenuous life, whose chosen medium of the novel was at odds with their message that bookishness and education were effeminate poisons that required a counterbalance of a rough-hewn masculinity in the form of fishing, hunting and camping. A faint echo of this ideology rings through *The Camper's Handbook*, particularly in Holding's warning that there is no time at camp for literary pursuits. Camping stiffens the sinews and tempers the spirit, but it is also a relief from the claustrophobia of the mind, which is as bad for the nerves as a crowded street. Muscular Christianity perceived nature as the countenance of God; to camp was to investigate His Divine works. Artifice was decadent. Healthfulness and simplicity were virtues. Dressed in hard-wearing tweed, a gentleman's Kevlar, Holding lay outside his candy-striped tent with carefully parted hair and a stern expression, his canoe, *Osprey*, at his feet. His relaxed posture says, simply, *This is all that I require.*

Camping was the townsman's holiday in the country, a break from civilization. Across the 1870s, cereal prices, undermined by increased imports of grain from the American prairies and Argentina, collapsed. The wholesale price of eight pounds of beef declined from five shillings and five pence in 1873 to three shillings and nine pence in 1896. By 1885, the acreage under wheat in England and Wales had fallen by a million. The countryside emptied as the workers headed to the cities in search of work. As fewer people lived in the countryside, memories of rural life became hazy and romanticized. 'A trickle of townsmen began to resort to the country for air, exercise, recreation and spiritual refreshment,' writes C. E. M. Joad. 'With the coming in the twentieth century of the second industrial revolution, the trickle broadened out into a river; for the second industrial revolution was a revolution in transport.'

The revolution in transport included, in 1885, John Starley's invention of the 'safety bicycle', so called because, with its equal sized wheels, it put the rider's feet within reach of the ground and so was not as treacherous to ride as the penny-farthing. In 1888, John Dunlop invented the pneumatic tyre for his son's bicycle, using rubber to make the ride less jarring. The bicycle put the countryside within reach of the average working man, and Thomas Hiram Holding was a pioneer of cycle camping. In the early 1900s, the car was a novelty. The bike was king. The roads were so safe that a *Boy's Own Paper*, published 26 May 1906, recommended for its readership of schoolboys a solo night bike ride from London to the Newhaven coast, passing through Caterham, Godstone, Ashdown Forest and the South Downs.

Holding's experience with cycle and canoe camping encouraged him to develop his own lightweight kit and tent, as the gear that was readily available was bulky and military. An accomplished tailor, Holding set about creating his own tent designs. His favourite was a small 'A' style tent that he called the Wigwam. Made from silk, it weighed just eleven ounces and could be carried in the coat pocket. For poles, it used walking sticks, its heavy steel pegs making up the bulk of the weight. Holding worked to improve on the Primus stove, invented by Frans Wilhelm Lindqvist in Sweden in 1892. His abiding values of compactness, space and solid packing led to the baby Primus, a paraffin-fuelled pressure stove.

Unlike Thomas Holding, Jerome K. Jerome's *Three Men in a Boat* were novice campers. The three men sail a camping skiff up the Thames with the hope of a wild and free time. The novel opens with the men feeling seedy and liverish, a malfunctioning liver being the source of all idleness. Published in 1889, two years after Thomas Holding's account of his journey around Connemara, Jerome's comic masterpiece satirizes Holding's muscular Christianity; the Christian virtues of camping are espoused by George, who wonders, as all campers do, why life could not always be like this, 'away from the world, with its sin and temptation, leading sober, peaceful lives and doing good'. Rain provides an answer. The three men start off comfortable enough, mooring their boat in a quiet nook, pitching the tent, cooking supper and smoking their pipes, but when the weather turns, pitching the tent over the skiff is such a struggle they opt for a hotel:

> The canvas wanted more putting up than I think any of us had bargained for. It looked so simple in the abstract. You took five iron arches, like gigantic croquet hoops, and fitted them up over the boat, and then stretched the canvas over them, and fastened it down: it would take ten minutes, we thought . . . You would not imagine this to be dangerous work; but, looking back now, the wonder is to me that any of us are alive to tell the tale.

The more experienced members of the Camping Club were men and women possessed of the practical skills to improve, with each trip, the efficacy of tent and kit. Members of the lower middle class with an industrial background, they were able to turn their ideas and designs into manufactured products. The Camping Club created a brand, Camtors, to market their products to members. Some of the camping gear had already been developed by the elite band of mountaineers known as the Alpine Club, men such as Francis Tuckett, who tested a prototype of the sleeping bag, and Edward Whymper, who gave his name to the mountaineering Whymper tent. The adventures of the Alpine Club and Edward Whymper pre-date Thomas Holding's camping movement by three decades. If camping was a suitably sedate nature pursuit for the liverish Edwardian, mountaineering was the exemplar of blithe, forceful and harsh Victorian masculinity.

The vigour of the Victorian camp drives *The Art of Travel* by Francis Galton, first published in 1855, a compendium of ruthless practical knowledge gathered from explorers, emigrants, missionaries and soldiers – people for whom camping was part of their profession. Galton was tall, slim and neatly dressed, a distinguished figure with a forehead that was likened to the dome of St Paul's Cathedral. His family were highly successful Quaker gun-manufacturers, and the death of his father gave Galton independent means. He quit doctoring. After consulting with the Royal Geographical Society, he embarked upon a two-year exploration of South Africa, his only motives being a love of adventure, discovery and shooting.

Galton's *The Art of Travel* begins by reassuring young men afraid of travel and camping that 'Savages rarely murder newcomers,' and continues on in that militaristic vein. There is a chapter on ammunition and what are termed 'hostilities'. On the activity of bivouacking – derived from the Swiss German word *beiwacht*, *bei* meaning 'by' and *wacht* 'watch', that is, to sleep outdoors in a rough sack or blanket like a watchman – he quotes Napoleon: the

French general preferred his men to bivouac because they slept with their feet to the fire, and the condition of the men's feet was crucial to the success of a campaign. Also he felt that the men's senses were keener when bivouacking, and not dulled by the false security of a tent's walls. As Galton notes, if there is danger, a bivouacking man will run into the dark like an animal rather than cluster around the tent's unjustified promise of protection.

What other camping advice does Galton offer? Well, he reminds us that when firewood is scarce, we can burn bones, like the troops during the Russian campaign in 1829 who ransacked cemeteries for fuel. On a lighter note, he recommends in a steady downfall of rain lighting a match for a pipe under your horse's belly.

Like Holding, he too offers counsel on the matter of women in camp, specifically the usefulness of the wives of natives. After an unsuccessful all-male camp, a chief advised him that not taking women was the cause of all their trouble:

> Women were made for labour: one of them can carry or haul as much as two men can do. They also pitch our tents, make and mend our clothing, keep us warm at night; and in fact there is no such thing as travelling any considerable distance, or for any length of time, in this country without their assistance … Women, though they do everything, are maintained at a trifling expense: for, as they always stand cook, the very licking of their fingers, in scarce times, is sufficient for their subsistence.

Galton's discussion of how to pitch a tent in the desert is instructive: bags of sand must be tethered to the end of guy ropes and then buried to a depth of a foot, thereby taking the strain of up to fifty pounds in weight. The landscape through which he camped was dangerous, and the appeal of the book to his contemporary readership lay in his heroics in the face of the inhospitable environment, people and wild beasts. The frontispiece is of a saddled horse immersed in a lake with our hero the adventurer, in top hat, coat and bandolier, clinging to its tail. Galton plays up to the myth of the rugged explorer, bivouacking under the stars. With Victorian machismo, he asserts that all a camper really needs is raw meat and a fur bag, and in this regard his modern equivalent is someone like Bear Grylls, the adventurer and television presenter.

The Art of Travel would go through nine editions in Galton's lifetime and it is a bracing, brutal read (it includes sections such as 'Proceedings in Case of Death', and under 'Seizing Food' Galton writes, 'On arriving at an encampment, the natives commonly run away in fright. If you are hungry, or in serious need of anything that they have, go boldly into their huts, take just what you want, and leave fully adequate payment. It is absurd to be over-scrupulous in these cases').

The violent camping practices of Victorian expeditions subside into the bucolic riverside camping of Edwardian England. Thomas Hiram Holding strips the armed expedition down into three cycle or canoe campers. In place of the life-threatening colonial adventure, there is canoeing in the Highlands and across Ireland, and cycling through Sussex, and this is enough for Holding's intended audience of city clerks. From the perspective of the solitary urban gentleman, camping had many virtues, which Holding lists:

- It teaches him no small measure of self-reliance.
- It gives him a new incentive to independence.
- It opens to him the possibility of personal resource.
- It teaches him patience when circumstances are adverse.
- It opens to him a new pleasure. It gives him greater freedom.
- It affords rest of mind.
- It is recreative.
- Repeated in another form, it is re-creating.
- It keeps old men young.
- It gives younger people experience that they would not have.

- It makes men more tolerant of the domestic life.
- [. . .]
- It teaches him patience and tolerance with other people.
- It takes him away from the toils of business.
- It opens to a man new society.
- [. . .]
- It revives his taste and love of the country.
- [. . .]
- It enables a man to get away from his family; or his family to get away from him for a spell.
- It allows a man to introduce his family to a new, and rough, and innocent pleasure.
- It produces in him a new individualism – for the better.
- It has a tendency to the extension of his geographical knowledge.
- It helps to harden his physical nature.
- It adds to his physical activity, and therefore tends to the lengthening of his life.
- It is an educational force, which would take a chapter to describe.

Over a hundred years later, Holding's list remains relevant. Campsites may be more proscribed than in Holding's time, and tents may benefit from cutting-edge technology and design, but the rudiments of the experience are unchanged. People continue to camp in a variety of ways and places, animated by much the same concerns as those that were prevalent in the Edwardian era. To Holding's list of the virtues of camping, we may add a few contemporary additions:

Why camp?

- It provides relief from the screens that surround us.
- Gaze into the fire. It will change you.

- It comes with low expectations. Anything above survival is a bonus.
- It is a negotiation between yourself and the environment. You can neither perfect nor control it.
- It gets your children out of the house and into nature. Nature is where children learn to take risks and where those risks have consequences.
- It puts you in a place where preparation is more important to well-being than money.
- It encourages you to discover the land and its moods.
- It teaches you how to train and use fire, and so control the element required for survival.
- It forces you to face your enemies: the rain, the mud, and the cold, cold ground.
- It helps you to realize you are neither helpless nor in command.
- It punishes greed.
- It confronts you with waste.
- It takes you out of domestic comfort.
- It opens you to a life with less stuff.

A list of reasons why not to camp is equally easy to draw up:

Really, why camp?

- Waking up in a small tent on a hot day is like waking up in a plastic bag.
- Most campsites are like suburbs, with neatly defined pitches, terrible bars, extortionate shops and fellow campers who are over-concerned with the condition of the toilets.
- Other people's faces first thing in the morning.
- Other people's feet.
- The first time a toddler runs through your tent wearing a pair of muddy wellies.

- Fires burn. Trees graze. Insects bite. If man had been made to camp, he would be born with an unfeeling hide.
- You need the toilet at three in the morning. It is cold out there. You lie still for an indeterminate time, stubbornly willing yourself back to sleep regardless of the pressure of your bladder. It is no use. You must face the night.
- The simplest of tasks becomes painfully complicated and protracted.
- Packing and pitching takes up most of a day; striking camp and unpacking takes a day. When does the holiday begin?
- It sounds like a lot of hard work.
- Have you forgotten the misery of a wet week in Cornwall?
- It is perverse and puritanical to deny yourself the advantages of civilization, or to pretend you are somehow outside of it.
- It is an undignified pursuit for adults.
- Campsites have so many rules, there is no freedom.
- It is not an escape from your stuff. Merely the migration of your stuff.

But then, remember: it is the coexistence of positive and negative that makes the camping experience vivid and telling. Sometimes a photograph captures an expression that is both a smile and a grimace; from that expression, you cannot tell if the person is happy or sad. For me, camping is the smile that is also the grimace. Just as we develop a taste for the sour, so I have grown to appreciate experiences that exist in a superposition, that is, proceeding in some unknown state, perhaps towards happiness, perhaps not; experiences that come with as many reasons to do them as to not. Stumbling around the American wilderness, the humorist Charles Dudley Warner captured the contrary pleasures and pains of camping, the grimace that is also a smile; even after being lost and rained out, his fellow campers remained in high spirits: 'For this straggling and stumbling band the world is young again: it has come to the beginning of things; it has cut loose from tradition, and is free to make a home anywhere: the movement has all the promise of a revolution.'

For a wry overview of twenty-seven years of camping, from 1886 to 1913, across the so-called Golden Years of British society, an era whose fair spirits and light humour trickle like a sun-dappled brook towards the chasm of the Great War, we turn to *Tales of a Tent*, the illustrated diary of an annual camp between Lodore Falls and Catbells Fell, in Manesty Woods, south of Derwentwater in the Lake District. It was compiled by Herbert and Agnes Winifred Valentine, a trained artist and cousin to Laurence and A. E. Housman, and her pen sketches depict the camping ideals of the time: a man in short-sleeved shirt and hat, on his knees, stirring a pot outside a small tent pitched before a tree; in another drawing, the same man, still cooking, but now with his mate in the background bringing a pail of water to the fire. A raised spit of land juts out into the lake, with a wood at its back, recalling Horace Kephart's description of the perfect summer campsite: 'an open knoll, a low ridge, or better still, a bold rocky point jutting out into a river or a lake . . . The best site for a fixed camp is near a river or lake, or on a bold wooded islet, with a bathing beach, boating and fishing waters.' Having found such an idyll not too far from home in Workington, the Valentine party revisited the site every year.

On arrival, the Valentine camp balloted for the role of cooks and scullions, and their order of duty – with two or three being appointed for each day. The cook's working day was a hard one, beginning at seven in the morning and not resting until it was time to tumble into bed. There was the fire to attend to, the potatoes to peel, vegetables to prepare and meat to roast, not to mention the matter of pudding. These campers were not content with baked beans and sausages served in a can. Crates of food were stored in a pantry tent, and when dinner was served, the gentlemen dined at the edge of the lake in shirt and tie, seated around a table with a tablecloth. Afterwards, the appointed scullions set to washing and drying the dishes as 'since the dog died, we have had to do the washing up ourselves.' The camp captain enforced bedtimes, a duty jokingly carried out with a 'mell', which in Cumbrian dialect is a large sledgehammer.

Chores were a great novelty to the Edwardian gentleman. Bertram Smith, a pioneer of horse-drawn caravanning, was keen on the way his pursuit elevated and ennobled sordid domestic jobs:

> I have often told myself that it cannot really be any fun to peel potatoes, or it would have been discovered long ago. And yet as I sit on the door-mat by the side of the stream with a pointed knife and a bucket I am quite unconscious of any lack of interest in my work. On the contrary, as long as potatoes continue to show the magnificent variety in substance and contour that I have always found in them, this is an engrossing pursuit.

He even confesses that, after travelling so much and picking up supplies in strange towns, 'by degrees, I have lost all shame about shopping.'

Every August, the Valentine party camped in a marquee tent that stood about fourteen feet tall. Five jacketless chaps, in shirt-sleeves and without waistcoats, sporting high-waisted trousers and white pith helmets, worked at the tasks allotted to them by the camp captain: here a fellow hauls a gnarled branch, while his campmate hangs a shirt upon the washing line. One man prepares the fire, another trims the veg. Each maintains an abundant moustache.

For two weeks beside Derwentwater, the campers fished on the lake, from five in the morning to nightfall, and walked through the woods at dusk, watching the squirrels and birds at work. There were singsongs around the harmonium and fiddle, strong tobacco to smoke in long clay pipes, wrestling matches and model yachting. They serenaded women further along the lake and, after dinner, debated politics. At bedtime, the campers retired to their camp beds by the light of an oil lamp. If the camp captain permitted them idleness, then a chap might take to the hammock, or administer a shave. They wanted for nothing. Summoning one another to dinner by bugle, they shared an abiding good humour. I envy the Valentine camp their golden years. I envy their freedom to make whatever use of the Lake District they saw fit, boating and fishing with impunity, unconcerned by restrictions concerning fires and the collection of firewood. (The current campsite at Manesty Woods does not even permit tents, allowing only caravans.) And then I remember that the diary ends in 1913. Within a year, on 7 August 1914, Lord Kitchener launched a recruiting drive, and an average of 33,000 men enlisted every day. The Edwardian camping idyll became serried ranks of bell tents in Aldershot and Tipperary, then on to the fields of Mons and Marne and slaughter.

The Valentine camping diary makes me nostalgic for freedoms I have never enjoyed. How girdled our lives have become with unnecessary rules, even in the Lake District, once the closest the English landscape got to the untempered life of the American wilderness. I also yearn for their division of labour: when Cath and I camp, there is no allocation of domestic chores – both of us must work at all times, we do not have the luxury of servants or drivers. 'I have just visited an ideal family camp,' writes Holding, in an ironic recollection that fills me with longing. 'It is on an island in a river. There was the eating tent, the sleeping tent, the servants' tent, the cooking tent for wet weather, and the overboat tent. Here the family and their servants were spending a "savage" holiday.'

There is an alternative to the captain of the camp: the bohemian camper, a romantic ideal composed of a fusion between the American Indian and the European Gypsy. The Gypsy was a familiar figure in Britain, first appearing in English literature in Thomas More's sixteenth-century description of a Gypsy woman who practises palmistry. In legends and in literature, in the writing of William Wordsworth, Jane Austen and George Eliot, the Gypsy is sometimes the originator of nefarious plots, sometimes a symbol of a lost and natural way of life. In 'The Scholar-Gipsy', published in 1853, Matthew Arnold associated Gypsies with the resistance to the 'strange disease of modern life', a representative of a life before industry and enclosure. 'Gypsies are the Arabs of pastoral England, the Bedouins of our commons and woodlands,' noted Henry Crofton. Writers and artists like John Ruskin and William Morris cultivated a yearning for a lost rural England, and the end of the Victorian era saw the envisioning of many utopias and New Edens. Artists were particularly drawn to the Gypsy and the promise of a way of life free from salaried boredom. Augustus John and John Sampson travelled the Gypsy encampments outside Liverpool, entranced by the idea of an existence free from the restraints of civilization. A photograph of Augustus John, taken in 1909, shows him bearded and striking in calf-length boots beside a caravan, playing the role of a Romany Rye, an English gentleman who adopted the image of the Gypsy to make himself appear alluringly idle, vagabond and unknowable. A citizen of the Open Road.

Lady Arthur Grosvenor, sister-in-law of the Duke of Westminster, spent the summer season travelling around the country disguised as a Gypsy. She assumed the name of 'Sarah Lee' and sold baskets out of the back of her van. In 1907, the *New York Times* caught up with her van as it clip-clopped through Oxfordshire on the way to Ascot: 'She gets up at 5 o'clock every morning, cooks her own breakfast, and usually takes the road at 8 o'clock. She may possibly write a book on her experiences of gypsy life.' Noting the second caravan of supplies trailing Lady Arthur Grosvenor, the reporter anoints her as the originator of the society trend for travelling by caravan, known as 'land yachting'. That

Lady Arthur Grosvenor assumed a different identity when camping and caravanning reminds us of the legends of Gypsies kidnapping an English child and raising him or her as one of their own, a fantasy of another life that Lady Grosvenor lived out as 'Sarah Lee'.

The Gypsy was a known quantity. The American Indian was more exotic, stranger, and possessed more violence than the typically passive image of the Romany male. As a consequence, the American Indian inspired more radical criticisms of society than Lady Arthur Grosvenor's Antoinette-style games of let's pretend. The writing of Edward Carpenter, a gay anarchist, who set up home with a young working man called George Merrill, held the example of the Indian up against the sickness of society. The customs of the Iroquois Indians were rigid, absurd and cruel, but at least, within those limits, the members lived peacefully together. By contrast, contemporary England was sick. Civilization had corrupted the unity of man's nature, with property ownership being the source of most of those ills; a house divides man against himself, and as he works against his will to pay the mortgage, it cuts him off from nature with walls and windows, and turns him against his fellows with a rivalrous status display of the home. Carpenter also wrote lovingly of sex outdoors. Only in the presence of nature, he eulogized, under the burning sun or the high canopy of the stars and surrounded by the fragrant atmosphere, could the meaning of sexual embraces be fully understood.

His book *Civilization: Its Cause and Cure*, published in 1889, was influential in the back-to-the-land movement. It questioned progress, the Victorian assumption that 'a sufficiently long course of top hats and telephones will in the end bring us to this ideal condition.' This ideal condition being, in Carpenter's polemic, a class of landless aliens, and various forms of the dominance of one class over another. From a contemporary perspective, in the economic aftershock of the disastrous house-price cult of the first decade of the twenty-first century, Carpenter's attack on property ownership gets a sympathetic hearing. His questioning of progress and the value of the primitive informs much of what comes next in our story about camping. But his passion for an alternative way of life led to an unfortunate fashion statement. He took to making and wearing sandals. Worse, sandals with socks.

Sandals were synonymous with liberalism across the twentieth century and beyond. In *The Road to Wigan Pier* (1937), George Orwell satirized alternative types as 'a dreary tribe of high-minded women and sandal-wearers'. Douglas Adams put his do-gooding angels in Dr Scholl's sandals and white socks. The whiff of the sandal persists today with the Birkenstock-wearing organic camper (there are two pairs of Birkenstocks in our shoe cupboard, and if I ever want to reduce Cath to the screaming cringes, all I have to do is slip them over my stockinged feet and parade around the house). The dreaded combination of sandals and socks is not merely aesthetically vile; the sock and sandal combination is a philosophical cop-out, a liberal refusal to commit either to the shoe or to the exposed foot. It's only at the dead of night, when I wake and want to see the stars, and step out of the inner tent, still wearing my socks, that I seriously consider slipping a pair of sandals on. Although I know that my vice will pass unobserved, I cannot bring myself to transgress, and laboriously lace up my boots instead. Once or twice I have experimented with sandals and socks and felt the indecent tightening of the leather strip caused by the extra padding around the foot. The feel of it sets the teeth on edge, like chewing polyester.

Carpenter's sandals, inspired by the Kashmir Indian, liberated the foot so that it could lead society to freedom. The shoe, that leather coffin, was one of the confining forces of European civilization, along with property ownership, capitalism and policemen. ('Imagine the rage of any decent North American Indians,' whispered Carpenter, 'if they had been told they required policemen to keep them in order.')

To Carpenter, American Indian society represented relief from class conflict. Nor did the American Indian suffer the marked contrast between rich and poor that was so evident in Victorian London. Like the Gypsy, the Indian offered a romantic counterpoint to sick, civilized man, and the images of both peoples beat at the heart of camping's mythology, images of their lives not as they were lived but as they were imagined and adored by the haplessly civilized. The romantic ideal plays its part in a persistent theme: camping is the promise of a new beginning, a revival in nature through reconnection with the values of a lost age and people. Youth turned to face the campfires of the Indian. Rudyard Kipling's poem 'The Feet of the Young Men', written in 1897 and dedicated to W. Hallett-Phillips, an outdoorsman also known as 'Sitting Fox', anticipates the camping movements to come:

> Who hath smelt wood-smoke at twilight? Who hath heard the
>   birch-log burning?
> Who is quick to read the noises of the night?
> Let him follow with the others, for the Young Men's feet are turning
>   To the camps of proved desire and known delight!

3

The Call of the Campfire

The Cumbrian landscape, with its crags and divots, its crumbling overhangs, lumpy sods and ancient, gnarly trees, presents handholds for the imagination; at night's approach, the woods withdraw into suggestive silhouettes and a distant copse forms one giant tree. The stream runs faster at dusk, and the first bat of the evening could almost be a scrap of charred paper on the breeze.

There are campfires across the field of Bowkerstead Farm. Campfires are the reason why we are all pitched here. The campsite rings with Lancastrian accents; the people of Blackpool, Burnley, Blackburn and Bury, the hearty *B*s of the formerly industrial North-West, have come to take advantage of the licence to set a fire and sit around it. Overexcited dads burn up fuel with spectacular, if short-lived, blazes, then hunt around for more flammables, tearing up wooden crates and gazing longingly at fences. Boys, unaccustomed to fire, become giddy and act the ass. On my way to the toilet, I pass one weeping girl, her parents distraught, her cheek scalded by a leaping, seething marshmallow.

The farmer sells stubby cylinders of compressed woodchip for us to burn. In the stillness between the fells, the smoke of two dozen campfires comes together in one low, flat, grey cloud. Aside from marshmallows, no one is cooking on the fires. The campers have barbecues and gas-powered stoves for that. The campfires are a decorative novelty, or a beacon of bawdy profligacy.

I want to use my campfire. I want the campfire to be the engine of our camp, to be its vital heart. The children watch me work, their eyes full of intense fascination as I scrape out the fire pit and set a circle of stones around it. Stones prevent the fire from spreading overground, they retain and reflect the heat, and shield the blaze from the breeze; too much oxygen and the fuel will be consumed too quickly. I explain this to the children, enjoying a moment of fatherly instruction. Campfires are an inefficient way of using the energy contained within fuel as so much of that energy is expended upon warming the earth and more is cast away upon the stars.

My campfire begins as a pyramid of kindling sticks fixed around torn and loosely clenched strips of newspaper set upon the flat side of a single log. Lumps of woodchip are placed against the tinder and they smoke noisily together. Gently, on all fours, I lean in and blow a long kiss; the flickering, bickering spirits of the fire respond to my affections. Once all the wood is burning, I add some coals so the fire will burn evenly for longer, making it easier to cook upon. I set a grill upon some foraged bricks, brown a shoulder of lamb over the fire, then swaddle it in foil so that it cooks through. Cooking over a campfire makes me fidgety, checking both meat and fire regularly but not – and this is crucial – interfering with them, as every prod and poke dissipates heat.

When the lamb is cooked, I set it aside to rest, then spread the burning coals across the fire pit, preparing to grill some breads. I explain all this to the children. But they are not listening to me, they are listening to the fire.

'We are the cooking apes, the creatures of the flame,' writes Richard Wrangham in *Catching Fire: How Cooking Made Us Human*. Wrangham suggests our evolutionary leap required the energy surplus provided by cooked food. He cites numerous cases of people who have, throughout history, tried to live solely on raw food and failed. Our bodies have evolved to require hot dinners. Cooking fires burn at the heart of humanity.

How ancient is our bond with the campfire? Clusters of burnt artefacts indicate campfires set somewhere between 690,000 and 790,000 years ago. Some archaeologists have proposed that man's mastery of fire is as old as one and a half million years, taking as their evidence burnt bones found at the Swartkrans site in South Africa. Even apes can make fires. The bonobo Kanzi was taught to communicate by pointing to symbols on a board; on a trip to the forest, Kanzi used these symbols to request twigs and marshmallows. He snapped the twigs into small pieces, lit them with matches and toasted the marshmallows – presumably without getting any stuck to his furry face.

Wrangham imagines how the campfire might have fostered tolerance: 'Among the eaters of cooked food who were attracted to a fireside meal, the calmer individuals would have more comfortably accepted others' presence and would have been less likely to irritate their companions.' Campfires meant that our ancestors no longer had to sleep alone in the trees for protection and that they could sleep together on the ground. Cooking around the campfire rewarded sociable individuals who 'would have been chased away less often, would have had more access to cooked food, and would have passed on more genes to succeeding generations than the wild-eyed intemperate bullies who disturbed the peace to the point that they were ostracized by a coalition of the calm'. I love that phrase 'the coalition of the calm'; it evokes the quiet wisdom of the group, the council of elders, the campers from whom we are descended.

Campfires are progressive, by which I mean they illuminate the needs of the majority rather than the greed of the few. To elaborate this grand claim, we must journey to the vast forests, lakes and high peaks north of New York State, to what was, at the beginning of the nineteenth century, an uncharted white space on the map of America, a terra incognita. An English map of 1761 designated it 'Dee Hunting Country', and early writers termed it 'the Mohegan Mountains' or 'the Black Mountains'. Mostly it was 'the Great Northern Wilderness' or simply 'the wilderness'. The first white man to see this wilderness was Samuel de Champlain in 1609, although he quickly fled after a skirmish with Iroquois Indians who claimed it as theirs.

In 1837, the geologist Ebenezer Emmons was dispatched by the New York State Legislature with the job of surveying the great wilderness of the north. His guide was John Cheney, a small, gentle man, an experienced hunter with a reverence for animal life. Together they ascended the mountain known as Tahawus, or Cloud Splitter. The distance between cloudscape and peak was not much more than that between the outstretched finger of God and the languid point of Man. Gazing down over the acres of virgin green forest, Cheney remarked, 'It makes a man feel what it is to have all creation placed beneath his feet.' In the High Peaks, untouched by the ravages of the logging industry, it seemed as if God's work was an ongoing process. The New World was Eden. The survey complete, Emmons suggested a name for this wilderness, the Adirondacks, after the Iroquois word for the tribes of the Algonquin.

It seems astonishing that the Adirondacks went unexplored and unnamed for so long by the early European settlers of America, although it's possible that they were simply too busy. Frontier life was punishing, and the wilderness was those areas most resistant to establishing a working community. The French historian De Tocqueville notes, in the second volume of *Democracy in America*, published in 1840, how late America was in adopting the romantic appreciation of nature that was rife in Europe:

> In Europe people talk a great deal of the wilds of America, but the Americans themselves never think about them; they are insensible to the wonders of inanimate nature and they may be said not to perceive the mighty forests that surround them till they fall beneath the hatchet. Their eyes are fixed upon another sight: the American people views its own march across these wilds, draining swamps, turning the course of rivers, and subduing nature.

De Tocqueville describes a poetryless frontier people, focused on expanding their dominion and quivering with what the historian Roderick Nash identifies as 'wilderness hatred'. Nature's bounty had neither limits nor rights, and existed solely as a resource to be bested and exploited.

But a change in attitude was already occurring among poets, intellectuals and artists. In 1836, Ralph Waldo Emerson's essay 'Nature' inaugurated the philosophical and literary movement of transcendentalism, which was to profoundly alter the American relationship with the wilderness. Nature would represent to America what history was to Europe: nobility. Across the landscape, a series of campfires was lit, each one a beacon towards a progressive American future. Unfortunately the first campfire of our story, set so carelessly by Emerson's friend Henry David Thoreau, spread to the surrounding bush and destroyed 300 acres of prime timber with a value of over 2,000 dollars. Despite this carelessness, Thoreau was considered sufficiently responsible to teach boys how to camp and how to scale the nearby peak of Wachusett. Thoreau's walk to Wachusett was the subject of one of his early essays, an account of a camping trip with his companion, Richard Fuller. In 'A Walk to Wachusett', the two men pitch their tent upon the summit, 1,000 feet above the village of Princeton. In the tent they read Virgil and Wordsworth, one an ancient poet, the other a romantic idealist of the Lake District, and wonder if their campsite will be as celebrated in poetry as Helvellyn or Parnassus. After their reading, the men forage for blueberries and eat them with milk. The song of the wood-thrush thrills the length of the ridge. Night falls. The moon is almost full. It shines brightly through the thin wall of the tent. The essay closes with a call to bring something back from a night on the mountains, insights that will elevate life on the plains; the idea of camping as philosophical retreat.

In 1845, Thoreau began to write *Walden*, an account of his time spent living alone, self-sufficiently and close to nature, in a cabin beside a pond. For two years and two months he dwelt apart from the nearby town of Concord. 'The mass of men lead lives of quiet desperation,' he decided, a scathing remark that reminds me of the faces of fathers in British sitcoms, the stifled longing and weary cynicism of Geoffrey Palmer in *Butterflies* or the exhausted liberalism of Hugh Dennis in *Outnumbered*; that is to say, Thoreau's diagnosis of the personal experience of the mass, of what your face looks like under capitalism, remains as true now as it was then: the marketplace, he felt, left man with no time to be anything but a machine.

Walden explores the moral potential of time spent alone in the wilderness; it builds into a rousing call to turn away from the imperatives of the mass, and obey the beat within, the often-quoted different drum. To hear that inner rhythm requires silence. In the American imagination, the journey into the wild, the camp, is a way to find that silence. It is an escape from oppression, obligation and the law in search of absolute freedom.

Thoreau writes of the restorative act of gazing into fire, how it purifies thought of the 'dross and earthiness which . . . have accumulated during the day'. In our homes, the television has replaced the hearth as the illumination into which we gaze. If the campfire and the TV both hypnotize the viewer and set him upon a thoughtless drift, the screen also cajoles, berates and disturbs; instead of purging oneself of the dross of the day, further dross is taken on. The screen opens on to a symbolic digital realm of layered windows and blinking cursors, cheerful icons and remorseless distraction, various nothings in various nowheres. Campfires can burn all that away.

Thoreau did not attend the 'Philosophers' Camp' of 1858, a distinguished party of ten men and their guides who ventured out into the Adirondacks, but Emerson did, along with the poet and editor of the *Atlantic Monthly*, James Russell Lowell, and the world-renowned scientist Louis Agassiz. The camp is detailed in the autobiography of journalist and artist William James Stillman, who was, of all the gentlemen, the most experienced in the ways of the wilderness. He visited it often to paint and seek out inspiration, impelled by a hope for 'new subjects for art, spiritual freedom, and a closer contact with the spiritual world, something beyond the material existence'. Stillman spent months in the wilderness, generally alone. In the silence, his imagination overheated. The mind is inclined to hear voices and see faces, to put a face on the moon and fill the night with hallucinations of humanity. The campfire exacerbates this tendency. Gaze through the flames and into the heart of the blaze, where the wood pulsates and seethes with transformation, and then suddenly look up into the surrounding trees:

> Over and over again, as I sat alone by my camp-fire at night, dreaming awake, I have heard a voice from across the lake calling me to come over and fetch it, and one night I rowed my boat in the darkness more than a mile, to find no one. Watching for deer from a treetop one day, in broad sunlight, and looking over a mountain range, along the crest of which were pointed firs and long level ridges of rock in irregular alternation, the eerie feeling suddenly came over me, and the mountain-top seemed a city with

spires and walls, and I heard bands of music, and then hunting-horns coming down with the wind, and there was a perfect illusion of the sound of a hunting party hurrying down into the valley, which gave me a positive panic, as if I were being pursued and must run.

Civilized man went mad if he stayed too long in the wild, or his intellect regressed to that of a dog. Stillman knew backwoods families, how they degenerated under the influence of the forest and the drink. The duration of a camping trip was sufficient to partake of the spiritual uplift. Any longer, and the struggle to survive would banish all higher contemplation. For the Philosophers' Camp, Stillman arranged for the transport of a company of distinguished men deep into his beloved wilderness. In place of the phantom voices of solitude, the discourse of the Enlightenment ranged across the campfire. Men of science and men of art hunted and fished together; removed from the distractions of town, they hoped that the particular conditions of a camp, its informalities and harsh practicalities, would inspire new ideas.

Stillman's painting *The Philosophers' Camp in the Adirondacks* captures a typical morning scene. Set in a sun-dappled forest, with the philosophers in the middle distance, each no more than three or four inches high, the painting emphasizes the diminished proportion of man to the surrounding great trees, particularly a striking maple that bisects the painting and for which the poet James Russell Lowell named the site 'Camp Maple'. Most of the men are observing rifle practice, while a few are grouped around the scientists Agassiz and Jeffries Wyman as they dissect and discourse on the anatomy of a fish. (On this trip, Agassiz discovered a new type of freshwater sponge; Wyman was a correspondent of Charles Darwin and supported his theory of evolution.) In the centre of the scene, singular and between the two groups, there is the poet Emerson.

In his journals, Emerson describes the campsite: 'Follansbee's

Pond. It should be called Stillman's henceforward, from the good camp which this gallant artist has built, and the good party he has led and planted here for the present at the bottom of the little bay which lies near the head of the lake.' There were no settlers within twelve miles of the camp, and Emerson notes, with some approval, that midges and mosquitoes protected the forest against tourism. The men constructed a shack with three walls of freshly peeled spruce bark, open to the east and the lake and supported by two large trees, with a fireplace and a bed made from layers of spruce and fir branches covered with fragrant cedar.

One evening, Stillman was in conversation with the poet Lowell, relating the hallucinatory experiences he had undergone in the woods, the voices and the strange music. Knocking the ash from his pipe, Lowell said that while he believed in the kind of spiritual world that Stillman described, it was purely subjective. These words resonated powerfully with the artist, and he was still shaking with exultation when the men took a boat out upon the lake at sunset. The mirrored surface of the water reflected the surrounding pines and ridges, an alternative realm. With the sun's decline, shadow took hold of the surroundings, darkening the clustered pine and encroaching upon the mountainside until only its peak snagged the last of the light. The shadow fell within Stillman also. Floating on the lake, in silence, the shadow within and without, he felt that he had become part of the landscape. He sensed a spiritual being hovering beside him, and heard it speak. Then, a gunshot was fired, the summons to return for dinner. Afterwards, the men slept side by side upon their bed of balsam and cedar boughs with their feet to the fire. Stillman remained awake, gazing out at the stars, which winked at him like fellow conspirators. Eventually he fell asleep but it was a peculiar sleep for, when he awoke, he did so with the sense that he had passed the night in conversation.

The following evening, when the others went out to fool around upon the lake, he sat by the campfire and resumed his conversation with the imaginary interlocutor, his daemon. They argued about the difference between dream and reality, the subjective and the objective, and the nature of spirit; imagine that there is a river of universal spirit, counselled the daemon, and your personality is an effect produced by immobility within that river, the same way a rock produces ripples in the water that runs around it. In a parallel to Christ's temptation by the Devil in the wilderness, the daemon refuted the orthodox view of God. Instead of an omnipresent Creator, the voice suggested something more like a Universal Law. When the daemon tired, Stillman asked the guides to turn the warm glow of the campfire into a blaze that scared the resting birds from the trees; in that reassuring heat, he fell soundly asleep.

This encounter is described in Stillman's essay for the *Atlantic Monthly*, 'The Subjective of It', a vivid and disturbing account of a spiritual experience and testament to the insight gained on the cusp of sleep beside a blazing campfire. The visionary potential of camping comes from being removed from home and placed all day and night outdoors until the self and the surrounding landscape seep into one another. The campfire seethes with knowledge and the promise of transformation, not merely a personal transformation, but also the discovery of ideas that could change society.

The Philosophers' Camp lasted a month. Not all the men stayed the distance. Judge Ebenezer Rockwood Hoar left early. In a letter to his wife, he wrote, 'I came in from the lakes and mountains yesterday – considerably browner and wiser than I went. Neither Mr Emerson nor I have shot the other, and Mr Emerson has passed for a very creditable woodsman.' He detailed the camp routine: the day commenced with a swim in the lake, with breakfast served at eight and dinner at six. The campfire kept off the mosquitoes and midges, and he observed, wryly, the effect of camping upon their respectable dress: 'Our party when assembled in costume were a remarkable-looking set, considering who

they were, and I think any one of them would have been con-
victed of piracy on very slight evidence, especially Mr Emerson.'

The artist and organizer Stillman felt the camp was a great success, and that it had created a unique bond among the participants:

> In such a great solitude, stripped of the social conventions and
> seeing men as they are, mind seems open to mind as it is quite
> impossible for it to be in society, even the most informal. Agassiz
> remarked, one day, when a little personal question had shown the
> limitations of character of one of the company, that he had always
> found in his Alpine experiences, when the company were living
> on terms of compulsory intimacy, that men found each other out
> quickly. And so we found it in the Adirondacks: disguises were
> soon dropped, and one saw the real characters of his comrades as
> it was impossible to see them in society. Conventions faded out,
> masks became transparent, and for good or for ill the man stood
> naked before the questioning eye – pure personality. I think I gath-
> ered more insight into the character of my companions in our
> greener Arden, in the two or three weeks' meetings of the club,
> than all our lives in the city could have given me.

Emerson's poem 'The Adirondacs', dedicated to his fellow travellers of August 1858, is a descriptive account of their camp life:

> We cut young trees to make our poles and thwarts,
> Barked the white spruce to weatherfend the roof,
> Then struck a light and kindled the camp-fire.

The poem includes his admiration of their ten guides, 'Sound,
ruddy men, frolic and innocent', but it does not throw its lot in
with the wilderness. This was a camping trip, by definition a hiatus
from everyday life. 'We flee away from cities, but we bring/ The
best of cities with us.' The wilderness is not superior to civilization.

> We praise the guide, we praise the forest life:
> But will we sacrifice our dear-bought lore
> Of books and arts and trained experiment,
> Or count the Sioux a match for Agassiz?
> O no, not we!

Camping revealed these great men to one another, it stripped away the pretence of town and city life to expose the essential qualities of its participants. The light of the campfire flickered over the true faces of all who huddled around it. But they could not stay, nor did they wish to. Progress demanded their return. Camping is temporary, and by its temporariness there is a drift to and from nature, between past and present. There can be no lasting return to lost ways of life. Camping promises nothing permanent. It is a way of trafficking between what was and what could yet be.

After the end of the Civil War, an economic boom opened up the Adirondacks with improved rail transport links. The tourists followed, diverted from their customary trips to the Catskills or the White Mountains. Previously the preserve of hunters and romantics, such a forbidding wilderness became associated with the idea of holidaying by a travel book, *Adventures in the Wilderness; or, Camp-life in the Adirondacks* by William H. H. Murray, published in 1869. William Murray was an energetic man and a powerful preacher, known for hunting for two days without sleep then returning to his congregation to deliver stirring oratory. Born in Guildford, Connecticut, in 1840 to a poor family, he supported himself through manual labour then attended Yale. After graduating he became a pastor and submitted accounts of his time camping in the Adirondacks to a local Connecticut paper. These were collected into his *Adventures*, published on April Fool's Day, which quickly went through ten printings before the end of the summer. The British Library holds a special tourist's edition that includes train timetables, notes on the character and trustworthiness of the local guides, and instructions on the gear and outfit required for the trip. Among the practicalities lie Murray's alluring descriptions of God's own country: 'From the summit of a mountain, I counted, as seen by my naked eye, forty-four lakes gleaming amid the depths of the wilderness like gems of purest ray amid the folds of emerald-colored velvet.' Wendell Phillips described it as a book that 'kindled a thousand campfires and taught a thousand pens how to write of nature'.

Murray attributes miraculous healing properties to the Adirondacks. He cites the case of a young man, a city dweller and consumptive, who, on the first of June, was carried in the arms of his guide into the forest, yet by the second week of November, 'he came out bronzed as an Indian, and as hearty. In five months he had gained sixty-five pounds of flesh, and flesh too "well packed on" as they say in the woods. The wilderness received him almost a corpse. It returned him to his home and the world as happy and healthy a man as ever bivouacked under its pines.' The Adirondacks were a retreat for city man suffering from consumption, the disease of Old Europe, and all he had to do was camp out and imbibe the healing vapours of forest, mountain, river and lake to return to town strengthened by an encounter that was considered to be truly American. Women would thrive too, argued Murray; whether they were delicate ladies or fragile schoolgirls, he guaranteed that they would gain a pound in weight a day during their trip. The hospitality of the Adirondacks to ladies and consumptives derived from its many rivers, which were easily traversed with the help of a guide and his canoe: 'It is the laziest of all imaginable places, if you incline to indolence. Tramping is unknown in this region. Wherever you wish to go your guide paddles you.'

Unfortunately, Murray's readers believed him. In the dour and rainy summer of 1869, a few thousand tourists arrived to find an area ill-equipped to accommodate them and too few guides to show them to the campfires they longed for. The tourists reacted with fury to the harshness of the environment, to the blackfly and mosquito and the long cart rides over tracks. For their stupidity, they became known as 'Murray's Fools'. Nevertheless, it was inevitable that the Adirondacks' proximity to New York and Boston would lead to its development by the tourist industry, and further travel books by its intrepid explorers.

One of the most influential guides to the Adirondacks was George W. Sears, better known by his assumed Indian name of Nessmuk. A small man with weak lungs, his letters in *Forest and Stream* magazine were published across the 1880s, and attracted renown. They popularized travelling light in the Adirondacks, and he was the man who more than any other taught America how to camp, based on his simple edict 'We do not go to the green woods and crystal waters to rough it, we go to smooth it.'

In the era of William H. H. Murray, canoes were a hybrid of the Indian canoe and the English rowing boat, on average fifteen feet long, three feet wide, sharp at both ends, ten inches deep, and weighing sixty to ninety pounds: a heavy burden for a burly, wide-shouldered guide and far too large for a man as slight, weak-lunged and old as Nessmuk. It was Nessmuk's demand for a canoe that he could carry that made the American wilderness accessible to the middle-income camper in much the same way that Thomas Hiram Holding and his canoe and bicycle introduced the countryside camp to the Edwardian middle class. Nessmuk did not write for the sportsman socialites of Fifth Avenue. His audience were 'mechanics, artists, writers, merchants, clerks, business men – workers, so to speak – who sorely need and well deserve a season of rest and relaxation at least once a year'.

Nessmuk was a lean and startled hare of a man with brown eyes and a beard and moustache that seemed poorly affixed to his small head. Just over five foot and rarely weighing more than 110 pounds, he was born George W. Sears in Oxford Plains, Massachusetts, on

2 December 1821, the oldest of ten children. At birth, he weighed barely four pounds. Home, as recalled in his gloomy memoir *Forest Runes*, was a 'gore', a triangular strip of land that was left out when the towns were surveyed. Near to this humble home, there was a reservation for the Nipmuck Indians (or Nepmug, as Nessmuk calls them) and an Indian camp on the shores of Nepmug Pond. Here a young man known as Injun Levi to the whites and Nessmuk to his tribe took to the five-year-old George Sears, and day after day carried him high on his shoulders around the lakes, teaching the young boy his woodcraft and love of the forest. Aged twelve, after four years of hard work at the local sawmill, Sears ran away to live with his grandmother in Cape Cod, beginning the restlessness that traces evocative routes across nineteenth-century America: Sears married, had three children and became a shoemaker like his father, but still he did not settle down. He would leave the family at home and walk from town to town, working as a cobbler for a few days before wandering on. With the outbreak of the Civil War, he enlisted in a regiment of lumberjacks, hunters and woodsman. Sears was thirty-nine when he went to fight and lasted only three months before being discharged after breaking his foot while drilling his company. His quest for fortune took him twice up the Amazon to cash in on the rubber boom, although his scheme was unsuccessful. He was a teacher in Ohio, a bullwhacker, a miner in Colorado, items editor of the *Tioga County Agitator*, a cowboy in Texas, and a camper and hunter in the Michigan wilderness; he estimated that, across his life, the aggregate of his time spent camping was twelve years. By the time *Forest and Stream* began to publish his letters, he was fifty-nine years old and unrepentant about the kind of man he was:

> To myself I sometimes appear as a wild Indian or an old Berserker, masquerading under the guise of a nineteenth-century American. When the strait jacket of civilization becomes too oppressive, I throw it off, betake myself to savagery, and there loaf and refresh

my soul . . . I love a horse, a gun, a dog, a trout and a pretty girl. I hate a pothunter, a trout-liar and a whiskey-guzzling sportsman. I smoke and take an occasional glass of wine and never lie about my hunting and fishing exploits more than the occasion seems to demand.

Suffering from pulmonary tuberculosis, he read William H. H. Murray's account of the health-giving properties of the Adirondacks, and the miracle cures it bestowed upon consumptives, and decided to try it for himself. Henry David Thoreau wrote that a person 'was rich in proportion to all the things he can afford to let alone', a high philosophical principle that finds succinct and practical expression in Nessmuk's advice when packing for a long solitary trip into the woods: 'Go light, the lighter the better.'

Nessmuk was one of many consumptives to seek a cure in the Adirondacks. Inspired by the success of Dr Brehmer's Davos centre in Switzerland, and having come to the forest himself to treat his own tuberculosis, Dr Edward Trudeau established a sanatorium beside Saranac Lake in 1884, with other sanatoria soon following. Prior to this, medical journals speculated on the benefits of camping for consumptives, some theories resting on the increase of appetite that came with life outdoors and how this alleviated the dyspeptic condition of consumptives. James Blake, writing in the *Pacific Medical and Surgical Journal* in 1860, insisted that the great outdoors was the only cure for the condition:

> . . . turn these dyspeptics out in the mountains, packing their blankets and their provisions on their backs, and in the course of a few days they will be able to digest, and not only to digest but to relish the fattest bacon that was ever made in Ohio: they will even be unwilling to lose the grease that drops from the luscious morsel as it broils before the campfire.

The Adirondacks treatment entailed fragrant woodland air, exercise, hearty meals of freshly killed venison and trout, and, most important to Nessmuk, the cheerful blaze of the campfire. 'An experience of fifty years convinces me that a large percentage of the benefit obtained by invalids from camp life is attributable to the open camp and well-managed camp-fire.' By open camp, he meant shelters made from felled trees and rain-proofed with bark and hemlock fronds, with their entrances facing the fire. He preferred earth warmed by a good campfire to a bed within a tent. In his handbook of anecdote and useful advice, *Woodcraft* (1884), he writes, 'A forest camp should always admit of a bright fire in front, with a lean-to or shed roof overhead, to reflect the fire heat on the bedding below. Any camp that falls short of this, lacks the requirements of warmth, brightness and healthfulness. This is why I discard all close, canvas tents.'

Nessmuk was a genius of the campfire. In *Woodcraft*, he dedicates an entire chapter to 'Campfires and Their Importance – The Wasteful Wrong Way They Are Usually Made, and the Right Way to Make Them'. A self-confessed slacker by temperament, he was always on the lookout for an easier way of doing something. On a trip with experienced hunters, whose campfire burned so hot that a man could barely light his pipe on it, nor sleep easily beside it without being roasted, he insisted that he could make a fire with half the fuel and less than half the labour of theirs, and which would maintain a steady heat through the night. The woodsmen mocked Nessmuk as a greenhorn and continued with their wasteful ways: 'Oh, you are a Boston boy. You are used to paying eight dollars a cord for wood. We have no call to save wood here. We can afford to burn it by the acre.' On arriving at another camp, the experienced woodsmen went off to dig up a large axe and some whisky, buried at the close of a previous trip, only to discover that a flood had swept away their marker. Without the axe, how could they make their campfire? Nessmuk promised that if he failed to make as good a fire as they had ever had, using only pocket axes, then they could tie him to a beech tree and leave him there.

He writes, 'We first felled a thrifty butternut tree ten inches in diameter, cut off three lengths at five feet each, and carried them to camp. These were the backlogs.' When green with sap, butternut wood burns slowly and lasts a long time. 'Two stout stakes were driven at the back of the fire, and the logs, on top of each other, were laid firmly against the stakes. The latter were slanted a little back, and the largest log placed at bottom, the smallest on top, to prevent tipping forward.' In front of these backlogs, a pyramid of bark stripped from a hemlock with a hand axe, knots and small logs provided a bright, high fire for when everyone was awake; with the onset of sleep, Nessmuk's method provided a slow-burning and steady fire fuelled by the 'night-wood', a dozen birch and ash poles from four to six inches across.

Nessmuk explained away his frugality as laziness, but there was a meaningful aspect to it, stemming from the Indian encounter of his boyhood. Indian campfires were small compared to the profligate bonfires of the settlers. A big fire demonstrated how ill at ease the white man was in the wilderness. Indian myths even castigated the spirits for burning too much wood: the Iroquois Indians had a legend about the aurora borealis, believing it to be the reflection of the light of the campfires in the Happy Hunting-Grounds. The legend chided the spirits for wastefulness in building so large a campfire and called upon them not to burn all the forests of the Great Spirits.

Throughout the pages of *Woodcraft*, Nessmuk counsels against waste. The forest was full of game, yet he followed Thoreau in advocating the moral rightness of killing only as much as you needed. As development of the Adirondacks advanced, he saw his old camping grounds destroyed and turned into tanneries, and regarded the desolation spread by industry as a violation of this principle: 'It is the same old story of grab and greed. Let us go on the "make" today, and "whack up" tomorrow; cheating

each other as villainously as we may, and posterity be damned.'
He had a low opinion of the rich and 'the weary devious roads by
which men attain to wealth and position'. Inspired by the American Indian, his camping methods were an early example of
environmental awareness, a consciousness that the abundance of
the New World was temporary, that man would quickly turn the
wilderness to timber and mill dams unless legal provision was
made to protect it.

Nessmuk died at home on 1 May 1890. In the last years of his
life, he could no longer go camping, so instead he and his family
camped in the yard. His obituary in *Forest and Stream* describes
the scene:

> The sad intelligence, which came to us last Saturday, announcing
> the death of 'Nessmuk', was not altogether unexpected. For sev-
> eral months past it had been known to his friends that Mr. Sears
> was in a very feeble condition . . . Last summer, too weak to make
> a camping excursion to the woods, yet powerless to withstand the
> longing for a taste of the old life, he pitched his tent beneath the
> hemlocks of his home yard and there with his grandson, 'played'
> at an outing. After the long and weary confinement of the winter
> just past, he craved outdoor life: and on the last day of April, sup-
> ported by loving arms, he went out for a while under the same
> trees. The next morning at 2 o'clock, May 1, he passed away. Last
> Saturday, in the spot he had selected beneath those same hem-
> locks, they laid him at rest.

Two years after Nessmuk died, the Adirondack Park was created,
conserving the area for future generations and legislating that it
remain 'Forever Wild'. Attitudes to the wilderness had shifted,
from the fear and loathing felt by the colonists to a zeal for nature.
The Adirondacks became the playground of the wealthy. Pluto-
crats built the so-called Great Camps, enormous mansions that
were their second homes. But what of the other natural wonders

of the continent, from the sequoia trees of the Yosemite Valley to the Grand Canyon? The question was: could the political will be found to check the onslaught of capitalism across the wild places of America? Could there be a progressive approach to the land?

A young Scotsman named John Muir liked to sleep under the great branches of the sequoia. He was born on 21 April 1838 in Dunbar, the third of eight children. As a boy, he spent Saturdays watching the North Sea thunder against the black headlands of East Lothian, then wandered along the seashore, inspecting the curious ways of eels and crabs. His family emigrated to Wisconsin in 1849. He studied at but never graduated from the University of Wisconsin, due to his inclination to study wide rather than deep, though he acquired sufficient knowledge of botany and geology to send him flying out into the meadows with wild enthusiasm. He walked a thousand miles from Indiana to Florida, and recounted the adventure in a notebook inscribed with his name and address: 'John Muir, Earth-planet, Universe.' Only a severe bout of malaria checked his plan to continue into the tropical jungles of South America, follow a tributary of the Amazon and then float downriver on a raft to the Atlantic. 'My plan was simply to push on in a general southward direction by the wildest, leafiest, and least trodden way I could find, promising the greatest extent of virgin forest.'

On these journeys, he did not exactly camp. He slept in the woods and open prairies without any blankets or supper and breakfast. His campfire was his kit and his companion; on a previous hike across the Canadian wilds, he heard wolves howl close by and had to be quick to stoke up the guttering flame. The thousand-mile trek enabled him to study the botanical riches of the less-travelled path. Footsore and exhausted, he was impelled onwards by a spiritual bond to the land, his strict religious upbringing giving way to an ecstasy in nature's abundance: 'How shall I ever tell of the miles and miles of beauty that have been flowing into me in such measure?' Muir was an avid reader of Emerson. Salvation could be found in nature. 'This is still the morning of Creation,' he cried, echoing John Cheney's amazement upon first gazing down upon the Great Northern Wilderness, the sense that, unlike in Europe, where Christianity was represented by ancient crumbling cathedrals, in this land, God was still new. America lived in Creation's unending dawn.

In-between his botanical treks, Muir worked in sawmills, and it was while he was working at a mill in Yosemite Valley, sawing fallen timber for cottages, that he met his hero Ralph Waldo Emerson, the great poet and veteran of the Philosophers' Camp. Emerson came to the Yosemite Valley on 5 May 1871, and at first Muir was too shy other than to loiter at the back of the meeting and did not approach his idol directly. Instead, he delivered an impassioned letter. Impressed, Emerson went out to the sawmill to meet his admirer. For the attention of his hero, Muir brought down many dried specimens of plants he had found on his travels and sketches of the mountain peaks and forest trees he had seen. Muir was thirty-three, Emerson was sixty-eight. Muir was the young exemplar of the old man's philosophy, living out the principles of the transcendentalists. Together they rode out to the great sequoia grove. Muir begged the poet to stay and camp with him, but the elderly distinguished gentleman was beyond camping, and he left Muir alone in the forest, to sleep in the crease of the great tree's bark. Muir was disappointed by his idol's failure to camp:

> But alas, it was too late, too near the sundown of his life. The shadows were growing long, and he leaned on his friends. His party, full of indoor philosophy, failed to see the natural beauty and fullness of promise of my wild plan, and laughed at it in good-natured ignorance, as if it were necessarily amusing to imagine that Boston people might be led to accept Sierra manifestations of God at the price of rough camping. Anyhow, they would have none of it, and held Mr. Emerson to the hotels and trails.

He met with Emerson for two more days, and continued to advocate that they camp together.

Camping was Muir's prayer to nature, and the centrepiece of that ceremony was the campfire: 'I pictured the big climate-changing, inspiring fire I would make, praised the beauty and fragrance of sequoia flame, told how the great trees would stand about us transfigured in the purple light, while the stars looked down between the great domes; ending by urging them to come on and make an immortal Emerson night of it.' But neither the poet nor his congregation could be persuaded to chance the cold night air. The transcendentalists had grown old and domesticated, 'as full of old-fashioned conformity as of bold intellectual independence'. They no longer heeded the call of the campfire, a call that Muir described eloquently in his journals:

> The glories of a mountain campfire are far greater than may be guessed . . . One can make a day of any size, and regulate the rising and setting of his own sun and the brightness of its shining. You gaze around at the illumined trees as if you never saw trees before. How marvelously the plumy fronds of the fir show out their beauty, as if the tree had ferns for branches. And each grass and daisy, now the attention is directed, may be seen for what it is, the shining corolla and panicles waving and nodding in sympathy with flashing flames . . . the bossy boles and branches ascend in fire to heaven, the light slowly gathered from the suns of centuries going again to the sun, in clear eddying sparks and flames of ever-changing motion, the very type of unweariable, elemental power . . . Sparks stream off like comets or in round starlike worlds from a sun. They fly into space in milky ways of lavishness, then fall in white flakes feathery and pure as snow.

But if Muir failed to persuade Emerson to share his campfire, he did not fail again when there was more than poetry and philosophy at stake. In 1903, John Muir camped for three days with

President Theodore Roosevelt, and around the campfire the two men discussed the preservation of the American wilderness.

Theodore Roosevelt was America's camping president. An asthmatic boy, he spent three summers at the Paul Smith resort in the Adirondacks, where he pursued his passion for birdspotting. Roosevelt had worked as a ranch hand, a cowboy, and, as colonel, led the 'Rough Rider' cavalry to decisive action in the Spanish-American War. When he was vice-president, he was camping in the woods below Mount Marcy (the renamed Mountain Tahawus, from whose peak Ebenezer Emmons and his guide John Cheney had gazed down upon the wilderness and declared it kin to the Creation) when the news came that President McKinley was dying. Across the rough roads, his guide Mike Cronin raced on steaming horses to fetch the new president from his camp in the woods.

In the spring of 1903, two years into his presidency, Roosevelt undertook camping trips with the two great naturalists of the time. With John Burroughs, he camped for two weeks in the north-east corner of Yellowstone Park. Before becoming president, Roosevelt had successfully lobbied to protect Yellowstone Park, for while it had been designated a national park in 1872, sufficient resources had not been allocated to protect it from commercial exploitation. In 1894, then-president Grover Cleveland signed a bill protecting the region. Roosevelt's return to Yellowstone Park with John Burroughs was an opportunity to bask in this victory. In his autobiography, he wrote that his intention was to show Burroughs the big game of the park. He went alone into the wilderness, tramping eighteen miles through rough country in search of a band of several hundred elk, which he wanted to see but not kill. The president elected not to fire a gun while camping in the park so that his trip did not become embroiled in a controversy about hunting, a sacrifice for a man who felt 'as if I ought to keep the camp in meat. I always have.' He merely ate lunch as close to the elk as he could get. He was disappointed that Burroughs was more interested in the bird life, and in the specimen of humanity represented by the president himself. In an essay for the *Atlantic*, Burroughs describes what it was like to sit around the campfire with Theodore Roosevelt:

> While in camp we always had a big fire at night in the open near the tents, and around this we sat upon logs or camp stools, and listened to the President's talk. What a stream of it he poured forth! and what a varied and picturesque stream – anecdote, history, science, politics, adventure, literature; bits of his experience as a ranchman, hunter, Rough Rider, legislator, Civil Service commissioner, police commissioner, governor, president, – the frankest confessions, the most telling criticisms, happy characterizations of prominent political leaders, or foreign rulers, or members of his own Cabinet; always surprising by his candor, astonishing by his memory, and diverting by his humor.

Next on Roosevelt's itinerary were the sequoias of California and John Muir. It was May 1903. John Muir was sixty-five years old and famous, leading hikes into the mountains with the Sierra Club that he had founded. In 1901, a collection of Muir's essays in the *Atlantic* advocating the expansion of national parks had been published, bringing him to the attention of the young president – Roosevelt was in his early forties upon taking office. By prior arrangement, the two men met at Raymond, Yosemite. Muir arrived wearing a new woollen suit purchased especially for the trip, and had a couple of packers and two mules to carry their bedding of army blankets and enough food for three days. The men separated themselves from the entourage and went off together on the Yosemite trails. In advance of the trip, John Muir had written in a letter that 'An influential man from Washington wants to make a trip into the Sierra with me, and I might be able to do some forest good in freely talking around the campfire.' The campfire and free speech go together because camping is a place where the hierarchies of normal life can be suspended. Muir spoke frankly to Roosevelt, in one instance confronting him about hunting with the remark, 'Mr President, when are you going to get over this infantile need to kill the animals?' Out in the woods, under the great sequoia trees, with one of his characteristic campfires blazing, Muir could be candid, and therefore at his most persuasive to a man like Roosevelt.

They camped at the Mariposa Grove under the Grizzly Giant, a sequoia with a branch six feet in diameter. Roosevelt describes the scene:

> The first night was clear, and we lay down in the darkening aisles of the great Sequoia grove. The majestic trunks, beautiful in color and in symmetry, rose round us like the pillars of a mightier cathedral than ever was conceived even by the fervor of the Middle Ages. Hermit thrushes sang beautifully in the evening, and again, with a burst of wonderful music, at dawn.

The men rode up to Glacier Point, the land five foot deep with snow and ice. Again they pitched camp, and Muir set the campfire, upon which he brewed some coffee and barbecued two fat steaks that he had packed for the occasion. It is hard to conceive of a more effective form of persuasion for the barrel-chested president than a hike, an astonishing vista and a brace of barbecued steaks. Around the campfire, the two men discussed the protection of the forests and Muir's glacial theory of the valley's creation. There was some difficulty in their campfire conversation as both men wanted to do the talking. Finally exhausted by the hike and the talk, the two men turned in under a pile of army blankets. The next day, they awoke covered in five inches of snow, the icicles jagged upon the branches of the silver firs. The president declared, 'This has been the grandest night of my life.' In a later letter, Muir confessed, 'Camping with the President was a memorable experience. I fairly fell in love with him.'

On the third day, the men descended into the valley, camping at the edge of a meadow. The tour revealed to Roosevelt the damage caused by the lumbering and tourism, and Muir spoke of the wanton forest destruction he had witnessed, and the frauds perpetrated against the government in the acquisition of the sequoia forests. Roosevelt asked John Muir what should be done. Muir insisted that the park be placed under federal control and its bounds expanded to Yosemite Valley. The president made no promises, but was keen that they should meet again. Their camping trip concluded, Roosevelt continued on to the more conventional politics of the West Coast, where in his address at Syracuse he recalled the camping trip:

> Lying out at night under those great sequoias was lying in a temple built by no hand of man, a temple grander than any human architect could by any possibility build, and I hope for the preservation of the groves of giant trees because it would be a shame to our civilization to let them disappear. They are monuments in themselves.

In the rhythm and grandeur of this speech, the wide-eyed exultation of John Muir's style can be discerned, a style that owed much to Thoreau – whose prose Muir studied assiduously – and to Emerson, whose poetry accompanied the Scotsman everywhere.

Theodore Roosevelt's term of office lasted until spring 1909, by which time more than 148,000,000 acres of forest reserves had been set aside, over 100,000,000 more than at the beginning of his presidency. He doubled the number of national parks and created sixteen national monuments, including the Grand Canyon. To better serve Yosemite, Muir's particular passion, Roosevelt signed the Yosemite Recession Bill in June 1906, which withdrew the Yosemite Valley Grant and the Mariposa Grove of Giant Sequoias from state control and placed them under federal protection, including them in Yosemite National Park. Roosevelt

remained close to John Muir, and after Muir's wife died, Roosevelt wrote to him and implored his friend to 'Get out among
the mountains and the trees, friend, as soon as you can. They will
do more for you than either man or woman could.'

Under the cover of dusk, somewhere in Derbyshire, two carloads
of dissolute, directionless twenty-somethings bump to a halt
down a track. I have no idea where we are, or what the plan is. I
get out to stretch my legs and discover a reservoir, midges and, at
the water's edge, the rusting skeleton of a burnt-out car. From
the boot, we remove what little gear we possess and carry it in
plastic bags as far as we can be bothered, and then pitch a wild
camp.

Wild camping is mostly forbidden in England and Wales.
Equally illicit is the campfire that we set and light. I am twenty-
five years old, perhaps younger. I know nothing about campfires
except that they are naughty. Sausages are cooked, and booze is
taken. So much booze that we take turns leaping barefoot over
the campfire, and run around laughing, and fall off logs. Para-
noid by habit and vice, I keep a watchful eye on a distant light,
convinced that its winks indicate that we are overlooked and will
soon be punished.

The next morning, I rise and set about exploring the wild.
Although I have neither woodcraft nor nature skills, and struggle
to identify any tree other than a pine, I have a yearning for sub-
limity. I seek a quiet forest grove where the light streaming
between coppiced beech is as sacred as the beams discoloured by
stained glass. My imagination howls at the indifferent wood,
romanticism that would only be diminished by factual knowledge of the trees and plants over which it swoons. Facts are an
impediment. Feeling is paramount.

On climbing a slope, I discover the limitations of feeling, especially when it comes to navigation, for our wild camp is, in fact,
beside the car park of a visitors' centre with gentlemen's and

ladies' toilets, a gift shop, bike hire and a coffee and ice-cream concession stand. To the surprise of the others, sat smoking roll-ups around a debris-strewn campfire, I return from my wild yomp with a tray of cappuccinos, accompanied by the ranger.

The ranger is unhappy about the campfire. He points to the forest in the distance.

'Do you see that forest?' he asks.

Yes, we could all see the forest.

'We've been working to create that forest for years. Do you know how much this campfire could have cost you?'

The gobby, insolent shrug of hungover young northerners.

He gestured again at the distant forest. 'Eleven million pounds.'

'Make it thirteen million,' came the baleful reply.

The ranger looks at me, expecting a more reasonable response; I am, after all, carrying cappuccinos. But what can I say? We are camped on the barren, treeless bank of a reservoir. Between the campfire and the forest there is in one direction a large car park and, in the other, millions of litres of water. I know it is against the rules to set the fire, but it would have taken a quite exceptional course of events for the campfire to spread.

Fifteen years later, on a trip south of Snowdonia to a small site called Gwalia Farm, I watch a gang of young men set their camp. They are no different than we were all those years ago in Derbyshire, compelled to come out into the country for some freedom and fire. Upon arriving, they discovered that the 35-hour-a-week shifts they put in consuming entertainment media had in no way equipped them for camp. They attempted to pitch their tent in a bog. Beside a wild pond surrounded by tall grass, they galumphed around for firewood, bringing back the greenest, dampest-looking branches; I suspect they tried to light the wood directly with a Zippo. A couple of hours later, they come to visit our camp, lured in by the smell of woodsmoke and the leg of lamb roasting over the campfire.

'I don't think we should have camped in a bog,' says one lad, shirtless and tattooed.

'The campfire's not . . .' His friend hesitates. 'It's not working.'

'You will need a campfire to keep the insects away,' Cath observes. 'Because you'll get a lot of midges and mosquitoes near that pond.'

Their disconsolate scratching is eloquent on this matter, even if they are not. Still, I understand how difficult it is to ask for help in setting a campfire (not that they asked directly for help; the lads presented their wounds like a dog with an injured paw, and hoped that I would infer what was required). It is embarrassing to admit that you cannot make fire, that the basic technology of humanity eludes you. I give them a couple of firelighters, some dry wood and a smouldering log. As they lope back to their sinking, midge-ridden camp, I briefly entertain the fantasy of a network of sites like Gwalia Farm spread across the country, rough and ready glades where young people can escape their bedrooms and the forecourts of late-night supermarkets and learn to build Indian shelters and set campfires.

The dream of setting aside wild places for the education of youth is not a new one; arguably its most influential proponent was an artist, writer and wolf hunter called Ernest Thompson Seton, a society figure in early twentieth-century New York whose woodcraft camps for local youth inspired Robert Baden-Powell's Boy Scout movement.

Ernest Thompson Seton's party trick was to light a campfire in the Indian way, without a match, using a bow-drill. In his novel *Two Little Savages*, he describes the process. Whittle a fifteen-inch pin of dry fir until it is three-quarters of an inch thick, pointed at both ends and roughly eight sided. To either end of this pin, tie a lace like a loose bowstring. Then trim a flat piece of balsam wood to about half an inch thick and cut a notch on the edge, and just above this notch, dig a little bowl. Into a half-inch-deep hole in the ground, lay a flat piece of pine punk (completely dry and rotten wood) and across this set the piece of balsam wood that is to act as the fire-board. The bottom point of the fir pin is placed in the pit of the fire-board. The top of the fir pin fits into a pebble with a socket hole in it (a hundred years later, foraging around woodcraft campsites in Sussex, we found one of these pebbles; it fitted snugly in the palm and had just the right-sized socket hole within it). Then, using a stick of about three feet in length, draw it back and forth across the bow, making the pin whirl in the fire-board. A brown powder will run out of the notch and on to the punk below. As the pit in the fire-board deepens, the powder darkens and forms a smoking heap atop the punk. The moment the powder smokes, fan it to stoke the heat. Remove the fire-board, and lift the punk from the pit, waving it in the air until the powder smoulders and bursts into flame. Add a tinder of cedar shavings and you have the beginnings of a campfire set in the ancient way.

The progressive nature of the campfire, its potential to civilize wayward souls and bring people together in a spirit of co-operation rather than competition, found its champion in Ernest Thompson Seton, another larger-than-life emigré from the old country and a crucial figure in our history of camping.

Seton largely devised the programme of the Scout movement. After dinner at the Waldorf Astoria, Baden-Powell declared Seton to be one of the real fathers of Scouting while he was 'only one of the uncles'. Long before the Scouts pitched up on Brownsea Island in Poole Harbour, Seton organized camps upon his own land for local and delinquent boys, and taught them to 'think Indian' in his programme of outdoor education called the Woodcraft Way. Only through camping and the campfire did Seton believe we could rediscover the association of the human spirit, our essential generosity to one another that was obscured by our day-to-day lives in the towns and cities. A dedicated observer of animals in the wild, and a highly successful nature artist and writer, he believed that competition, the so-called survival of the fittest, was less important than co-operation. The law of mutual aid as practised around the campfire was more important to our survival than the law of mutual struggle.

Seton was born Ernest Evan Thompson in South Shields, Durham, on 14 August 1860. His mother, Alice Thompson, named him for the romantic novel she was reading at the time, *Ernest Maltravers*, written by Edward Bulwer Lytton. The novel's hero is a 'wild, enthusiastic, odd being . . . bolder and madder than most . . . whatever was strange and eccentric had an irresistible charm for Ernest Maltravers.' The story of Ernest Thompson, and the Woodcraft Way that he founded, is also a bold and mad one, a trail that leads to the well-trodden path of the Scouting and Guide movement, then veers off in its own peculiar direction.

Ernest was one of eleven surviving sons. After a downturn in fortune, his father, Joseph Thompson, took the family to Canada in 1866, purchasing a hundred-acre tract of forest so that the family could build a new life. The Thompsons lasted four years as farmers before selling the land and moving to Toronto, where Joseph got work more suited to his temperament as an accountant. 'From 1871 to 1879, the Toronto marsh was my loved, ever-rewarding resort,' writes Ernest Thompson Seton. He also played in Don Valley, a landscape of wooded ravines and grassy meadows to the north of the city. He followed wild geese on their arrowed flight north, climbing through thick forest walls until he came to a dale bordered by hemlock, birch and pine. Here he built himself a secret cabin that he named Glenyan. The shanty was rudimentary, five feet high and six feet long with a roof of bark and twigs. Fashioning a bow and arrow, and a scalping knife from an old putty blade, he imagined himself a wild man, an Indian, and danced naked around the fire in the blazing sun.

Reality intruded when the shelter was taken over by three tramps. They snapped his home-made necklaces and used the shells as poker chips, burned his bow and arrow for fuel and despoiled the place. The shock to young Seton was terrible; his health suffered, and he was sent to a farm to recuperate. Later he was to use this period of life as the basis for *Two Little Savages*, a tale of outdoor adventure and adapted Indian woodcraft wisdom that owed its fictional form to the intervention of Rudyard Kipling; in 1898, Seton and Kipling, both known for their animal stories, met and Kipling advised Seton to turn a manual of woodcraft into a story, believing that would be more inspiring.

Two Little Savages reveals Seton's troubled relationship with his father, Joseph, whom he hated. The hero Yan's obsession with nature is opposed by his father. 'His father was in poor circumstances. He was an upright man of refined tastes, but indolent – a failure in business, easy with the world and stern with his family. He had never taken an interest in his son's wildwood pursuits; and when he got the idea that they might interfere with the boy's education, he forbade them altogether.'

Yan goes out into the woods and meets a stranger, a Scottish naturalist who teaches him the ways and names of the birds. 'Yan saw that [the man] had hair like his own – a coarse, palaeolithic mane, piled on his rugged brow, like a mass of seaweed lodged on some storm-beaten rock.' The rugged naturalist is an ideal father, a replacement for the poor, uptight man at home; not only can he teach Yan the ways of the woods, he is also Scottish, corresponding to the Thompson family claim upon the ancestral Scottish line of the Setons. Joseph Thompson believed that he was descended from George Seton, the fifth Earl of Winton, a seventeenth-century aristocrat who lived out his life in exile in Rome for his part in the Jacobite Rising of 1715, and for which treason he was stripped of his title. Although history states that George Seton died childless, it seems that he did have a son, Charles Seton, born in Northumberland. A casket of heirlooms documented by the contemporary descendants of Charles Seton affirms Joseph Thompson's lineage, and therefore the right of his son Ernest to take the Seton name.

In a later memoir, Ernest Thompson Seton would dismiss his father as one of the greatest scoundrels who ever lived, putting Joseph Thompson in a trinity of evil along with St Paul – blamed for devising the doctrine that condemned Seton's devout mother Alice to the rule of such a husband – and General Custer, condemned for his crimes against the Cheyenne and the Sioux. Joseph Thompson was 'a worthless loafer, a petty swindler, a wife-beater, and a child murderer', a verdict contested by Ernest's siblings. *Two Little Savages* is his quest to unparent himself, to become an Indian boy with a noble Scottish heritage.

After shaking off the influence of his father, he took a while to decide upon what he should call himself: Ernest Evan Thompson, Ernest Thompson-Seton, Ernest Seton-Thompson, Wolf Thompson. His second wife called him Chief, and to his woodcraft boys he was Black Wolf. The taking of a new name is a recurring motif in the woodcraft movement. It marks the transfer of allegiance from town life to the wild, and it emulates the American-Indian practice of naming; and perhaps it has its origin in one man's hatred for his father.

In 1879, at the age of eighteen, Seton arrived in London to study art. He rented a room near Regent's Park and lived a solitary, hungry but happy life, mainly due to his discovery of the British Museum library and its wealth of naturalist illustrations and observations. Too young to be admitted entry into the library, he petitioned the museum trustees, the Prince of Wales, the prime minister Disraeli and the Archbishop of Canterbury, and within a few days received a polite reply from each and a lifetime membership.

During this solitary period of his life, he practised various modes of unbeing: Zen meditation, vegetarianism and celibacy. Thus starved, Seton began to hear voices. The call of the wild. The backwoods of North America wanted him back. He obeyed and returned to Canada without completing his studies. When he arrived home, at the age of twenty-one, his loathed father presented him with a bill for 537 dollars and 50 cents, the total amount the Thompson family had spent upon his upbringing, including the doctor's bill for his birth.

Seton's most famous animal story is 'Lobo, the King of Currumpaw', included in his collection *Wild Animals I Have Known*, which sold several hundred thousand copies between its publication on 20 October 1898 and the author's death. 'Lobo, the King of Currumpaw' tells the true story of Seton's hunt for an old grey wolf and its pack. First published in *Scribner's Magazine* in November 1894, the tale was described by the ageing Leo Tolstoy as 'the best wolf story I have ever read'.

Seton's interest in wolves first took shape in 1892, when he returned to his art-school studies in Paris at the Académie Julian. Inspired by a story in the Paris newspapers of a woodsman who went missing while hunting wolves, Seton painted a gory panorama of a wolf gnawing on a man's remains as the other members of the pack stood sentry. Originally entitled *The Triumph of the Wolves* (and dreadfully retitled as *Awaited in Vain*), the magisterial canvas, four and a half feet high and seven feet wide, thrills at nature's revenge. The wolf strains to fit the head of a man between its jaws, its incisors skittering over the curve of the skull. The painting was rejected by the salon for anti-humanism, and Seton returned to Toronto and exhibited it first in his father's home and then at the back of a local jewellery store. The furore against the painting continued in Canada, where it was attacked for its blasphemy against the sanctity of man.

To escape the scandal, Seton accepted an assignment to exterminate wolves in New Mexico, and it was here he undertook the capture of Old Lobo in the valley of Currumpaw. His story relates the capture in detail. The wolves refused to touch poisoned meat, no matter how painstakingly baited. They killed sheep for sport but ate so many of the finest cattle that the bounty upon the head of Old Lobo was a thousand dollars. The old wolf evades traps and disdains all the trappers' cunning schemes as if they were the product of an inferior species.

Seton's style is the naturalistic observation of the wolf, rather than the broad anthropomorphism of *The Jungle Book* and its ilk. He was not always scrupulous with the facts, and the American naturalist and writer John Burroughs was to publish an excoriating essay on the confabulations of the nature writers, in which he cited numerous instances from Seton's work, including the supposed instance of a fox feeding her cubs poison to spare them captivity, and that same fox escaping from a pack of hounds by hitching a ride on the back of a fleeing sheep. Citing such anomalous behaviour, Burroughs's essay, published in the journal the *Atlantic*, archly suggested retitling Seton's book from *Wild Animals I Have Known* to *Animals I Alone Have Known*. Criticism of such storytelling excesses received congratulation from US president Theodore Roosevelt, who was particularly upset by the tendency of the nature writers to assert the truthfulness of their account in the opening lines. Only weeks after the accusing article appeared, Seton met with Burroughs at the annual literary dinner hosted by Andrew Carnegie. Accounts of the dinner weigh in Seton's favour, with Burroughs appearing both penitent and on the verge of retracting his accusation, at least as it concerned Seton. When it comes to the tale of Lobo, the essential facts are undisputed: above the fireplace in Seton's final home in New Mexico was hung the hide of the great Lobo along with a rusted wolf trap and the torn noose of Seton's lasso.

Come the onset of the twentieth century, the success of his nature stories and his investments meant that Seton was a rich man, with a fortune estimated at 200,000 dollars. His wife Grace Gallatin Seton, a feminist and suffragette, was also wealthy. They took an apartment on Fifth Avenue and he became a charter member of the Camp Fire Club, a society of businessmen and artists united by the conviction that animals had a right to life regardless of their usefulness to man. Seton's membership was an indication of his stature as an East Coast gentleman of renown, and he was an eccentric society figure into his old age (at the age of seventy-one, he responded to a barking dog by getting on all fours and leaping at the dog, seizing its throat between his jaws). The ethos of the Camp Fire Club anticipated the animal rights movements to come, although it is hard to imagine today's advocates for animal welfare marching around the ballroom of the Hotel Astor behind two whole roast pigs, as occurred at one annual meet.

On 12 June 1910 the Camp Fire Club met on Seton's estate, Wyndygoul, 150 acres of lake and splendid forest near Greenwich in Connecticut. Wyndygoul, named by Seton after an English country estate he believed his ancestors had owned, was a property patched together from a few farms. He bought the land cheap, and designed and dammed the marshes to create a lake that was a third of a mile long and contained fifteen islands. He named the lake Pipestave Pond and stocked it with trout. Into the surrounding plantings of birch and pine, he imported squirrels, otters, fox, waterfowl and skunks. At the entrance to the estate were two stone pillars upon which iron bulldogs stood guard, each marked with a baronial *S*. Wyndygoul was an ideal camp-site, and a testament to an era of high-society excess in which the successful New Yorker could imagine himself a lord. The estate was an artfully simulated wilderness:

> In a woodland of two hundred acres, the boundaries do not crowd or obtrude. There is room for the privacies and mysteries of the forest itself. The wild creatures who inhabit there, guarded but unspoiled by a protection which is not thrust upon their notice, find ample space to choose their own most fitting resorts, whether of deep swamp-thicket, or high, rocky brush-tangle, or overhanging bank by the brown water, or grassy glade sun-steeped at noon. There are seclusions within seclusions, so that the shy and various inhabitants of Wyndygoul are not forced into associations of other than their own choosing.

The meeting of the Camp Fire Club at Wyndygoul was fuelled by a ten-gallon keg of cider, and included various woodcraft tasks such as competitive fly-casting, a revolver match, a rifle contest and trap shooting. In the afternoon, there was a canoe race with portage and a campfire. The contestants had to carry their canoes 150 yards over land, then paddle across the lake before lighting a fire and boiling water. Each team was issued with an axe, a hunting knife, a tin pail and one match. Next came the flapjack campfire cook-off, in which the various lawyers, bankers and doctors who made up the 100-strong meet were given a log of firewood, a camp axe, a frying pan, a slice of pork, flour and baking powder, a fork, a spoon and a vial of maple syrup, and challenged to be the first to split wood, build a fire, mix a batter and make a flapjack. The flapjack cook-off took place beside a totem stone surrounded by buffalo skulls, at the foot of a sharp knoll overlooking the lake, Spy Hill, Seton's Indian camp for boys and a crucial site in the history of camping.

The story of how Ernest Thompson Seton founded the woodcraft movement begins with his renovation of Wyndygoul, and his fencing of the land. The fences annoyed local boys who had previously hunted and played on the farmland, and so they tore them down, shot Seton's animals and painted graffiti on his gateposts. He knew who the young vandals were, and instead of punishing them, he marched into their schoolhouse and invited the boys 'to come up to the Indian village on my place' and camp during the Easter break. The boys were to bring two blankets each. On Good Friday, April 1902, forty-two local boys attended the camp. After a swim and a meal, the boys gathered around the campfire to hear Seton sing the praises of the red men, the noble Indians who had been wiped out before their time. Seton was at the height of his fortune, a tall, handsome, robust man with a shock of long, heavy black hair. He began the council by lighting the campfire without the use of a match. The performance never failed to draw gasps from its audience. That weekend, boys donned feathered headdresses, took up bows and arrows, and went either bare-chested or wrapped in a blanket before a blazing campfire and against the backdrop of a tipi. Here was Seton's boyhood dream, his Glenyan, revived.

Seton recognized the campfire's power as a civilizing force. Instead of seeking punishment for the vandals of Wyndygoul, he trusted in the power of the group around the fire, bonded by ersatz American-Indian ritual and the experience of camping, to keep wayward instincts in check. Only Indian names were permitted at camp and, crucially, the boys would be their own authority. He insisted the boys elected chiefs and councillors from among their own number while he would act as their medicine man. Adults would offer guidance but would not be in charge, relinquishing control to the boys. The movement rejected formal religion and discipline; instead the gang instinct, 'the real religion of all boys between eight and eighteen', would be the governing force. 'Power and possibilities are found in the instinct of initiation,' wrote Seton, 'the habit of giving nicknames, the love of personal decoration ... the compulsion of atmosphere, the power of little ceremonies, the love of romance, the magic of our camp-fire.'

Seton's woodcraft programme combined aspects of various Indian ways of life: from Pacific coast cultures, he took totem poles; from the Iroquois he took tribal government; from the Plains peoples he appropriated the Omaha Tribal Prayer and the concept of coups, which were honours awarded to warriors for feats of bravery such as touching the dead body of an enemy. The Boy Scout badge is descended from the coup. The universal campfire Seton developed into the council fire. During the next five years, annual summer camps were held at Wyndygoul, the young campers becoming known as either 'Woodcraft Indians' or 'Seton's Indians' depending on the reporter. Through Seton's accounts of their exploits in the *Ladies' Home Journal*, the woodcraft movement spread across America, promoting the virtues of the outdoors as an improving force, its progress only impeded by the whiff of Seton's progressive ideals and his fetishization of the American Indian. Each year saw a new edition of the handbook *The Birch-bark Roll of the Woodcraft Indians, Containing Their Constitution, Laws, Games and Deeds*, which Seton wrote to guide the movement.

This was a time, noted Seton in his introduction to *The Birch-bark Roll*, when the whole nation was turning to the outdoor life, and the culmination of that outdoor life was camping. Seton noted that camping had become unpopular because it was associated with intrepid solitary adventures in the wilderness. This error, wrote Seton, had come about because camping as an art was not understood: 'It is a cheap and delightful way of living as well as a mental and physical savior of those strained and broken by the grind of an over-busy world.' He proscribed a cure of one month's camping a year in groups organized along tribal lines.

There are only ten laws in Seton's Woodcraft order. The first is 'Don't rebel'; the second is 'Don't kindle a wild fire.' These two laws add up to one principle: stick together around the campfire. (Law 5, 'Don't bring firearms of any kind into the camps of those under fourteen. Bows and arrows are enough for their needs,' is a wry reminder of the disparity between our confidence in children then, and our fear for them now, a disparity that grows almost alarming when you discover, on the official contemporary website of the American Boy Scouts, detailed instructions concerning 'risk management' and the accompanying encouragement to use camp stoves rather than campfires.)

Seton's art of camping included star-craft, sign language, recognizing animal tracks, map reading, and triangulation of one's position upon the earth. The boys were motivated by personal decoration for personal achievement, challenged by time and space rather than by their fellows, the aim being to raise the skills of the many rather than to make champions of the few. Broadly, Seton devised a programme to build character and manhood through intellectual, physical and spiritual means – at camp in Wyndygoul that ethos translated as 'something to think about in the woods, something to do in the woods, and something to enjoy in the woods'.

Seton was right. There was a cultural yearning for a boys' movement; but his Woodcraft Indians, with their tribal structure and lack of adult leadership, were too subversive for the mainstream. Seton's notions of communal living were inspired by the anarchist Peter Kropotkin, whom he met in Toronto, and the two men agreed upon the moral instruction that nature could provide for men. While capitalists cited 'survival of the fittest' to suggest that free markets emulated the bloody competition of nature, Kropotkin refused to accept that competition was the primary mechanism for the survival of species. On his travels through the wilderness of northern Manchuria, he closely observed the activities of the animals he encountered and concluded that, within a species, mutual aid was more important to survival than competition. 'Nature has . . . to be recognized as the first ethical teacher of man,' he wrote. The attitude of Indian mythology to animals, conferring great wisdom upon them, accorded with the beliefs of the Russian anarchist, and it was Seton who made that crucial synthesis. Not only did this advocacy of mutual aid undermine the propaganda of the nineteenth-century capitalists, it also led to pacifism, seeing the drive to war not as a born instinct but as a product of civilization, an unnatural act. Seton made anti-capitalist declarations such as 'Our system has broken down. Our civilization is a failure. Whenever pushed to its logical conclusion, it makes one millionaire and a million paupers. There is no complete happiness under its blight.' In 1905, sensing that the Woodcraft Indians and their subversive leader were not going to fit the bill for America, one of his colleagues in the Camp Fire Club, Daniel Beard, set up a youth movement called the Sons of Daniel Boone, taking as its model the American frontiersman rather than the contrary and problematic figure of the Indian. But events were already underway that would overwhelm the efforts of both men, thanks to the opportunism of the English war hero Robert Baden-Powell.

Baden-Powell's reputation as the founder of the Boy Scout movement and war hero of the siege of Mafeking has come under attack in a series of biographies and studies since his death. Michael Rosenthal in *The Character Factory* (1986) examines the origins of the Boy Scouts and how much Baden-Powell's supposed invention owed to the woodcraft camps at Wyndygoul. Baden-Powell's *Scouting for Boys* plagiarized Seton's *Birch-bark Roll*, removing the problematic figure of the Indian and replacing it with the militarism of the fading empire, with Christianity usurping Seton's nature-worshipping pantheism. Crucial aspects of the woodcraft programme, such as the awarding of coups for feats of strength or good character, were adapted into the Boy Scout badge system. Before he met Seton, Baden-Powell circulated a vague idea of adapting the scouting programme he had encountered in Mafeking for the benefit of Britain's boys. (Although he took credit for organizing the 'boy scouts' of Mafeking, according to *The Character Factory* these scouts already existed before his arrival, and were used as messengers by Baden-Powell's second-in-command, Lord Edward Cecil.) Through acquaintances, Seton and Baden-Powell were made aware of their mutual interest in establishing an outdoor group. Seton sent Baden-Powell a copy of his woodcraft handbook, *Birch-bark Roll*, and they met that same year, 1906, at the Savoy, as Seton was undertaking a lecture tour of Great Britain. During this lunch, Seton persuaded Baden-Powell that, instead of continuing to graft his Scouting programme on to the existing Boys' Brigade, he should establish a new youth organization based on woodcraft.

Baden-Powell's Scouting movement was an international overnight success. The first Scout camp took place at Brownsea Island in August 1907, a year after Seton and Baden-Powell met at the

Savoy. Of his influence upon the Scouts, Seton wrote, 'My ideas [were] taken, all my games appropriated, disguised with new names, the essentials of my plan utilized, and not a word of acknowledgement to me, or explanation why I should be left out of a movement that I began.' The handbook *Scouting for Boys* followed in 1908, and by 1910 there were 100,000 Boy Scouts in Britain.

Here our history of camping divides into two trails. We could follow Baden-Powell down the right-hand trail, in which camping harks back to its soldiering past, turning away from nature and dedicating itself to the furthering of God and nation. At the end of this trail we would encounter the American icon of the Eagle Scout, a rank attained by men such as Neil Armstrong, Steven Spielberg and Donald Rumsfeld, an honour that in the twenty-first century has been caught up in the partisanship of the American culture wars: in protest at President Clinton's sexual excesses, the Boy Scouts of America did away with the tradition of the president of the United States signing the Eagle Scout certificate; then, in 2000, the Supreme Court debated the legality of the movement's insistence on barring gays from leading Scout troops. The court upheld the right of the Boy Scouts of America to exclude homosexuals from positions of leadership.

Rather than embark upon that path, we will follow Seton, down the left-hand trail of the Woodcraft Way, where we will encounter the progressive movements of the twentieth century, from nudism to vegetarianism, from feminism to eco-awareness, pausing at the socialism of the campfire while out in the woods lurk crankier beasts, theosophy and the occult, and the terrible temptations of fascism. The fork in the trail is a choice between Ernest Thompson Seton or Robert Baden-Powell. 'My aim was to make a man,' said Seton; 'Baden-Powell's to make a soldier.' Seton was Chief Scout in America, a position he was relieved of with the Great War. His views were considered untenable for a nation gearing up for battle. But if his woodcraft ideas were considered too soft for boys, they were suitable for girls.

The Camp Fire Girls of America was a movement founded in 1910 by the educators and social reformers Luther and Charlotte Gulick (Luther Gulick was also involved in the invention of basketball, asking a young YMCA instructor to devise an indoor team sport). Their camp took the pseudo-Indian name of Wo-He-Lo, representing the central tents of Work, Health and Love. The girls made their own ceremonial dresses and bead headbands decorated with symbols they had chosen to represent their character. The central tenet of the Camp Fire Girls was service; 'The bearing and rearing of children has always been the first duty of most women,' wrote Luther Gulick, 'and that must always continue to be. This involves service, constant service, self-forgetfulness, and always service. I suggest that the fire be taken as a symbol of the girls' movement, the domestic fire – not the wild fire.'

Tasks for the Camp Fire Girls included the ability to make ten standard soups, recognize three types of baby cry and keep a daily account book. The programme may sound conservative but it was founded ten years before the ratification of the Nineteenth Amendment that gave American women the right to vote. Grace Gallatin Seton, first wife of Ernest, and Lisa Beard, the sister of Daniel Beard, promoted woodcraft in the Camp Fire Girls. Beside the wooded banks of Lake Sebago, the girls gave disciplined displays of rowing before leaping joyously backwards off their Indian canoes. They made their own jewellery and pottery, decorated oars with Indian art, learned to ride a horse and keep bees. They danced holding hands in a circle around the campfire, part ersatz-Indian ceremony and part half-remembered folk dances from Old Europe. They made pancakes and cooked stew over the campfire, then bivouacked down under the shelter of an overturned canoe. The Camp Fire Girls were, in the words of their matriarch Charlotte Gulick, 'hard as nails and dipped in sunshine'.

When the war ended, some of the senior Scouts who had survived the trenches dropped out of Baden-Powell's movement, disgusted by its cheerleading of slaughter. These fierce, idealistic and battle-scarred young men returned from the war bent on regenerating society and razing the ruins of the old ways; they didn't want to give up the outdoors life, but they had outgrown a boys' movement. They returned to Seton's progressive ethos to found new youth movements and, following the emancipation of women, and the success of the Camp Fire Girls, those movements would involve women as equals. And so the progressive light of the campfire was passed on, to radical camping groups such as the Order of Woodcraft Chivalry and the Kindred of the Kibbo Kift.

4
Activities in Camp

'Jerkin and Hood. Tents in a half circle. Pitched at sundown, gone in the morning. Outlaws . . . ?'

From the pamphlet 'The Kibbo Kift: Its Aims and Ideals'

The figures marched up the Long Man of Wilmington, a chalk giant inscribed into the steep Windover Hill. The men wore knee-length shorts, brown leather belts, jerkins and pointed green cowls in imitation of the forest outlaws Robin and his Merry Men. The women wore Arabian keffiyeh-styled head-dresses to protect against the sun and one-piece knee-length dresses tied with leather belts. On the flap of their grey Bergen rucksacks, a mark was painted – a large letter *K* beside the curling smoke of a campfire and a single green fir tree. The men and women greeted one another with the salute of the open palm, right hand raised high, and a cry of 'Huh!' All the hikers carried rough ash staves, which pushed against the earth as they ascended the Long Man, singing a song of their own devising, 'The Kindred is Coming'.

The Long Man stands 200 feet tall. Today, the outline is defined with concrete, and the Long Man is visible to the traffic passing on the A27 between Lewes and Eastbourne. But at the time of the hike, August 1929, the figure outlined in the long grass was a mystical watermark on the hillside.

Windover Hill and the surrounding area are rich with remnants from England's ancient past: Neolithic flint mines, Bronze Age burial barrows and a Roman terrace way. The hikers marched up the steep hill and, at the heart of the Long Man, performed a brief ritual of dedication. Their voices echoed in the distinctive acoustics of the concave slope. Thus they reached back, far, far back, into the void-faced hood of prehistory. Mankind's evolution has been a progressive degeneration, with alienation at every stage. First, man was alienated from oneness with his god, then cast out from the harmony of Nature. The process of separation is remorseless, each severance placing another partition between man and the world. He lost his link to his ancestors. He grew apart from others, from his community and fellow man, until even his wife and his own children were alien to him. Each cut was made by the instruments of capital and industry, two scissor blades cutting in unison. The final divorce, the ultimate decree nisi, was issued by Freud: man was alienated from his own self. The hikers reached through the void and into the hood, searching for the rough hand of Neolithic man, their ancient guide to living in harmony with the subtle, undulating forms of the Downs.

Ritual completed, the hikers continued up over the featureless head of the Long Man to the top of the hill. There, they looked down over the South Downs, a cumuliform landscape of whale-backed hills and verdant valleys founded on a bank of chalk. Cloud shadows passed over ploughed wheatfields. In the distance, coastal bays and the glittering English Channel, and the seven peaks of the chalk cliffs known as the Seven Sisters. Each Sister is the measure of a terrifying eternity: trillions of coccolithophores – nano-plankton – lived and died in a deep warm sea, leaving behind their scales of calcium carbonate to build up over time into the gleaming white cliffs. On the beach, a stunning everywhere of light as the high sun was reflected by these geological mausoleums.

The South Downs, its name derived from the Saxon word *dun*, meaning 'hill', was one of a number of English landscapes stalked by these strange hikers. Their rituals combined the teachings of the world's religions with the ancient British pagan tradition, the Albion of menhir, tor and cromlech, Silbury Hill and the White Horse of Uffington. These ancient sites throbbed with dormant meaning. For a joke – in the Freudian sense that there is no such thing as a joke – one of their men stripped naked and squatted at the root of the enormous phallus of the Cerne Giant, as if drawing the sexual potency into himself. Such ancestor worship sounds preposterous now: in the twenty-first century, Stonehenge is a tourist attraction at which the passing traffic on the A303 slows to gawp, before speeding on to holidays in Dorset. But in 1929, the sites of English prehistory retained sufficient mystical charge to inspire this select group of hikers and campers as they sought to change the direction of Western civilization. They were the most intriguing of English reform movements, an elite cell a few hundred strong, already nine years into their existence come the occasion of the dedication to the Long Man of Wilmington; they were the Kindred of the Kibbo Kift.

On 8 September 1914, John Hargrave left the office of the *Scout* magazine to enlist in the Great War. Slight and fiercely fit, with abundant dark hair, the twenty-year-old Hargrave was one of the earliest members of the Scouts, joining in 1908, the year *Scouting for Boys* was published. The son of two artists, he left school when he was fifteen years old to become an illustrator and author. When he was nineteen, he published his best-selling book *Lonecraft* (1913), which brought the idealism of the Scouts to the country boys who lived remote from organized Scouting groups. The book was noticed by Baden-Powell, who invited him to become staff artist at the *Scout*. He was known as White Fox or, to his friends, simply 'Fox'.

Lonecraft includes Hargrave's instructions on how to make a simple, lightweight tent. Take a sheet of square canvas of 7 x 7 feet; insert four one-inch curtain rings into the corners, add a triangular patch and rope that suspends the tent from a tree branch, then secure the remaining three corners to the ground with three pegs. The tent sleeps one. *Lonecraft* was the work of a fierce individualist, a manual for self-reliance and self-control. Live pure, speak true, right wrong, follow the trail. Don't be a waster. Be silent and ready to act. Don't talk. Do something. The stoic, wise American Indian stands shoulder to shoulder with British heroes: St George, King Arthur, Captain Cook, Robinson Crusoe. This manual attracted followers: the young King George VI and his brother Prince Henry, Duke of Gloucester, were taken to one of the lonecraft camps by their tutor. If Hargrave was sufficiently charismatic for the future king, you can appreciate the influence he wielded over the young Scouts who followed him.

In 1914, beside the beech woods of Buckinghamshire, on Mayhall Farm overlooking the River Chess, Hargrave said goodbye to his own troop of Scouts. Then he went home to say farewell to his beloved father. Gordon Hargrave was an artist and Quaker who had taken his family from his son's birthplace in Midhurst, on the Sussex Downs, to wander around Westmorland and Cumberland, 'amid the purple heather and the sunset in peat-moss puddles'. With his son, he shared a passion for anthropology and the countryside. Born in 1894, Hargrave spent his early childhood in the birthplace of English Romanticism, the land of lakes and mountains where the boy Wordsworth slipped out, stole a boat and sailed by moonlight under the looming oppression of jagged night mountains. A land where boys ran free.

After enlisting, John Hargrave served with the 32nd Field Ambulance 10th Division of the Mediterranean Expeditionary Force. He gave up his lonecraft for a bell tent in Aldershot shared with twenty-two other men. In row after row of military tents, the men waited for training. The bell tent had no groundsheet, and when it rained muddy streams ran where the men would have slept, had there been sufficient room. The air was thick with foul language and twist tobacco. Hargrave was like a caged animal. A self-sufficient, artistic individual, he found that this forced proximity with his fellow man did nothing for his disdain for the masses. The men were transferred to Tipperary barracks where Hargrave threw himself into the soldier's life, training his sixty-two men in semaphore and instructing them in the Scout craft of hiding. He had the voice and bearing for drill. He taught the men to crawl on their stomachs and to take cover behind clumps of vegetation or ridges in the ground. The training ground, it seemed, offered a chance for a Scout to excel. But would Scouting be enough when faced with the horrific reality of war?

Suvla Bay is on the coast of the Gallipoli peninsula in Turkey. On the night of 6 August 1915, a series of landings was launched to break the deadlock of the Dardanelles campaign. John Hargrave watched the Suvla Bay landings from his ship. In his account published in 1916, he wrote:

There was no glory. Here was Death, sure enough – Mechanical Death run amok – but where was the glory?

Here was organized murder – but it was steel-cold! There was no hand-to-hand glory. A mine dispersed you before you had set foot on dry land; or a high explosive removed your stomach, and left you a mangled heap of human flesh, instead of a medically certified, healthy human being.

Mechanical Death wavered and fluctuated – but it kept going. If it slackened its murderous fire at one side of the bay, it was only to burst forth afresh upon the other.

Hargrave landed on Suvla Bay in a lighter boat. The searching zone of the ambulance division lay along the Kapanja Sirt, a ridge to one side of a horseshoe of mountains, a desolate, rugged wasteland. Under shellfire, the ambulance division worked their way up to the firing line in the hills and then carried the wounded back to the dressing station. The men slept little more than an hour or two a night. Time became jumbled and fragmented. Bullets sang. Hargrave distracted himself by drawing the explosion of every type of Turkish shell. He even filed a column for the *Scout*, written under fire on 26 August, which draws a veil across the horror: '. . . the sights I have seen during the last few days are too awful to bear description. This is the seamy side of war – and it is too gruesome to dwell upon.'

The small band of men slept in dugouts on the edge of the bay, bathing and swimming together in the sea, and Hargrave grew to love their company:

I have slept and lived in every kind of camp and bivouac. I have dug and helped to dig dug-outs. I have lain full length in the dry, dead grass 'under the wide and starry sky'. I have crept behind a ledge of rock, and gone to sleep with the ants crawling over me. I have slept with a pair of boots for a pillow. I have lived and snoozed in the dried-up bed of a mountain torrent for weeks. A ground-sheet tied to a bough has been my bedroom. I have slumbered curled in a coil of rope on the deck of a cattle-boat, in an ambulance wagon, on a stretcher, in farmhouse barns and under hedges and haystacks. I have slept in the sand by the blue Mediterranean Sea, with the crickets and grasshoppers 'zipping' and 'zinging' all night long.

But our dug-out nights on the edge of the bay at Buccaneer Bivouac were the most enjoyable.

These experiences at Suvla Bay validated the worth of his Scouting. Under shellfire throughout August and September, his lonecraft ensured his survival. He tracked along dried watercourses and took cover behind thorn bushes, all the time sought out by the sniper's bullet. The Turkish soldiers were 'born scouts' and only those soldiers who had been trained in the cunning and craft of the savage Scout came out top in the Great Failure of the Great War. Officers unable to find the North Star could not make their way at night, nor could they read maps drawn on too small a scale to be of practical use. Entire companies of men were cut up because they lost their way, unable to read the lay of the land. Baden-Powell's best-selling manual promised *Scouting for Boys*. On Suvla Bay, it was no boys' game.

When his division was evacuated from Suvla Bay on 30 September 1915, John Hargrave was the only surviving non-commissioned officer from his section. He was twenty-one years old. The Allies suffered 18,000 casualties at Suvla Bay and at Anzac Cove in the August offensive. Although his survival proved the value of Scouting, the war itself indicted the leadership of Baden-Powell's movement, ageing examples of the same contemptible officer class who had failed the men of Suvla Bay: veterans of the Anglo-Boer War (1899–1902), an inglorious campaign in which it took three years for nearly half a million men to defeat 40,000 Boers.

The Great War was the end of the Age of Empires: the legitimacy of a civilization and a right to rule shredded by machine-gun fire. Something new had to follow. It was impossible to imagine the same old order persisting. Hargrave came out of Suvla Bay riddled with body lice and with 'heart strain'. He contracted malaria and was invalided out of the war. Survival convinced him of his natural authority and destiny, and his columns filed under fire made him a prominent figure in the Scouting movement; Baden-Powell knew he was trouble. In a letter to his advisor Sir Percy Everett, he confided, 'My only doubt about Hargrave is his ultra views and possibility of going off at a wrong tangent, but, ensconced under your eye and mine he should be – I think – a very valuable agent.' On 6 December 1917, John Hargrave was appointed by the Scouts as commissioner for woodcraft and camping. But he would not be so easily assimilated. With no appetite for Baden-Powell's patriotism and militarism, he resolved to find a new trail.

After being invalided out of the Great War, Hargrave returned to his lonecraft camp and set about cleansing himself of the conflict, retreating into silent communion with the earth. He practised meditation and studied the religions, myths and legends of the world. To survive the prolonged terror of infantry conflict was to be transformed. Soldiers often attributed their inexplicable cheating of death to – in the words of Paul Fussell – 'a plethora of very un-modern superstitions, talismans, wonders, miracles, relics, legends and rumors'. Trench warfare was a baptism of fire; the soldier was initiated into a secret shadow realm of death and visions. It is ironic that the modern industrial slaughterhouse of the war inspired in some of its veterans a mystical, medieval and pastoral way of thinking.

As a war hero, Hargrave's standing within the Scouts had increased even while his regular columns for the *Scout* developed ideas contrary to the leadership of Baden-Powell. In an article published in the summer of 1917, still three years before the formation of the Kindred of the Kibbo Kift, he wrote of a camp he ran for about thirty boys in five or six tents, pitched in an English park, 'an open and wild place, with great tracts of forest land and sweeps of verdant greensward'. He shares the basic routines of camp with his readers. First, the boys dug latrines, then pitched tents and lit the cooking fire and the council fire. On Sunday, he and the boys stripped for bathing parade, turning the cold hose on one another. Then, a nature hike wearing only shorts and a singlet, barefoot and bare-legged. A fortnight after this expedition, Hargrave set out for his youthful audience his belief in the imperative of human evolution along Scout lines. In an essay entitled 'What's Bred in the Bone', he wrote:

> We must continue to evolve. We're helping to evolve a New Race of Scout Men – we're the beginning of a new off-shoot of evolution – we're making ourselves something different from the old civilized boy – we're trying to become more healthy, and fit, and alert and keen – and we shall hand on our Scout training 'from one generation to another'.

If the Great War was the work of an old and degenerate civilization, regeneration required youthful vigour, honed in wild camps and on long hikes. In December 1917, in a column entitled 'A Prophet in His Own Country', he predicted that the education of boys in the future would become more like a Scout education, and that outdoor school would rid society of the sickness that led to the terrible events of Suvla Bay: 'People in general – the public – will discover that the mode of life they lived before the war was not life at all but simply mental and physical stagnation, and they will go in for scouting as a cure for this disease of civilization.'

By wiping out a generation between the young and the old, the Great War created a generation gap wider than any previously. The terrible experiences of the war, the slaughter of family and friends, needlessly, in a conflict that Europe seemed to sleepwalk into, put everything open to question. Hargrave offers answers to these questions in his polemic *The Great War Brings It Home: The Natural Reconstruction of an Unnatural Existence*, published in 1919. The cover has an illustration of a baby in a stiff-backed Indian cot hanging from a single branch. Off to the left, three shadowed figures are in discussion around a campfire.

Hargrave articulated what was becoming a truism among the youth. Civilization had overdeveloped our intellect while neglecting body and soul. Civilization may advance, but what of us? He saw degeneracy in every class of society, a decline in fitness caused by the enervating effects of urban life and the extermination of the country's finest young men in the war. The cure for degenerate civilizations, historically, had been the sacking of the cities by nomadic tribes, such as the hordes of Genghis Khan. Technological advance gifted an insurmountable advantage of force to urban societies. If the barbarians could no longer storm the gates, where would renewal come from? His answer was that civilization must produce its own stock of barbarians.

John Hargrave was twenty-five when *The Great War Brings It Home* was published. Its ambition is outrageous, fuelled by the authentic rage of youth. 'Everyone – rich and poor, men and women – are dissatisfied, discontented, "fed up" with the old system.' To his credit, Hargrave did not offer up a scapegoat. 'Every man must realize that everyone is more or less to blame for the rotten state of our civilization.' Some of his ideas concerning eugenics were of their time. He proposed that by improving society and standards of education, men and women would be so proud and potent that they would voluntarily forge suitable partnerships. There would be no need for breeding certificates to be issued by the government. Natural eugenics would arise from fit and intellectual men and women seeking one another out. Everything would be voluntary. Camping education was so self-evidently the right and natural way to go, he felt, that there would be little opposition to it.

Hargrave proposed setting aside tracts of English countryside to act as national training grounds for his programme of outdoor and woodcraft activities and camps. The New Forest would be one, as would Epping Forest, the North and South Downs, the Chiltern Hills, the White Horse Hills, Salisbury Plain, the Mendip Hills and the Cotswolds. The aristocratic landowners would, he imagined, gladly rent out their lands for such a purpose. 'We have some of the finest camping grounds in the world,' he wrote, 'we have scenery which, for wild and romantic grandeur, cannot be surpassed, and we have all this within a few hours of every great industrial city in our land.' At each training ground, yogis of camping, tramping and meditation would lecture and train the youth in the disciplines of the intellectual barbarian. Private family camps would be set aside for parents to train their children in the summertime. If a boy did not pass his test of initiation then he would not be admitted to school. And if a youth did not pass a test of manhood, he would neither be able to vote nor marry.

Diminished potency was a prevalent anxiety throughout the staggered fall of the British Empire. Baden-Powell's *Scouting for Boys* was published in a mood of national crisis concerning the security of the empire and the strength of its men. In 1903, an Interdepartmental Committee on Physical Deterioration was established. After the Great War, the decline of the British Empire, and the concomitant rise of America, was apparent.

Hargrave had no wish to preserve empire. What the Great War brought home, he argued, was the end of the legitimacy of the existing class structure: 'The upper classes have realized that the "masses" really are human beings after all – and the "masses" have realized that the "upper ten" are really just the same as they are.' With this change in perception of the classes, new social relations could be forged. He did not identify with the working class or with the bosses, and was neither right nor left wing. He was a pacifist, albeit a muscular one who demanded physical feats of stamina and strength from his followers. Equally, this was an era of mass enfranchisement, and Hargrave's rejection of democracy can be seen as a revolt against the prospect of mass rule. The Representation of the People Act of 1918 enfranchised women and the poor, transforming an electorate of 7.5 million voters into more than 20 million people. Hargrave would not be ruled by a committee. He envisaged a new elite, one determined not by birth but by fitness, intellect and camping, with himself as unquestioned leader.

★

In spring 1919, Hargrave was holed up in his Caravan Camp, at Mayhall Farm. Every moon, his patrol of Scouts (all seventeen years old or older) met around the council fire, and practised their woodcraft at weekends, or as often as work in London permitted. In a green-and-orange showman caravan, Hargrave wrote and painted, then bedded down in his A-type Canadian tent, handmade for him by his friend 'Wanderwolf'. Weighing about ten pounds, the tent was fashioned from Egyptian cotton and bamboo poles with a flysheet that came down to the ground. This camp attracted followers, as his camps always did. In late March, the *Punch* review of *The Great War Brings It Home* admitted his ideas for renewal were sound, 'but not for those of us who, even in a case of great national urgency, cannot get away from the tyranny of convention'. The positive critical response to his polemic increased his sense of manifest destiny as a leader. He continued in print to rail against the direction of the Scouting movement, demanding stiffer tests and fewer badges, real outdoor scouting rather than indoor games and lectures, less drill and more tribal tradition, more scouting and less shouting. His lobbying for a training ground for Scouts came to fruition with the establishment of Gilwell Park Camp in June 1919. As commissioner of woodcraft, Hargrave was the natural choice to lead the training ground but Baden-Powell passed over him and appointed Francis 'Skipper' Gidney as Gilwell camp chief instead: Gidney was described by Baden-Powell as 'the perfect Boy-Man', an epithet we must assume to be a compliment.

Being passed over in this way contributed to Hargrave's alienation from the Scouting movement. That August, he was visited at the Caravan Camp by 'Little Wolf', C. J. Mumford. They talked all night and formed Lodge Ndembo, consisting of seven men, whose purpose was to 'precipitate' the woodcraft element out of the Scout movement.

In the same month, he travelled to the newly formed Scout training camp of Gilwell Park and was appalled by what he saw there, setting down his wrath in an article for the *Trail*. Under the pseudonym of 'Our Red Hot Bolshevik', Hargrave lambasted the behaviour of the Scouts, who ran around blowing bugles when they were meant to be stalking rare birds. The emphasis on parade over the survival skills of woodcraft demonstrated the Scouts had learned nothing from the Great War.

By October, he was even challenging the role of Christianity in the Scouts. 'The Woodcrafter takes the trouble to study the comparative religions of the world,' he wrote, 'in order that he may acquire wisdom from all the Great Teachers. This Woodcrafter considers "compulsory religious worship" (such as forced Church Parades and closed troops) not good.' The climax of *The Great War Brings It Home* calls for the establishment of a world religion, a synthesis of the major religions and philosophies, stressing their similarities rather than their differences, as the worship of one great power – the force of life and nature, the Great Spirit.

As Hargrave's confrontation with Baden-Powell entered its final phase, he was busy recruiting sympathetic Scouts. Throughout that October, a Scalphunters club met every Wednesday to which new members were brought. In November, Hargrave married his long-term love Ruth Clark, the leader of the Merrie Campers and author of *Camp Fire Training for Girls*. Her woodcraft name was Minobi, meaning Glad Heart, and she brought her own followers to the nascent movement. By the end of 1919, the Kibbo Kift was gestating, as was John Hargrave's first and only child.

What do the words 'Kibbo Kift' mean? John Hargrave explained the etymology:

> The words Kibbo Kift are Old English (Cheshire) meaning 'Strength' or 'any proof of great strength'. They are connected with the old dialect words 'kebbie', a cudgel, club or rough hook-headed stick or staff, and 'kifty' meaning sound, good, genuine, OK, correct, proper, 'good form' or in the tradition.

The triple *K* of their name appears, to modern eyes, to be drawn directly from the Klu Klux Klan, whose resurgence also took place across the 1920s. If the Kindred were aware of this connection, they made no mention of it.

After sunset on 18 August 1920, the Kindred of the Kibbo Kift were formed at Denison Hall on Vauxhall Bridge Road. The Kin covenant, drawn up by John Hargrave and witnessed by his wife Minobi and Little Wolf, Cecil Mumford, attracted disaffected Scouts, left-wing politicos, former suffragettes, theosophists, vegetarians and artists. The seven-point covenant was as follows:

1. Open Air Education for the Children – Camp Training and Nature Craft
2. Health of Body, Mind and Spirit
3. Craft Training Groups and Craft Guilds
4. The Woodcraft Family, or Roof Tree
5. Local Folk Moots and Cultural Development
6. Disarmament of Nations – Brotherhood of Man
7. International Education based on these points. Freedom of Trade between Nations. Stabilization of the Purchasing Power of Money (in all countries). Open Negotiations instead of secret treaties and diplomacy. A World Council.

The covenant proceeds swiftly from education to a reorganization of capitalism and the founding of a new global political authority. You cannot fault the Kindred for a lack of ambition. Combined with the promise of co-educational camps, the Kin covenant convinced ex-suffragettes like Emmeline Pethick-Lawrence to join. Like Hargrave, she was raised a Quaker and had spent the Great War campaigning for the Women's International League for Peace. Denison Hall was known for its radical gatherings. Two years earlier, Emmeline Pethick-Lawrence attended a discussion on the Problem of Population at the hall, specifically consideration of the new woman in the creation of the future race. The essays of sexologist Havelock Ellis were under discussion: 'In the eyes of the new morality, the ideal woman is no longer the meek drudge but the free instructed woman, trained in a sense of responsibility to herself and to the race, determined to have no children but the best.' The Kindred promised an elite training for women and their children.

Emmeline Pethick-Lawrence's experience of working with youth groups went back to the nineteenth century. She lent her standing to the Kibbo Kift and was joined by her activist partner, Mary Neal, a tall, lean woman with striking blue eyes, described by Pethick-Lawrence as a pragmatist with a cutting wit who 'brought into the atmosphere the sparkle of a clear frosty day'. In 1892, the two women took the girls of the Mission's Working Girls' Club away for a week together, pioneering seaside holidays for the working class. In 1901, Mary Neal joined Cecil Sharp in reviving folk dances and Old English folk songs, which they would teach to the poor young people in their charge at a dressmaking co-operative in Somers Town, King's Cross.

Among Mary Neal's contacts was the future prime minister Clement Attlee. Then Mayor of Stepney, Attlee chaired a committee called the Camelot Club in Poplar dedicated to building up a youth wing for the Labour movement. Mary Neal secured Hargrave membership of this committee, giving him access to mainstream activists. Attlee had also served in the Dardanelles campaign, and perhaps this made him inclined to support Hargrave. Youth workers from the South London co-operative movement were drawn in by Attlee's stamp of political legitimacy, and so the ranks of the Kindred grew.

By the second meeting of the Kibbo Kift, held at the large house of Emmeline and Frederick Pethick-Lawrence in October 1921, there were 200 individual members of the movement, drawn mainly from London and the Home Counties. In his essential sociological study of the Kibbo Kift, *Social Movements*

and Their Supporters (1997), Mark Drakeford provides a sophisticated and insightful analysis of how the shared ideals of the
various groups forming the Kindred provided sufficient centrifu-
gal force to bind them together in their early years. The Kindred
encompassed such diverse figures as the formidable May Billinghurst – a paraplegic former suffragette who fought back
ferociously against the doctors who tried to force-feed her during
her hunger strike, and whose wheelchair is visible in photographs
of the Kindred's camps – to Baron von Pallandt, a Dutch aristocrat with a deep interest in theosophy. Such a gathering of radicals
and oddballs soon attracted the interest of the Home Office and
Special Branch, who watched the Kibbo Kift very closely in these
early days. They detected a faint communist influence but concluded that 'the leaders can, however . . . be fairly described as
cranks.'

Special Branch may have declared the Kibbo Kift to be mostly
harmless, but the Scouting movement disagreed. John Hargrave
continued his attacks on their hierarchy, writing in a left-wing
journal, *Foreign Affairs*, that 'They have earned their bread by
war, got promotion and higher pay from war – and they are
war.' In January 1921, a resolution was passed at the annual general meeting of the London Scout Council to prohibit White
Fox from addressing any Scout meeting or contributing any
further articles to the *Trail*. In a letter in *Headquarters Gazette*,
John S. R. Pankhurst objected to the resolution, describing it as
reactionary. But the running battle between Hargrave and Baden-
Powell had reached the point of irreconcilable break. The Scout
movement would continue to belittle and attack the Kibbo Kift
in its formative phase, painting it as communistic and therefore
entirely unsuited for young people. White Fox may have imagined he held sway over hundreds of thousands of young minds,
but there was no hope of overcoming such an immense power
as the Scouts. The Kibbo Kift would not become a mass movement to rival Baden-Powell's. Nor would it become a Labour

youth movement, as Attlee and the Camelot Club hoped. Its destiny was far stranger than that.

The Kindred camped four times a year, in tune with the seasons. Their camping grounds included Crystal Palace and Bradenham Common in High Wycombe, and they also gathered in Matlock in Derbyshire, Missenden in Buckinghamshire, and Old Sarum, an Iron Age hill fort and site of ancient Salisbury. They were always in search of new places to camp. 'The camping years have become one long camp,' remembers former member Leslie Paul:

> Only the sites have changed, and what flawless ones we chose: their very names are immemorial England! At Princes Risboro' under the enormous cross carved on the chalk hillside of Whyteleafe; by Magpie Bottom in the downs above Shoreham valley; by the Hammer Ponds, near Horsham; close by Steyning, or underneath Chanctonbury Ring; within sight of Stonehenge; staring at the Long Man of Wilmington; on the banks of Coniston Water; a walk from the Swannery at Abbotsbury; under dreaming Christchurch Minster; at Timberscombe by Haslemere; at Hangman's Cove; in the meadows of the giant curve of the Wye, under the brow of Symonds Yat; or in that tiny hamlet with the Norse name of Garth, high up in the Welsh hills, not far from Llangollen, looking across the rich Cheshire plain on which in the early mornings all the clouds of England lie pillowed.

At Whitsun, the great meeting of the Kindred took place. Named the Al-Thing, from the Old Norse name for the gathering of the millennia-old Icelandic proto-parliament, it was a group camp of men, women and their children. At the Al-Thing, there were wrestling contests and the performance of plays and mummeries. Here the Kindred held their council meetings at which disputes were aired and resolutions made. Whole sheep and ox were roasted and giant loaves baked with a symbolic *K* marked in the dough. Activity was divided between intellectual and physical training, between the writing of songs and poetry, the playing of music, embroidery of banners, the fashioning of puppets and masks, and trials to harden the spirit and stiffen the sinews. The men and women exercised in a costume based upon the garb of the American Indian, with loincloths for the men and short skirts for the women. Some of the Kindred survived solely on rations prepared the previous winter to test out their preparedness for a state of emergency. Their formidable company of archers honed their skills.

The Kinlog of the Kibbo Kift records their official history, an illuminated manuscript that begins with the birth of John Hargrave and concludes with his death at the age of eighty-eight on 21 November 1982. Its pages are beautifully illustrated by Kindred member Blue Falcon, the art reflecting the eclectic interests of the group: Egyptian hieroglyphs, futurist watercolours, *Metropolis* meets the Middle Ages. The costumes and artefacts of the Kindred of the Kibbo Kift are held at the Museum of London and include their ceremonial dress. While typical camping clothes and staffs were used for hiking, more striking and secret outfits were used for ritual. These include the tabard of Hawk the gleemaster, with its outsized straight shoulders and potent central symbol. The appliquéd felt imagery is bold, simple and symbolic: an upturned tomahawk, pine trees under night and day, wavy lines denoting water. The colours are decisive and energetic. Hargrave dictated the style: 'the vital man uses vital colour – red, yellow, blue and gold. Heraldic, primitive, full-blooded, vigorous.' A photograph shows Hawk, a strikingly handsome man called Frank Dixon, with dark hair and an amused glint in his eye, calling the group to attention with a twist of his ceremonial noisemaker. This was how the otherworldliness of the Al-Thing was summoned.

At the Al-Thing over a hundred tents were pitched in a semicircle on a large flat common bordered by woods. A man dressed in a leopard skin beats a drum. He enacts a tribal hunting dance with a woman dressed in what appears to be an enormous Shredded Wheat. A solemn procession of barefoot men in shorts and hooded jerkins follows a caped man carrying a tall staff. Four hooded adolescent boys carry between them an ark of some sorts, its poles resting on their shoulders, and atop the ark a totem: a kneeling wooden figure holding aloft the Great Mark of the Kibbo Kift. The Great Mark is a single *K* with an extended vertical, making the letter appear like a leafless winter tree. A curl of woodsmoke from a campfire bisects the mark, the sinuous symmetry of the yin-yang. Kibbo Kifters frequently posed for photographs by making the symbol of the *K*, their upright posture forming the vertical line of the *K*, their arms completing the letter. It was an ancient gesture of supplication to the sun, adapted by the Kindred to demonstrate their reverence towards a different light, that of knowledge. To make the sign of the *K* was to bow down to art, science and philosophy. All of Hargrave's symbols and rituals were layered with meaning. The badge of the Kindred was circular to symbolize eternity; the campfire also represented the flame of life. When a man stood naked on the hillside and made the mark of the *K* with his arms, he was not merely worshipping nature or the sun, he was acknowledging the intellectual and spiritual inheritance of humanity.

Artistic talent and craftsmanship were celebrated, evident in the individually painted tents of the campers and the ceremonial costumes. Over in the glade, an Indian woman led the meditation surrounded by mystical maidens. Plays were performed, such as *The Great Taboo*, as staged by the Woodlanders at the fifth Al-Thing of 1924. There is something primal and scary about the Mummers' outfits: one small figure is hooded with black cloth, a skull painted over the face and a large crossbones over the chest; another actor poses behind a large mask of a deer's head, his hands as precisely arranged as in an Egyptian hieroglyph. The Kindred were talented and disciplined in their art.

There was also plenty of socializing, sitting around a campfire, drinking tea from cups and saucers. There was a general air of fecundity: pregnant women and babes-at-arm alike camped at the Al-Thing. 'All the best girls were in the KK,' maintained Hawk the gleemaster. The Kibbo Kift was not a free-love movement, nor did it embrace naturism. It was a camping movement of fit young men and women, and that was shocking enough. Many people met their partners there. Angus McBean, the great photographer, married a fellow Kibbo Kifter; only later did he become the lover of Quentin Crisp and serve two and a half years hard labour for buggery.

A reporter attended the Kindred camp in Bradenham Common, Buckinghamshire. The air of freedom made him light-headed with sexual fascination. He noted the long hair of the men and the short hair of the women. The reporter writes:

> When I reached their camp which is discreetly hidden in the heart of a wooded hill, I felt inclined to make an apologetic retreat . . . As I tentatively entered I got an impression of very short skirts, bare sunburnt legs, bobbed hair and bare arms. For a moment the impression was overpowering. As I hesitated I noticed a man in a sort of glorified Boy Scout costume suddenly raised his arms toward another dressed in the same garb, and shouted 'Huh!' at the top of his voice. Two young girls also raised their arms and shouted 'Huh!' This was not exactly reassuring . . .

After eavesdropping on a meeting of the Kindred, the reporter found his way to John Hargrave. When asked what the movement was all about, Hargrave said, 'It's simply that we want to live to be left alone, to be fit and to enjoy things. In a thousand years we shall conquer the world. Everyone will be on our side. There will be no more wars. We are the survivalists. We insist on living.'

After sunset, the campfire ceremony began. The keeper of the council fire, dressed in a grand scarlet costume with snaking gold flames, swung a censer and intoned, 'Energy, energy, ceaseless energy . . . Microcosm and macrocosm. One, One, One is One.' Then the Kindred played the night game, a version of Capture the Flag with burning torches. Leslie Paul remembers playing the game around the back of Hargrave's house on a timeless evening:

> The glimmering torches were flying still in all directions, in graceful curves, lighted and then obscured, like darting fireflies. And as the night wind blew fragrant from the spring meadows it was like Greece, I thought, with the torches of the priestly rabble scouring through a wood on the slopes of Mount Hymettus to a dawn ceremony.

Members were given a new name by their friends within the organization. The naming and costume severed the link with the class-bound life outside camp, allowing each member to create themselves within a new order. Men took the names of animals, women the names of plants and herbs. The Kibbo Kift fulfilled the transformative promise of camping.

Vera Chapman first met John Hargrave at a party in Kings Langley in 1919. He was wearing evening dress and 'He looked like Mephistopheles somehow, and I was rather fascinated by him. He had a sort of Byronic air about him.' Vera Chapman attended the Al-Thing at the invitation of May Billinghurst, who knew her from Oxford. She remembered the camp as:

> . . . full of exuberance and excitement. You were lifted right out of this world. There was the mystique of totems and so on. The meeting began with quite a little bit of mysticism, ritualism . . . you made your camp fire and made your invocation and that definitely set up a feeling of belonging to the other world. It was a magical and religious atmosphere. It was the religion of the spirit which you could not deny, out there under the sky.

Vera Chapman would go on to found the Tolkien Society and write medievalist novels. She later joined the Order of Bards and Druids, and some of the occult rituals of the Kibbo Kift seeped into that movement too. In short, she was an extremely impressive individual who regarded her time in the Kibbo Kift as the fundamental experience of her life, a common attitude among the Kindred. When Mark Drakeford interviewed surviving members in the 1970s, some met him in their costume, and husband and wife referred to one another by their kin names. Frank Dixon was always known as Hawk Dixon, even to his wife, who had never joined the Kindred and had no time for it. Being part of the Kibbo Kift was to be transformed by an ideal that lasted a lot longer than a weekend of camping.

In 1924, the fifth Al-Thing was held at Bradenham Hill Farm in West Wycombe, Buckinghamshire. Over the previous year, the ranks of the Kindred had expanded to nearly 500 members, with most of the growth coming from those groups who wanted to create a Labour youth movement. John Hargrave was too autocratic for these members. In modernist fashion, the centre could not hold and things began to fall apart.

A resolution critical of John Hargrave's leadership was put forward at the 1924 Al-Thing. Hargrave had refused to counter-sign the covenant of a local group, the Brockleything, formed from Kinfolk in Camberwell, Deptford and Lewisham. He had also exiled Kindred member Eric Peake, known as Wanderwolf, for 'treachery' without giving him opportunity to defend himself. 'Trial in the absence and without the knowledge of the accused is a betrayal of elementary civil liberty,' the dissenters claimed. 'We do not believe that a decent man or woman can tolerate it or remain associated with an organization which tolerates it, for a single moment.' Furthermore, Hargrave's pronouncements embarrassed them. His intention 'if the Moveable Dwellings Bill should pass into law, to break the law at every opportunity' was

cited as an indiscretion, as was his continued needling of the
Scouting movement, calling them 'Scout boys' and insisting they
were bad campers. The breakaway group objected to Hargrave
making grand public claims concerning the power, influence and
achievement of the Kindred, which they felt only made the movement look ridiculous. Fundamentally, they reacted against
Hargrave tightening his grip upon the movement and seeking
greater obedience from its membership. The censure of Hargrave was not extended to the rest of the Kindred. The resolution
made it clear that 'We regard Kibbo Kift as a free association of
individuals, tribes, lodges, rooftrees and things, bound only by
virtue of their signature of a common covenant. To this covenant
we continue to give the fullest possible assent.'

One of the signatories to this resolution was Leslie Paul. As
much as the document marked a schism in the Kindred of the
Kibbo Kift, it was also the inauguration of the Woodcraft Folk,
the movement the splinter group went on to found, the leftist
youth movement Attlee and the Camelot Club had signed up for
years earlier. The Woodcraft Folk continue to this day. In his
autobiography, *Angry Young Man*, Leslie Paul regretted that this
feud meant that more experienced and brilliant recruits within
the Kindred moved on, leaving him and Hargrave to their 'impassioned puerilities' as the heads of rival youth movements.

Vera Chapman was present when the resolution was put forward. The weather was bad. A cold and wet Whitsun. Once
the motion of censure was on the table, Emmeline Pethick-
Lawrence insisted that it be debated before discussion of any
other items. The weather forced the debate into a nearby
deserted barn. Twenty-two members took part in this tremendous argument, as the wind raged through the loose and rotting
timbers, and rats scampered and squeaked away from the
candlelight. The dissenters demanded representation but Hargrave simply did not want to run the movement along democratic
lines. The censure vote was defeated by eighty-eight votes to

fifty-five. With typical Kindred theatre, Leslie Paul and other dissenters marched directly out of the camp. The Kinlog records
the schism as the righteous rejection of mass rule and democracy: 'Long waged the word-fight. Yet held at last The Kindred
To the way Of English folk – Their fathers – Free men Willingly
By chosen chief Led From their midst Democrats With scorn
Thenceforth They sent.'

The Kindred's anti-democratic tendency stemmed from pacifism and the ideas of H. G. Wells, who was named on their
advisory committee. Wells had written of the need for a new
governing class which he termed 'Samurai', a class of intellectual, unelected rationalists, men and women who had achieved
something exceptional and had passed a test or induction of
some sort. The Samurai were also expected to journey alone
into the wilderness for a week to maintain their physical and
spiritual hardiness. This non-hereditary, voluntary ruling class
was superior to a democratically elected one because, in a
democracy, Wells felt that the only way to be voted in was to
play on patriotic sentiment, and the cultivation of nationalism
led to war. Wells, in a lecture, also floated liberal fascism as a
way to achieve a liberal society; in other words, the means of
authoritarianism and force would be used to achieve progressive
ends. Under Wells's influence, the Kibbo Kift quietly refused to
be a democratic movement.

In his autobiography, Leslie Paul was less critical of John Hargrave's decision: 'Having in my turn failed just as dismally to
build a Labour Scout Movement after years of effort just as
intense, I cannot blame him for deciding in advance that it was
not worth trying.' Yet the man's manner still irked. 'I recall him
in those days as tall, with sharp, almost Romany features, an aqui-
line nose, and a mass of wavy black hair . . . Hargrave always
spoke as though possessed of an absolute and even insolent certainty of where he was going and what he was doing.' For Leslie
Paul and the woodcraft movement, the story of the Kibbo Kift

ends there. However, for those who were left behind, the schism of the 1924 Al-Thing bonded them together all the more.

Charles A. Tacey was sixteen years old when he joined the Kindred in 1927, the year of the publication of *The Confession of the Kibbo Kift*, John Hargrave's public manifesto for his movement. Tacey was in the Third Putney Scouts and wrote articles about camping for *Boy's Own* magazine. Returning from a cycle-camping trip to Dorset, he called in at Sandy Balls and encountered the Kindred, who were camping alongside another progressive group called the Order of Woodcraft Chivalry, who we will encounter in a subsequent chapter. That year, he was initiated at the Al-Thing and took the name Will Scarlet.

To find out more about Charles A. Tacey, I visited his son, Jon Tacey, in a village north of Andover in Hampshire. His mother, Ella, was also a member of the Kindred and took the name Briony. Jon was conceived in a tipi in the woods of Surrey in 1933, a unique claim. On the kitchen wall, a paper model of a Buckminster Fuller dome attests to an ongoing interest in camping. Jon has devised a tent he calls the Yurpi, a cross between a yurt and a tipi, and as we chat around the kitchen table he fashions, out of paper, a small tent that follows the specifications laid down in Hargrave's *Lonecraft*. A golden sickle hangs on the wall. I recognize its occult significance, and point to it.

'Does that mean you are a Druid?'

'It was a gift from some friends,' he explains. 'Yes, I was a Druid. Now I am a non-practising Druid.'

The artist Olivia Plender is also sat around the table. In 2005, she presented a project about the Kibbo Kift at the Coniston Water Festival. A video, *Bring Back Robin Hood*, wove her research into the Kindred around present-day stories concerning gentrification and economic crisis. Her filmed interviews showed that historians and former members each had a different take on the movement. At the festival in Coniston, a small band was dressed in replicas of Kibbo Kift ceremonial outfits and marched through the village singing.

Jon shows us his father's herald stick, and explains the symbols carved upon it: here is a mouth representing the role of Kin herald, and there is the mark of the Kibbo Kift and the mark of his lodge, Wandlething, intricately worked and painted upon an elder branch.

'I thought I'd lost this,' says Jon, the look on his face showing us how much finding the stick meant to him.

'My parents married in 1933 and I was born a year later, much – I suspect – to their annoyance. My first memory of camping with them was at the Al-Thing in High Wycombe, in 1938. I slept in their little triangle tent. "Don't touch the sides. Make sure the groundsheet doesn't slip out from under the edge of the tent." All that stuff. After dark, everyone gathered around the campfire in a chalk pit and sang the old songs of the Kindred of the Kibbo Kift.'

By 1938, the Kindred of the Kibbo Kift was a different movement from the one that Charles Tacey had joined over a decade earlier. The Kibbo Kift was transformed by an idea called 'social credit', a new economic system that John Hargrave embraced as the cause they had all been training for. Social credit was devised by Major C. H. Douglas. Douglas believed both consumers and producers were unnecessarily burdened by debt; consumers had to borrow from the banks to buy goods that were priced high because the producers had to borrow from the banks to stay in business. High prices meant that consumers couldn't purchase all the producers' products, and so new markets abroad had to be opened up, and this was the cause of war. To reduce the gap between production and consumption, credits would be allocated to the population. To a pacifist, social credit promised to check the violent consequences of capitalism's expansionism. It was also a way of cutting the banks out of the system. From 1924, study of social credit was compulsory for the Kindred. It was added to the third clause of the Kindred covenant in 1927, at the same time as Charles Tacey was initiated.

Up until the incorporation of social credit, the Kindred was a youth movement whose members camped and studied to train themselves to be a physical and intellectual elite. It took up a lot of time, which was fine for the young, but was more difficult to accommodate with the demands of career and family. With the embracing of social credit, this period of training was over, and now it was their job to carry ideas out into the population and make things happen. The Kindred had trained for a crisis. They had a 'Noah's Ark' plan to cope with social collapse. With the Wall Street Crash and the doubling of unemployment in Britain, the crisis was upon them. On 3 January 1931, John Hargrave inaugurated a reorganization of the remaining Kindred along paramilitary lines. The movement metamorphosed into the Social Credit Party, known as the Green Shirts, their numbers swelled by a 'Legion of the Unemployed' from the Midlands. The emphasis shifted from camping to marching. Many members left, new members joined and a few remained, Charles Tacey among them.

As leader of the Social Credit Party, Hargrave modelled his presentation upon the demagogues of the era. The Green Shirts marched with a hundred drummers, a ferocious, street-stopping act of theatre. He always maintained that the green shirt was a costume, not a uniform. The Green Shirts were a parody of Oswald Mosley's blackshirts and the communist redshirts. Off duty, there was no deference to him from the other leading members who had come over from the Kibbo Kift. On duty, spreading Green Shirt propaganda, he was their unquestioned leader. Ezra Pound, writing through the miasma of his madness, touched upon the Green Shirts performing the role of a street movement when he told Hargrave that he was all dressed up but he didn't know where he was going. The Green Shirts were Hargrave's intervention into 1930s politics with the purpose of breaking through the pitched battles between far left and far right. They performed regular provocations: in 1938, on Guy Fawkes Day at midnight, Hargrave's followers burned an effigy of the Governor of the Bank of England, Montagu Norman, outside the Bank of England. On Budget Day, 25 April, a car with an effigy of Montagu Norman squatting on the back of a soldier in full fighting kit drove through the City of London. The sides of the car bore National Service posters and the legend 'Conscript the Bankers First'. At noon on 29 February 1940, R. J. Green, a member of the Social Credit Party, dressed in a green jacket, shirt and tie (with a policeman at his elbow), fitted a green arrow to his bow and let it fly at a window of No. 10 Downing Street. The arrow shaft carried this message:

END HITLERISM – WAR DEMANDS A DEBT-FREE BRITAIN – SOCIAL CREDIT THE ONLY REMEDY – SOCIAL CREDIT IS COMING

Hargrave had been critical of Hitler as early as 1925. In a letter to Rolf Gardiner, who, in the early 1920s, acted as go-between for the Kibbo Kift and German youth movements, Hargrave rejected 'the kind of nationalism developed by Hitler, which, viewed from a distance, is more like third-rate comic opera'. But his adoption of social credit and his attack upon the banks aligned him with the anti-Semitic rhetoric of the fascists.

'Ah, that,' says Jon Tacey. 'There was the sense that the whole banking system was run by Jews, but John Hargrave was not anti-Semitic. He struggled to get people not to think, "Oh, they are all horrible Jewish bankers and they are screwing us."'

Hargrave was keen to distance himself from racially driven ideologies. A chapter in *The Confession of the Kibbo Kift* is entitled 'Racial Absurdities and Nordic Nonsense'. But social credit was an idea that fascists approved of. In their correspondence concerning the Green Shirts, a letter from J. A. Macnab of the British

Union of Fascists to Ezra Pound states, 'Sir Oswald Mosley has always welcomed the attack on orthodox finance made by the social creditors . . . and he was glad to observe that a large body of intelligent people had at any rate seen through the old financial ramp.' But, having established this point, Macnab goes on to complain about the conduct of the Green Shirts, and a fight between them and the fascists at a meeting in the north of England. The Green Shirts would disrupt meetings of communist and fascist alike by forming a line down the centre and drumming. Macnab has realized that although blackshirt and green shirt shared a dislike for international finance, the Green Shirts were allied against fascism:

> Green Shirts to my certain knowledge, from personal observation in London, had been and still are identifying themselves with the Red Front. They have joined in practically all the so-called Peace demonstrations right through the Abyssinian campaign, speaking from a common platform with the Communists and Socialists, denouncing Italy as a warmonger and aggressor, joining in the demand for sanctions both economic and military, and in general making common cause with the so-called United Front against Fascism.

The originator of social credit, Major C. H. Douglas, was exposed at the end of the thirties as a raging anti-Semite. Hargrave and the Green Shirts had to disown the originator of their founding idea. With the onset of war, Charles Tacey asked Hargrave what he should do. Hargrave told him to sign up and do the best he could, because after the war the Green Shirts would need people in positions of influence. Charles Tacey did very well in the war; he returned a colonel and was awarded the OBE. But the Second World War was the end for the group, although Hargrave felt that rationing owed something to his proposed system of social credit.

After the war, Hargrave ran for Parliament on a social credit platform in Stoke Newington. 'I was there for that,' remembers Jon Tacey, 'John Hargrave liked to appear dramatic. He walked almost on tiptoe, like the American Indian. I travelled in cars with him and he could be normal enough. But he was self-centred in conversation. He wanted people to listen to him. He could get on his high horse. His whole life was spent trying to be special, trying to get his ideas adopted in some sense.' When the votes were counted, Hargrave lost his deposit. In the years that followed, his old supporters did what they could to keep him in money. Charles Tacey commissioned him to write the *'Paragon' Dictionary* for his company of educational supplies. Hargrave became a healer by the laying on of hands and he painted healing art. He married again, an actress called Gwendolyne Gray, and he renamed her Diana. He went to ground in a flat in Fortune Green Road, West Hampstead.

In the 1970s, musician Chris Judge Smith wrote a rock musical about the Kibbo Kift and was surprised to discover, towards the end of the process, that John Hargrave was still alive. Hargrave and his wife Diana invited him to dinner at the flat, and after the pleasantries, Hargrave asked the young, somewhat intimidated Chris Smith, 'Right, what is this all about?'

'I spent the last year writing a musical about you, but I didn't realize that you were still alive,' replied Chris, who was soon to be renamed Judge Smith by John Hargrave. Judge and his musical partner returned and sang the musical about the Kibbo Kift to Hargrave and Diana after dinner. They approved, even though it depicted the hero leaving the movement upon its transformation into the Social Credit Party.

'John Hargrave was the most extraordinary person, certainly the most compelling person I have met in my life,' says Judge. 'He had an enormous presence. Very sharp intellect. He was quietly spoken but fascinating. Dapperly dressed, great blade of a Roman nose and careful with his appearance; he wanted to be an impressive person. I sat there like a snake in front of a mongoose.

He was quite deaf at that time in his life, which suited him, as he could talk without interruption. He spoke discursively; he could snake off from a topic and bring it back to the original stated subject at the end of an hour. I used to go over there every few weeks for an evening. Our conversations were more about mystical politics than about the outdoor life. After the KK became the Green Shirts, he didn't carry on camping into middle age.'

In 'Plan of Action of the Kindred in the British Isles', Hargrave writes, 'We have to dispel the overhanging feeling that "Britain is played out."' The Kindred existed at a similar moment in history to our own, a time of cultural exhaustion and political pessimism following a financial collapse. They responded to contemporary ills with intellectual and physical courage, men and women alike, an energetic, creative community, with ideas above their station, bonded by camping and ersatz ritual; taking names such as Seeonee Wolf, Little Lone Wolf, White Chief, Little Elk, Wappo and Little Owl, they lived the extraordinary dream of their leader, their head man, in robe and cowl of brilliant white edged by a four-inch purple border, John Hargrave.

The Kindred were swimming in the same current of ideas as fascism: anti-democratic, one charismatic and unquestioned leader, regeneration of the race, 'a vicarious expectation of an idealistic revolution', an assault on the bankers and international finance – all hallmarks of National Socialism. The differences are equally important: pacifist, anti-nationalist and against anti-Semitism, and fighting fascists in the streets. In the early 1920s, John Hargrave's woodcraft manual *Tribal Training* was a significant influence on the German youth movement, and there was considerable traffic between English and German groups throughout the decade, largely thanks to the efforts of Rolf Gardiner, a self-appointed conduit. Gardiner was to make some unwise alignments with National Socialism in the 1930s from which his reputation never quite recovered, as we shall see in a later chapter. By 1926, Hargrave and his followers were being demonized by Nesta Webster, a prominent fascist conspiracy theorist whose work built on the notorious forgery *The Protocols of the Elders of Zion*. She linked the Kibbo Kift with communists and socialists in a worldwide fraternity with the devil.

Like many intellectuals of the modernist era, John Hargrave was revolted by the masses and regarded democracy as a sham. Pragmatic, if possessed of a wildly contradictory philosophy, the Kibbo Kift were agrarian-futurists, H. G. Wells-inspired intellectuals who also mythologized England's ancient past as a mystical Albion. Their union of the ancient and the futuristic in which technology permits a deeper connection to nature reoccurs throughout the history of camping. It is camping's radical idea.

A prehistoric track stretches across 250 miles from the Dorset coast to the Norfolk Wash. For over 5,000 years, people have walked or ridden the trail. The first section we know as the Ridgeway, a chalk ridge beginning in the uplands of Wessex and bisected by the River Thames at Goring Gap, rising above the low ground and valleys that once would have been treacherous with woods and marshes, wolf and boar. At Ivinghoe Beacon in the Chiltern Hills, the second part of the track commences, the Icknield Way, a narrow corridor and ancient line of communication between South-West England and the East coast, a path worn steadily by traders, travellers and invaders as far back as the Bronze Age.

On a night hike returning to his encampment in Latimer overlooking the River Chess, John Hargrave crossed the Icknield Way, inspiring the closing address of *The Confession of the Kibbo Kift*. Entitled 'The Spirit', this evocation of English mysticism is the closest Hargrave's writing comes to the achievements of his modernist peers. Rolf Gardiner, an acolyte of D. H. Lawrence, recognized the genius in 'The Spirit', describing it as 'a truly magnificent exhortation, the authentic voice of the seer crying in the wilderness of stupid wayward men; it is the voice of the gods in the soil of Britain'.

Hargrave knew yoga and meditation. He synthesized Eastern ideas – the clarity of unbeing – with the sensual being of D. H. Lawrence; 'when the mind and the known world is drowned in darkness everything must go.' The night hike was a way into the deep knowledge buried beneath civilization. The charged, adrenalized sensation of being alone with nature, every sense alive to predators – this was being! This was life! No wonder scholar David Bradshaw has seen something of John Hargrave filling the red trousers of Mellors, Lady Chatterley's lover, himself.

'The Spirit' closes with a call for the great men to go into isolation and prepare themselves for the work to come. It was read at the funeral of Charles A. Tacey, Will Scarlet.

I shall go where the great trees stand, deep into the half-light of the woods whelming upon the giant bodies of the beech. I know the place where the afterglow shines like a pale halo upon the hill, and there the ash and the elm take hold upon the earth, flinging their strength into the sky. And over the summit of the hill on slanting ground a crab tree and a crooked thorn crouch and clutch each other.

I shall come around them uneasily and pass under the ash and the elm with an intaking of breath, and so down the valley to the track that runs into the pine wood where the darkness closes in, and the feet tread noiselessly, and the lungs are filled with the scent of the hanging curtains, the needled carpet and the cones . . .

Tread softly over the grass that springs out of the blood and bodies of old heroes of the Icknield Way long since gone to dust.

Back to the place of dwelling, to the encampment.

5
Camping Mystics

'What is real camping, anyway?' asks Mick Tutt. 'Is it real camping if you sleep in a tipi that you made yourself? Is it real camping if you get up in the morning and dress in a loincloth and moccasins that you also made yourself?' Mick camped with a man who did just that, Logan, the leader of a Czech woodcraft group who fashioned his tent and outfit by hand. There is always someone better than you. There is always someone more real.

'Logan parks his car out of sight of his tipi. He does not want to see the car for the duration of the camp.'

'Because the car is not real?' I ask.

'Is it only real camping if you take the train? Or should you always hike to the campsite?'

Mick and I are in the Woodside bar of Sandy Balls Holiday

Park. Mick is a permanent resident of the campsite, living in a tidy chalet nearby with his wife, Sue.

I improvise my definition of real camping: 'Real camping is any day and night you spend in a tent that gives you the mystic charge of being outdoors. Real camping is a technique for making strange. The fewer familiar domestic trappings you have, the greater the defamiliarization, opening you to the uncanny stars, the gibbous moon, the September chill, the dawn chorus. That is what constitutes real camping, for me.'

Even as I am hesitating my way through this speech, I am thinking, Could I make my own loincloth? And would Cath let me wear it? How would a big man in a skimpy loincloth go down in the Orchard, the field of gravel pitches in which we have camped upon our visit to Sandy Balls in the New Forest? It is late September. Blackberries are on the turn, and the first caravans of retired people have emerged from their hibernation during school holidays. Caravanning is definitely not real camping. Caravanning and camping are very different pursuits, and lumping them together on one field is like pitting a cricket team against a football team. The equipment is different. The rules are different. The state of mind is profoundly different. The art of caravanning is miniaturization; instead of leaving the domestic realm behind, it is shrunk and towed along. To enter a caravan is to step into a wonderland of diminished scale; here is the small telly, the small microwave and a little fridge. Admire the ingenious uses of space: the toothbrush holder that is also a spice rack, the table that turns into a bed, the bucket in a cupboard that thinks it is a toilet. My parents started out as campers, but went over to the other side in the early 1980s, the catalyst being an injury my father, Eddie, sustained in the Toxteth riots. It was my job, at the age of eleven, to guide the caravan into its berth or usher it on to the tow bar. I unwound the legs, checked the electrics, fetched the fresh water and emptied the waste water. Of the holidays themselves, I remember only card games and homesickness; sleeping in a miniature version of the family home made me pine for the real thing.

One of the early pioneers of leisure caravanning, Bertram Smith, decided that the special charm of a caravan was its 'complexity and completeness, the whole fun of it is to bring with you a dwelling fitted out in every detail, even to shoe-horns and paper knives'. The caravan is an object of pride. In the Orchard field of Sandy Balls, I watched the man on the opposite pitch polish his Swift mobile home in the same way that he groomed his expensive dog. The caravanner is tethered to their status symbol: pedigree dog and little house. I eavesdrop upon their chat of dogs and traffic. Caravanners fear the low bridge, the narrowing road and the snake. Oh, how they fear the snake! My mother speaks of snakes in a low, superstitious voice: 'They got a snake going downhill on the A303' or 'He came off the motorway too quickly and started to snake.' Rapid change of direction or speed, side winds, or a bow wave from a lorry cause the caravan to swing out. If the driver over-corrects the steering, inertia causes a shift in the opposite direction. The wheels lose their grip as the van oscillates on its tether across the road. If the driver cannot bring it under control, the snake lashes. The caravan jackknifes. The car loses control. The tail wags the dog. The dog wags the owner.

'Is it real camping if you have an electric hook-up and a satellite dish?' I wonder.

Mick had this very debate with Logan in the Czech Republic. Afterwards, Logan went out in his handmade loincloth and moccasins, and returned with a satellite dish made from branches and grasses. He stuck it on the side of his tipi. Mick Tutt slaps the table and laughs at the memory.

'Is it real camping,' he asks, 'if we spend all day at our tents, cooking over a fire, chopping wood, going on hikes and then, at night, go back to a hotel?'

'That's a day out,' I reply. Sleeping in a tent is the first principle of camping, never mind the rarefied condition of real camping. The rest is open to debate.

From the late 1960s until the late 1990s, Mick was an active member of a camping group called the Order of Woodcraft Chivalry. One of his daughters continues to camp with them. As a young man in his early twenties, Mick founded the Phoenix Lodge within the Order. The Phoenix represented his attempt to get back to real camping in a movement that, since its inception in 1916, he felt had drifted away from its authentic origins. Its reality.

'In the early 1960s,' he explains, 'the Order decided to expand its membership through these "family camps", where visiting families could get a taster of the Order of Woodcraft Chivalry experience. It wasn't real camping, more like Butlins under canvas. It was regimented and meals were taken communally. I wanted to cook my own food, but that disrupted organized activities because people were eating at different times. Some of the older members, who had been there at the beginning, supported me. They understood that I was trying to get back to the sort of things they had hoped for in the 1930s.'

In its name and imagery, the Order of Woodcraft Chivalry harks back to the medieval ideal of the knight, taking as its symbol a shield bearing the St George's cross laid over two upturned axes. The name is problematic, and somewhat comic, and the Order has made concerted but unresolved efforts to change it. When the name was coined, in 1916, it was an earnest if bungled attempt to fuse three different ideas, two of which – the religious order and the chivalric code – belonged to the cluster of ideas known as medievalism, a yearning to restore lineage to the way of life broken by the Industrial Revolution, to roll back capitalism and return to a system of guilds. A shield painted with the St George's cross appears to be a lament for a lost Albion and the simpler, rural way of life. But don't be misled. At its height in the late 1920s, the inner circle of the Order was concerned with progressive education, experimental thought and frank sexual discussion.

I leave Mick Tutt in his chalet and follow signs for a River Walk. The path is lined with tall pines and groves of timber chalets and leads to a rough track twisting down to the River Avon. Much work has been done to manage the surrounding woodland, thinning the foliage on the Sandy Balls themselves, waxing the testicular hillocks that have inspired a century's worth of double entendre. (Eggs are rolled down the Good Friday Ball every Easter, celebrating its fertility.) Turning right at a Sandy Ball, I follow a sign to the Folk Moot, or meeting place, and find large logs arranged in two concentric circles around a charred patch of earth. This is where the Order of the Woodcraft Chivalry still holds its annual council, its 'moot'. The keeper of the fire takes ash from the fire and adds it to the next one he or she sets; the eternal campfire. I have seen old photographs of this place, dating from the 1920s; woodsmoke rises over the Order of men and women, bare-legged and sprawled around the fire. Serried ranks of Woodcrafters on terraces of banked earth. Rhododendron bushes crowd against their backs. The wood appears to be pushing against their presence. The shield of the Order is born aloft, the same shield that, today, is kept in a rusting container on the grounds of Sandy Balls. In the old photographs, there are no log circles. The trees stand like lieutenants beside the chieftain in his ceremonial cape. Set furthest back, a gaggle of white-hatted children observe the adult mysteries.

From the circle, I follow the path further down towards the river and arrive at Greenwood. This glade has another fire circle, and a pair of Portaloos. Beyond the bushes, the wide and lazy progress of the Avon. There has been camping at Greenwood for a hundred years, with campers, young and old, beginning each morning with a thorough dousing in the bracing waters of the river. In the 1930s, young unemployed men were trained at Greenwood to live self-sufficiently; they built bunk houses and dining rooms, manufactured looms and wove their own cloth, grew vegetables and milked goats. Known as the Grith Fyrd (Anglo-Saxon for 'peace army', *Fyrd* pronounced 'feared'), the work camp stayed in Greenwood for eight years. The men of Grith Fyrd also made their own camping kit, which they used during long camping trips exploring the state of the nation, the farms and factories, Stonehenge and slums that constituted England in the interwar period. Greenwood was also used by the Forest School, an educational experiment in the pedagogical benefits of camping. Both the Forest School and Grith Fyrd grew out of the progressive educational nature of the Order of Woodcraft Chivalry, a dedicated band of men and women who did not merely yearn for a lost authentic era, but used camping and woodcraft to experiment with a different way of life. But all of this is to come; first it is time to meet the founder of this movement.

Ernest Westlake is buried on Woodling Point, a singular peak that gazes out over Greenwood and into the town of Fording-bridge. His coffin was fashioned from fir trees with the bark still on them. In place of brass handles, there were leather straps, and instead of a plate on the breast of the coffin lid, his name was carved into the wood. How quickly his woodcraft coffin sped his remains into the churning cycle of decomposition! The tumult of earth, the scampering woodlife and teeming ferns make this spot feel more like a junction than a resting place. The raging forest fires of 1976 left scars on the bark of the surrounding pines but did not mark the wooden arch that stands over the grave. Carved into the arch, the symbol of the Order of Woodcraft Chivalry and an inscription:

Here on Woodling Point overlooking his native town lies the body of Ernest Westlake 1856–1922 [the engraver was in error, he was born in 1855]. Founder of the Order of Woodcraft Chivalry, its first British chieftain and honoured as father of the Order. His fore-sight and public spirit preserved Sandy Balls for lovers of natural

beauty and for the training of youth in his great inspiration the
Forest School.

The epitaph contains the final line of Sappho's poem 'To
Evening', which is dedicated to Hesperus, the evening star, son of
the dawn. In the poem, the arrival of the star brings all that the
day has scattered – the sheep, the goat and the tired child – back
home. The final line can be translated as 'Thou bringest the child
back to its mother.' This was the motto of the educational ethos
of the Order. Scored over a grave, it has a pagan suggestion of
death as a return to the source.

Ernest Westlake's mother, Hannah Westlake, died from tuberculosis when he was eighteen months old. He was raised by his
aunt, Agnes, whom his father married in 1863. The Westlakes
were a respected family of Southampton Quakers who could
trace their ancestry right back to John Westlake, converted by
George Fox, founder of the Society of Friends, in the seventeenth
century. Ernest's childhood was reclusive. As soon as the doors to
the nursery were flung open, he went into the woods surrounding their home in Fordingbridge and made platforms high in the
trees to spend his days swinging in the summer breeze. He dug
out caves in chalk and sand; the timeless allure of the cave to the
boy was at the centre of his later educational programme, which
sought to awaken and recapitulate the primitive within the child.
Seven or eight years old, on the way to a family camping trip in
the South of France, I remember gazing avidly at the nooks and
caves in the white cliffs of Dover. I yearned to set up home there,
to leave the family and run with the pack. It was this instinct that
the Order of Woodcraft Chivalry was devised to foster and
metabolize, so that the child would be ready to join civilization
without unresolved primitive yearnings.

After university, Ernest Westlake joined the Society for Psych-
ical Research as an investigator. A typical mission was a trip to the
village of Ham to look into the case of a poltergeist. The ghost

hurled boots and chairs around a room and even threw the cat into the fire. Ernest detected that, contrary to the testimony of the local clergyman, it was all the work of a disabled little girl. Soon after joining the Society, he married his cousin, Lucy Ann Rutter, and they had two children, Aubrey Westlake, born in 1893, and Margaret Westlake, born in 1896. Tragically, Lucy Westlake died in 1901 at the age of thirty-six, during morphine treatment for pleurisy. Ernest Westlake's modest fortune had been lost in a series of unlucky investments, and he lamented that 'I am now left fortuneless, homeless, wifeless with two motherless children to support, and now the family wish to take my children from me – but I will not let them go.'

Ernest Westlake travelled around the New Forest in his Gypsy caravan and wore sandals, a clear signal of progressive intent. He compiled a bibliography of dowsing and read the likes of John Ruskin's *Sesame and Lilies*, which called for the reconstitution of chivalry, and other influential anti-modernist writers such as Charles Kingsley, whose muscular Christianity influenced Thomas Hiram Holding. In the view of these writers and thinkers, the Industrial Revolution had destroyed the social harmony and landscape of Albion and replaced it with filthy cities and a degenerating citizenry. Westlake considered the questions of the age: how could the ruinous course of civilization be diverted? How could England be saved? The educational theory of recapitulation provided an answer.

'Recapitulation theory' was devised by G. Stanley Hall and inspired by the fearsomely named 'biogenetic law' of Ernst Haeckel. The biogenetic law proposes that the foetal growth stages match our evolutionary progress from sea creature to ape to *Homo sapiens*. 'Ontogeny recapitulates phylogeny' was Haeckel's formula; ontogeny (the growth of the embryo) mirrors the evolutionary history of the species (the phylogeny). The theory is now discredited, but it was highly influential both in science and in philosophy, and inspired Carl Jung's theory of the collective unconscious. Educational theorist G. Stanley Hall proposed that we should view the healthy development of the child as one that recapitulates the history of human evolution. If, in the womb, the foetus goes from amoeba to fish to *Homo sapiens*, then, once out of it, the child must progress from Stone Age to Bronze Age to Iron Age and so on before being 'born' into adulthood. Adolescence was the point of crisis in psychological and physical development:

> The child from nine to twelve is well adjusted to his environment and proportionately developed; he represents probably an old and relatively perfected state of race-maturity . . . At dawning adolescence this old unity and harmony with nature is broken up; the child is driven from his paradise . . . he must evolve a more modern story to this psycho-physical nature . . . It is the most critical stage of life, because failure to mount almost always means retrogression, degeneracy and fall.

The answer was the indulging of instinct. The animal in man was as much a gift of God as vaulted reason. For children, in whom instinct remained strong, that ability to discern and act upon ancient imperatives made them closer to God. Those instincts were best expressed while camping.

Recapitulation theory provided pseudo-scientific justification for putting real camping at the heart of education. Ernest Westlake's solitary childhood of climbing trees and digging into caves, along with his amateur study of the artefacts of primitive man, meant that he was intellectually and emotionally disposed to believe in the theory. His son Aubrey Westlake took up Scouting in Cambridge in 1914, and Ernest saw that a youth movement with camping could put recapitulation into practice. As Quakers and pacifists, the Westlakes could not stand for the Scouts' military drill. But if Ernest Thompson Seton's woodcraft practice and ethos were combined with symbols of Englishness, then a new movement could be founded. Westlake contacted Seton, and the old dog agreed to act as grand chieftain for the proposed Order.

Ernest Westlake devised the name 'The Order of Woodcraft Chivalry' to evoke a religious order from the medieval era. Addressing a meeting of the Baha'i, a progressive faith founded in the mid nineteenth century, Aubrey Westlake explained that the Order would satisfy the need for a 'social religion, one which is carried into every detail of life, one which embraces every field of activity. This religion we seek is already in every child.' This was an articulation of the Quaker belief that the light of the Divine resides in everyone, and churches are not required to mediate between Man and God. The blueprint of the progressive camping sect owes much to Quaker principles of direct experience of the Divine and the integration of religion and everyday life, to learn by doing. Although they borrowed a great deal from Seton in the early days, including their rallying cry of 'Blue Sky!', the Order of Woodcraft Chivalry did not look to the American Indian for meaning. Authenticity lay within, and required the psychological archaeology of ritual to discover it.

G. Stanley Hall recommended setting a time and place for children to let loose their barbaric instincts. In his *Adolescence*, he advised that 'Every adolescent boy ought to belong to some club or society marked by as much secrecy as is compatible with safety. Something esoteric, mysterious, a symbolic badge, countersign, a lodge . . . give a real basis for comradeship.' The Order of Woodcraft Chivalry would be all that and more. Women too were welcomed into the movement. But the education of adolescents was not the limit of the Order's ambition. Ernest Westlake felt that civilization itself needed to undergo a period of recapitulation if it was to progress healthily. 'Civilization is comparable to a tree,' said the young Aubrey Westlake, 'whose height and extension is strictly limited by the strength of its roots and lower limbs.' For society and for the individual, a healthy future required a revival of the past through ritual and the indulging of instinct.

The Order of Woodcraft Chivalry was a product of the Great War; Westlake's plan was supported by the Quaker movement as a programme for peace. The youth were to be inculcated with the chivalric creed of service, and with camping and recapitulation they would express and thus purge the instinct to fight prior to full adulthood. At the request of the headmaster of Sidcot School, Aubrey Westlake organized the first instruction in the Order in the summer term of 1916, overlapping with zero hour of the Battle of the Somme.

We open up the container at Sandy Balls and there, propped up against a corrugated iron wall, is the heraldic shield of the Order of Woodcraft Chivalry backed by inverted crossed green axes and painted with the St George's cross. At the back of the container, a stack of the manuals published by the Order in the 1920s and 1930s under the imprint of 'The Woodcraft Way'. The theories of the Westlakes are scattered across these publications. The majority of the Order was never confronted with one single cohesive expression or manifesto of the movement, which was a blessing, as it made the Order more accessible to the mainstream Quakers and well-meaning middle classes that constituted its membership.

I retrieve a copy of *How to Run Woodcraft Chivalry: Deeds, Trials and Adventures* from the store, a small orange paperback printed in 1922 and unopened since then. The St George's cross continues to bother me; it is now largely associated with football tournaments, and in the months of anticipation building up to any international football tournament involving England, supermarket shelves groan with opportunistic me-too marketing, beer cans and cakes and crisps all flying the St George's cross in a pretence of belonging. Millions of St George's crosses churned out in Chinese factories are affixed to car aerials and draped out of bedroom windows. The St George's flag is a defiant yawp from John Bull, the Confederate flag of these Isles. Englishness as a shared grievance. (On a campsite outside Hastings, the caravans were arranged around the perimeter, each one hedged with windbreaks and all flying the St George's flag: patriotic wagons circled around the flagless, creedless middle-class campers pitched in the centre of the field.)

Ernest Westlake chose the red cross to evoke medieval chivalry. For him, it was not a symbol of nationalist defiance. In fact, for a movement that takes the St George's cross as its emblem, there is a surprising dearth of patriotic or nationalistic rhetoric in their publications. My unease at the use of the St George's cross stems not from the Order itself, but from the associations of camping in general with nationalism. No, let's be honest, the association of camping with fascism.

The British youth movements of the interwar period owed much to their forerunners and contemporaries in Germany: the Wandervogel, active from 1896 to the Great War, and the Bünde, a catch-all term for a diverse collection of camping and hiking groups that thrived throughout the 1920s until Hitler folded their ranks into the Hitler Youth in 1933. Writing about Nazi Germany under the remit of a history of camping is awkward, but unavoidable. After the Great War, youth movements took it upon themselves to change the direction of society. The question of whether that altered course led directly to National Socialism is a complex one, but it must be addressed. If we are to celebrate the simple pleasures of camping, that feeling of being close to the land, the unspoken but palpable sense of community, the camper's exultation in doing rather than passively consuming, then we must consider the monstrous iteration of those ideas in Germany from the beginning of the twentieth century to Hitler's assumption of the role of chancellor in 1933.

The revival of chivalry did not begin with Ernest Westlake. The historian Walter Laqueur observes that for the Wandervogel, 'The Middle Ages became the great ideal: the manly virtues and poetic love, true faith and loyalty had disappeared with the age of chivalry.' This idealization of chivalry survived the destruction of the Wandervogel in the Great War and passed into the Bünde, the German youth movement that succeeded it. Leaving an Easter camp of the Bünde in 1927, Rolf Gardiner observed that 'there emerged from these young men a clear desire for Einsatz [opportunity] in the national destiny and focusing of their lives, almost along the lines of an Order of Chivalry.' Chivalry became an active sequence in the DNA of Nazism. Hubert Lanzinger's painting *Der Bannerträger* (*c.* 1934–6) depicted Hitler as a knight in shining armour riding a black steed and bearing a swastika flag. The SS saw themselves as a new Order of Knights. Ideas replicate, spread and mutate in defiance of our intentions.

The Wandervogel was a countercultural youth movement founded in 1896 by a shorthand study circle at Steglitz grammar school. The students went rambling. They liked it. They hiked through the Harz Mountains, they camped across the Rhine, they wandered through the mountains between Bavaria and Bohemia. A leader emerged, the brooding and not particularly bright Karl Fischer. In 1901, the first association of the Wandervogel was formed, consisting of ten boys. Unlike Baden-Powell's Scouts, there was no adult leadership and no central programme. Other Wandervogel groups sprang up, some were left wing, most were right wing, all were reacting against the constraints of the era. The Wandervogel rejected the stultifying social order of turn-of-the-century Wilhelminian Germany, and its atomized mechanical life, for a life of rambling, singing (the Wandervogel songs have entered the popular German songbook), dancing and camping. Mainly drawn from middle-class families, they sought authentic reinvention in the German landscape, in the same way that contemporary bourgeois youth seek out the real in gap years in Africa or India. Long-haired and bare-legged, rootless, free and without a plan, the Wandervogel were vague but alluring; their first decade saw steady growth, along with the usual secessions and conflict that characterize youth movements. Their early leader, Karl Fischer, whose countenance was likened to an approaching thundercloud, was rejected for being autocratic; he formed a splinter group, the Altwandervogel, before disappearing to China in 1906.

Although each group of Wandervogel developed its own distinctive identity, there were certain common traits. Members were between twelve and nineteen years old, with a leader a few years older who wielded absolute authority. Each group consisted of a minimum of seven or eight members and up to a maximum of twenty – or about as many as could comfortably fit around a campfire. Their dress was cheap and flamboyant, their hats decorated with a jaunty feather. In his book on the origins of bohemianism, Richard Miller describes the life of the Wandervogel: 'They pooled their money, spoke hobo slang, peasant patois and medieval vulgate. They were loud and rude, sometimes ragged and dirty and torn by briars. They carried packs, wore woollen capes, shorts, dark shirts, Tyrolean hats with heavy boots and bright neck scarves. Part hobo and part medieval they were very offensive to their elders.' They were often described as proto-hippies, and their habit of greeting one another with '*Heil*' was the 'Hey, man' of its time, until it was adopted by the Nazis. They were part of the wider Life Reform movement, a platter of nudism, vegetarianism and sun worship with a side order of theosophy.

In 1907, girls took part in Wandervogel outings for the first time. Accusations of free love followed, and groups such as the Jungwandervogel were notoriously homosexual. The similarity between the Wandervogel and the hippies is most evident in the artwork of Hugo Höppener, known as Fidus, or 'the faithful'. Fidus's paintings were rediscovered by the 1960s underground. His painting for the cover of the Hoher Meissner report, an account of a pivotal gathering of the Wandervogel, depicts a naked phalanx of men with leonine manes, swords, scabbards and hairbands, their hands joined, their faces gazing into the middle distance; at their feet, two naked maidens cavort draped in vegetation. A high sun fires psychedelic swirls over them all; the cover of an album by the Incredible String Band, if the Incredible String Band were newborn Nordic clones. Fidus's psychedelic swirls express the intensity of the Wandervogel experience, as mind-expanding and transformative as the LSD trips of the hippies. 'The authentic and deepest experience of the youth movement is difficult to describe and perhaps impossible to analyse,' writes Walter Laqueur. 'The experience of walking at night and at sunrise, the atmosphere of the camp fire, the friendships that sprang up ... Very deep emotional chords were struck.' Real camping eludes definition; it is a deep feeling shared by the campers, instinctive and primal.

The Hoher Meissner meeting of October 1913 was an attempt by the various bands of the Wandervogel to reach consensus. Camping seemed to be the only thing they agreed upon, until a declaration was made to ban nicotine and alcohol. Eventually, after some rousing songs around the campfire, it was agreed that youth should be tolerant and respect everyone's opinion so long as it was sincere and the result of a search for truth. This formed the basis of their Meissner formula: 'Free German Youth, on their own initiative, under their own responsibility, and with deep sincerity, are determined independently to shape their own lives. For the sake of this inner freedom they will under any and all circumstances take united action.'

The Great War extinguished any hope of putting this formula into action. After the war, the youth movement was radicalized towards the left, and saw an influx into its membership of German Jewish soldiers. The Wandervogel was succeeded by a movement referred to as the Bünde, the second phase of the German youth movement, which lasted from 1919 to 1933. Less individualistic and certainly less harmless than the Wandervogel, the Bünde reacted violently against the liberal democracy of the newly formed Weimar Republic.

The ideas and methods of the Kibbo Kift were adopted by a

large part of the Bünde. John Hargrave's books were popular in German translation; his call for economic reform and world peace, and his programme of mental discipline, solitude and meditation, physical fitness and spiritual awareness, helped to mould the Bünde in the early to mid 1920s, his influence waning through the decade as the Bünde became more pragmatic. Via John Hargrave's writing, the Indian mythology of Ernest Thompson Seton was fused with German Romanticism, providing another example of the unexpected iteration of ideas through these movements. When the youth movements rejected conventional politics, they reached instead for a grab bag of countercultural ideas that became conflated in alarming ways. Seton's mythical Indian and his close relationship to the land mixed with the Volkisch mythology of blood and soil. Walter Laqueur defines Volkisch as 'not folkish but indicates a specific trend in German right-wing thought and politics. It is not synonymous with nationalism, since it puts people (or, to be precise, the race) above state and nation as a supreme good.' 'Woodcraft Folk' are named after the German sense of 'volk' to mean people, and not in the 'fairy' or 'arty crafty' sense of the word. Even the seemingly innocent educational principle of 'learn by doing', a central tenet of woodcraft, has a correlative in the instructive camps of National Socialism, where there was an emphasis on 'education through the act'. Once you deny the validity of democracy, and devise an ethos that could be characterized as wilful romantic delusion, ideas swarm and agglomerate, and are liable to fall under the manipulation of someone with a powerful agenda. As John Hargrave observed, 'Lack of maturity – Youth – [while] essential for impetus can never be a policy.'

Ernest Westlake wanted land. He wanted a place where he could establish the Forest School and put his educational ideas into practice. But he had no money. When he saw that ninety-four acres of woodland and a small gatekeeper's cottage were for sale at Godshill near his home at Fordingbridge, he submitted a bid.

The story of how Ernest Westlake acquired Sandy Balls is one of a few moments of magical thinking that pepper the Westlake family story. He was outbid for the land by a local timber merchant, Mr Ormond. Rather than give up his dream, he dispatched an agent to offer the merchant a couple more hundred pounds. Mr Ormond agreed, although later that afternoon he showed up at the Westlakes in an agitated state, unable to say why he had agreed to sell the land on. Could he be released from his commitment? He could not. Aubrey knew there was no money to pay the interest on the mortgage, but his concerns were met with his father's serene response: 'Everything will be all right.'

At the same time as Ernest Westlake was mortgaging himself up to the hilt, Aubrey was starting a medical practice in Bermondsey in partnership with another young doctor, Dr Alfred Salter. Aubrey introduced the local London boys to the Order, recognizing that they would benefit from a camp at the newly acquired Sandy Balls. In 1920, Aubrey took twelve London boys there for a month (the Order's educational programme required a longer camp than was normal among the Scouts).

Aubrey Westlake's woodcraft name was Golden Eagle, in recognition of his formative role in the Order as well as his striking red and gold hair. Whatever misgivings he had about his father's investment in Sandy Balls, the camp was a success. More children joined the lodge in Bermondsey, both boys and girls. Winter was spent as it always has been for campers, in preparation for the coming camping season. Prior to the mass production of kit, this meant the sewing of lightweight tents, uniforms and rucksacks, and the writing of letters to persuade parents to allow their children to attend.

Come the summer of 1921, seventy members of the Order camped at Sandy Balls. Ernest Westlake lit the ceremonial campfire. The smoke was fragrant. Between the gently stirring branches of the pines, the shadows deepened. The gathering was silent, the faces of children and adults determined to experience mystery and reverence. The grey-bearded chieftain, serene in his eccentricity, began with Socrates' prayer to local deities: 'Beloved Pan, and all ye other gods who haunt this place, give me beauty in the inward soul, and may the outward and inward man be at one. May I reckon the wise to be wealthy, and may I have such a quantity of gold as none but the temperate can bear or carry. Anything more? That prayer I think is enough for me.'

A year later, returning from a folk meeting, Ernest Westlake rode with Aubrey on his motorcycle and sidecar. A car squeezed them towards the roadside. The sidecar turned gently over. Ernest struck his head on the kerb and never regained consciousness.

In the bar at Sandy Balls, Clive Bowen hands me the first issue of *Pine Cone*, the journal of the Order of Woodcraft Chivalry, priced sixpence. Clive, burly and bearded and inclined to whittle idly with the point of his Opinel knife, constructed a totem pole that depicts the history of Sandy Balls. It stands off to the side in the piazza, by the bike rental place and within view of the pizzeria. Clive is married to Lynden Bowen, granddaughter of Aubrey Westlake. To commemorate her grandfather, a golden eagle is perched atop the totem pole.

Sandy Balls changed throughout Aubrey's lifetime, mainly in ways he did not agree with. He wanted the site to be self-sufficient and for all the campers' food to be grown in his daughter's garden. A small organic farm with a herd of Jersey cows was established in 1949 but was closed in 1961. The shop was modernized and electric hook-ups were put in for caravans, initiatives implemented by Aubrey's son and Lynden's father, Martin Westlake, along with his colleagues, to make Sandy Balls work as a business.

Campsite business often calls Lynden away during our conversation. 'It's like working on a farm,' observes Clive. 'She's always on call. She's always needed.' I ask her if she felt that being raised on a campsite made her different from other people.

'I can remember being laughed at,' she says. 'The people in the village thought that we were witches. They used to hear about the parties that happened down here. This place acquired a reputation of being a nudist camp, which it never was and never has been.'

I feel that reputation was partly due to the copies of *Pine Cone* laid out on the bar table. The first issue, dated July 1923, marks the passing of Ernest Westlake with an obituary written by Aubrey, but it is dominated by the obsessions of its editor, Harry 'Dion' Byngham, a keen nudist, occultist and hack who changed his name to Dion in honour of the god Dionysus. Byngham's editorial is distinctly inappropriate for the launch issue of a journal of a Quaker-based children's woodcraft movement. He explains the title of *Pine Cone* as representing both the pine cones strewn around Sandy Balls and the head of the penis, via his beloved Dionysus, 'a wild-souled and supple-bodied youth who carried a wand or thyrsus as the symbol of his will, love and power. To the top of the thyrsus was fastened a pine cone, the ancient symbol of Life; around it were twisted branches of ivy and of vine.' In a way, because Byngham had changed his name to Dion, *Pine Cone* was the head of his penis, spurting generative seed directly into the minds of the young readership. As he would later write, the Order of Woodcraft Chivalry 'should be proud to regard itself as the erect Penis of the social organism (nation or civilization) of which it is a part'.

Dion Byngham's brief tenure as a man fit for a position of responsibility came to an end with the contents of issue four of *Pine Cone*, published in April 1924. There on the inside front cover is a photograph of Dion and his girlfriend posing in a naked tableau entitled 'The Dawn Dance of Spring'. Byngham lies on the ground, one leg crooked to retain some modesty, playing the pipe as Mary Perkins cavorts clutching vegetation and showing one bare breast. 'Here we are – alive,' declares his editorial. 'We might as well live then. We are sure it is good to be alive.' The naked dancing is, it seems, joie de vivre. 'Living abundantly, therefore, means acting abundantly. And the one purpose of acting abundantly is that we should earn a more abundant Life.' And so on. Byngham's prose cannot stand much quotation, but it conveys the emphasis upon action and the distaste for reflection that were in the air. As for the rest of the issue, there was talk of the Order acting as the bridge between Man and the Nietzschean supermen. Byngham also published a theatrical scene written by Victor Neuberg, occultist and associate of Aleister Crowley. Meanwhile at meetings, Byngham pushed for the Order to commit to mixed nude bathing at Sandy Balls and he was adamant on the need to appal the villagers of Godshill: 'We must shock and hurt some people . . . The clothing of both sexes should be reduced to the minimum.'

Conservatives within the Order took a stand against Byngham's attempt to transform it into a Dionysian cult. It wasn't just the nudity, or the phallic imagery, there was also his toxic eugenicist rhetoric:

The future of humanity depends on a few. Not only the kind of future depends on these few, but, almost, the possibility of any future at all. They will have to counteract somehow the influence of the great sub-human class, which might include feverishly active financiers, inane 'aristocrats', various grades of the smugly respectable and the smirkingly vulgar, as well as inept hordes of the degenerate and the unemployable. To save ourselves from the menace of the sub-man we must consciously select, and select again.

Byngham had sex with his girlfriend at camp and defended himself by pointing out that as the rest of nature at Sandy Balls was engaged in procreation, why shouldn't he? Finally he was suspended from the Order for prancing naked around a Sussex field with a girl-friend and with various members of the press in attendance. To be fair to Byngham, his eugenics rhetoric was not atypical of the mid 1920s, and he was later horrified by what he saw of the Hitler Youth movement, witnessing first-hand their military rhetoric at a youth camp in Bavaria, what he called their 'intensive death-culture'.

Throughout all this scandal he remained friends with Aubrey Westlake and together they attended a garden party at Kelmscott House, William Morris's former residence in Hammersmith, in the summer of 1925. Gertrude Godden, an author who described Mussolini's regime as the 'birth of a new democracy', reported her distaste to Special Branch about this gathering of various radical groups; their names make the garden party sound like a conference of superheroes: there were delegates from the Guild of the Citizens of Tomorrow, the World Federation of Young Theosophists and the Order of the Round Table. The principal speaker was Harold Bing, a conscientious objector who spent three years in prison and witnessed the suffering, madness and death inflicted upon those who refused to fight. In the words of Godden, he was 'the virile, golden-haired, simple life type – sun-burnt, and full of force; the driving power of the meeting'.

Gertrude Godden moved through the throng until she encountered Aubrey Westlake, whom she engaged in brief conversation, insisting that they had met previously at an Al-Thing of the Kindred of the Kibbo Kift. Aubrey was adamant that they had not. Byngham was beside him. Both are described as repulsive types, with Byngham in particular being an 'over-developed animal – exactly illustrating the cult of the body which marks these Movements'. There was something of the matinee idol about Dion Byngham; shorter than his fellow chieftains, with slicked-back hair, his collar open and his camper's shorts held up by a leopard-skin belt.

At the garden party, the songs of the Wandervogel were sung, and militant pacifism espoused. In a report dripping with prejudice, Gertrude Godden nonetheless astutely diagnoses the danger facing these groups: 'The real menace of the Movement lies in the fact that it is revolutionary propaganda, in romantic disguise, subtly preaching to immature youth the "ecstasy of demolition" of the foundations of civilization.' 'Ecstasy of demolition', a phrase George Bernard Shaw coined in an essay on education, expressed the survivalist fantasy embedded in the British and German youth movements. Both the Order and the Kibbo Kift discussed a Noah's Ark strategy of hiding out at Sandy Balls in the event of societal collapse. (The survivalist fantasy continues to be part of camping's appeal. In the Age of Terror and Anxiety that followed 9/11, I was bedevilled by regular daydreams about dirty bombs in London, and planned my escape along the Eurotunnel with our trusty tent balanced on a pushchair.)

On the August bank holiday of 1924, Theodore Faithfull travelled with his son Glynn and the children from his experimental school in Norfolk, the Priory Gate School, to Sandy Balls. Some of the children went by train, some in Theodore Faithfull's Model-T Ford, the boot full of tents and camping equipment, and others – including the twelve-year-old Glynn – went by bike. Faithfull was interested in how the Order divided its members into age groups according to phases of growth and development, a scheme he had adopted to organize the pupils at his school. In the Order, children from five to eight years old were 'Elves', whereas from eight to twelve years old they were 'Woodlings'. Early adolescents from twelve to fifteen were 'Trackers'; later adolescents from fifteen to eighteen were 'Pathfinders'. The groupings continued into adulthood. Young adults were Waywardens. At the age of twenty-five they became Wayfarers, a phase that lasted until sixty. Anyone over sixty was Witana.

In the autobiography of his granddaughter, Marianne, Theodore Faithfull is described as a sexologist who ran off with a circus dancer and set up a commune. He was mercurial, highly intelligent and in thrall to Freud's ideas, which he followed rather loosely, as befitting his profession of vet. In the 1960s, his contributions to countercultural newspaper *International Times* and his invention of the 'Frigidity Box' ensured that he cropped up in Germaine Greer's *Female Eunuch*. His Freudian take on sex led to some questionable assertions; he even supported the old saw about masturbation causing blindness, stating that 'Boys often transfer the worries about the unsuitability of their sex organs to the eyes and in doing so distort their vision.'

At the folk moot, he encountered Norman Glaister, who had brought his three children to the Order camp. Glaister's wife, Irene, had died in the flu epidemic of 1918; as with Ernest Westlake, the loss of a spouse had turned his energy and concern from the focus of the family and towards the greater good. Throughout the camp, Glaister and Faithfull were deep in conversation about the meaning and possibilities of the 'New Psychology'. Glaister also met Dorothy Revel, whom he would marry at a controversial ceremony during the folk moot of 1930.

Norman Glaister had been looking for a social organization sympathetic to his theories of individual and group development. He was a crucial influence upon the Order, using them as a living laboratory to test his concept of the resistive and the sensitive. He characterized the infant as being 'resistive', that is, believing that the world will fit into their needs and desires and, when it fails to, resorting to tried and tested methods to get what they want. Healthy individuals are also capable of making adjustments to themselves to adapt to external reality, and this was a 'sensitive' modification. The ideal mind synthesizes both approaches to cope with the future.

Glaister's influence over the Order was consolidated when they accepted a reorganization according to his theory of dual governance, that is, allotting roles within the Order that corresponded to the resistive and sensitive approaches. The structure of the Order already embodied part of his duality principle:

authority was shared between the grand chieftain and his grand marshal, with the more pastoral spiritual remit assigned to the keeper of the fire. The keeper of the fire sought out new ideas, creative possibilities and spiritual counsel; the chieftain and the grand marshal represented tradition, the way things had always been done. In 1929, after much debate, Glaister succeeded in grafting his theory on to the leadership. Upon his election as chieftain, Aubrey Westlake would belong to the resistive tendency of the movement while Glaister, appointed keeper of the fire, was sensitive. This resistive-sensitive approach to leadership unlocked creativity, which led to the Order's most sizeable contributions to general society, the Forest School and the work camps of Grith Fyrd.

In 1929, Ernest Westlake's ambition for a Forest School was finally realized in a small bungalow in the pine forest of Sandy Balls. The headmaster was Cuthbert Rutter, Aubrey Westlake's cousin and a primary-school teacher in Bethnal Green. Marjorie Westlake, Aubrey's wife, acted for a time as housemother at the school. The children were outdoors as much as possible, for meals and lessons, collecting wood and playing in the river. Every morning the headmaster emptied the children's pisspots and set the fire. There were earth closets and no running water. There were uniforms, albeit ones the children were expected to make themselves at compulsory needlework classes. The three Rs were replaced with the three Hs – heart, head and hand, meaning the cultivation of the whole individual through the head (analytic reason and theory), the heart (emotional well-being and political and social savvy) and the hand (practical skills, making and doing). Montessori's ideas on the value of play were influential, as was the belief in nature as a good teacher. Three pupils enrolled in the first year, all of whom came down with scarlet fever. Despite this difficult start, the school went on to attract children of progressive intellectuals, such as the poet Robert Graves, as well as those who were resistant to conventional education.

Camp can be a classroom. It is more instructive to sit with a child and show them the progress of rain clouds over the mountains than to explain the actions of relief rainfall via diagrams upon a chalkboard. But the education it offers is more than an extended field trip. Nature is only one of the subjects. The camps of the Order involved the whole family, and exposed the children to the influence of the mother and the father, a rare experience in the 1920s and 1930s for children under the age of five. Also, the Victorians had educated their children to take their place in the empire, a certain and stable future that was no longer on offer by the mid 1920s. An uncertain future, it was felt, required an education that cultivated improvisation.

Camping was an integral part of the Forest School curriculum. Each child had their own decorated tent, a blanket and a groundsheet folded up in a home-made rucksack. Children were expected to put up their own tent, set a campfire and cook their own food upon it – mainly fish they had caught themselves from the river with a bent pin. Marjorie Westlake was so confident in the aptitude of her three children that when they were seven, nine, and ten and a half years of age, she left them camping in Greenwood for six days without adult supervision. She and Aubrey returned at noon on the sixth day and found an orderly camp, with washing strewn over bracken to dry, and the youngest cleaning himself in the river. The children prepared lunch for their parents, serving an apple pudding and an inedible onion salad. The experiment was declared an unqualified success.

Norman Glaister acted as a director of the school, duties he carried out at the weekend while continuing with his London psychiatric work through the week. His wife Dorothy Revel was senior mistress at Forest School. She set down her experience and wisdom in her book *Tented Schools: Camping as a Technique of Education*. The tented school is a technique where children learn by living and doing and not by hearing or reading alone, she asserts. Geography and physics are easier to grasp when such theories can be observed in action upon a river. Growth requires freedom. In Ernest Westlake's phrase, the kids needed to go 'knocking about the world'. Dorothy encouraged the boys to hit back; how else would they learn courage? She helped one boy overcome his timidity by giving him some matches and paper to burn. The experience of playing with fire gave him confidence. When another boy set upon him, hearty blows were exchanged. 'At this point,' writes Dorothy, 'I rose and opened the door into the garden because the school room is an unsuitable place for fights.'

She is full of sound advice about camping with children, which she regards as one of many helpful ways in which a child encounters life with 'a minimum of cotton wool and trimmings'. Before taking children camping, they should be shown a map of the intended site and the route along which they will travel. This allows the child to build up a picture of the place in their imagination beforehand. An adult leading a children's camp needs a few qualities: knowledge of a few songs; a cheerful disposition and some camping expertise; the ability to play music and to dance, to tell stories and to swim; but, most importantly, the possession of an encyclopaedic knowledge of everything in general so they can answer all the children's enquiries about the world around them.

Each age group required a different camping experience. For the Woodlings (eight to twelve years old), camping was a practical education in how to do and how to be, to enjoy the elements, to forage and cook food, make shelter and keep themselves warm, happy and entertained. For the Trackers, aged twelve to fifteen, their restlessness and herd instinct meant they should be encouraged to hike and camp. Trackers wanted to hunt, and so Dorothy set them the task of killing vermin such as rats, mice and rabbits. In the long summer hikes organized by the school, a Tracker tribe could cover as far as 320 miles in a month, learning first-hand how and where ancient man lived. 'The boys were in many ways little savages,' remembers Jean Westlake in her memoir. 'They killed adders with forked sticks and for some unknown reason they had developed a taste for formic acid and delighted in eating the swollen abdomen of the wood-ant. One boy ate hemlock and had to have his stomach pumped, and this was hushed up.'

Writing in 1934, Dorothy Revel also has a premonition of the problems that the Internet would present to parents. It was a contemporary truism that in the future, industrial advance would remove the need for labour and lead to an idle age of plenty. One of the purposes of the camping movements was to devise useful ways to fill up the leisure time that was our destiny. In the future, she writes:

> . . . it will be possible for children to tap all the resources of civilization which are available to the touch of a button . . . There is likely to be an increasing number of the so-called 'amusements' of civilization on tap . . . It is questionable how much of all this clever stuff of ours is good and helpful to a child . . . how if all of it is easily on tap, are we to limit his opportunity of pressing a button?

Camping was also essential training for revolutionary-minded adults. It would provide:

> . . . a background to his courage if it should ever become essential to defy the power behind the big bank balance . . . In times of widespread instability like the present, a set of people capable of living comfortably in light-weight tents and of taking their homes on their backs and trudging on their own two feet wherever they determine to go are less likely to lose their heads in a national or world-wide emergency, than those who have never known what it is to break contact with houses.

Dorothy Revel also suggested that a young couple before marriage should go away and camp together in a remote spot, 'as a trial of readiness for marriage and an insurance against mistaken alliances'.

Sex education was for all members of the Order, young and old. For the children, sex education meant frank answers to all questions without any prudishness, but taking care not to speak outside of the child's understanding. Love affairs between children of differing ages and between children and adults were absolutely taboo. Communal nude bathing would satisfy children's hunger for knowledge about their bodies. The Fathers of the Order would be on hand to ensure there was no impropriety. Pupils recall Dorothy Revel putting the operetta *Orpheus in the Underworld* on the gramophone, stripping her clothes off down to her large brogue shoes, then dancing. When it came to sex education, the children weren't the problem. It was the adults, specifically the inner circle of Wayfarers.

Eighteen members of the circle were selected to act as 'sensitive brains' in accordance with Norman Glaister's theory of resistive-sensitive. The circle met every fortnight to explore progressive ideas around sex, religion, alcohol and war, much of which challenged the Quaker foundations of the movement. The activities of the circle were kept secret, which only increased the scandal and shock when their debates were disclosed. For the consideration of the inner circle, a series of reports on sex were drawn up, invariably by Dr Harold Dinely Jennings White. Like Theodore Faithfull, Jennings White was a published sexologist; his paper 'Psychological Causes of Homoeroticism and Inversion' had come out under the imprint of the British Society for the Study of Sex Psychology, a society founded by Havelock Ellis and Edward Carpenter. Jennings White's reports for the Order questioned chastity prior to marriage and marriage itself. He devised a system of group marriage with regularized promiscuity, though there is no suggestion that anything so untoward was actually put in practice by the Order. He did make suggestions for 'Some Sex Adventures for the Order', and his description of his own sexual technique anticipates the works of Luther Vandross: 'It is not necessary for the woman to take any initiative if the man knows how to rouse her. The man should play upon the woman as an artist on an instrument . . . Personally I prefer to take from one to two hours over the complete symphony.' The Order's edict of 'learn by doing' was used to goad the more prudish elements.

These reports were too much for some members. The Lewes group of the Order resigned, feeling that the inner circle had turned highbrow and evil. The prospect of the ideas of Dion Byngham or H. D. Jennings White being mailed to the homes of parents or brought home from a camp was a real risk.

The prominence of psychologists and doctors in the Order ensured that reform would not be stifled by prudence. In 1930, Jennings White had the temerity to argue against the notion that masturbation caused fits. Conservative members of the Order were appalled, pointing out that 'the whole chapter on masturbation is calculated to lead young people not only to think that there is no harm in it, but definitely to make a practice of it.' A proposal was put forward that the Order of Woodcraft Chivalry teach that sex was the sole preserve of married couples. Aubrey Westlake submitted a ferocious reply. At his practice, he had seen the real immorality, 'the lives thwarted and crushed in the sacred name of morality'. These were not licentious individuals engaged in promiscuity. Changing the mores of sex was a moral imperative. Dion Byngham noted, with some amusement, the seriousness of their sex exploration: 'we have committees of solemn middle-aged folk discussing the sex "problems" and sex demeanour of the adolescent.' Norman Glaister and Dorothy Revel's marriage ceremony at a folk moot in full Order of Woodcraft Chivalry dress was a further indication to the conservative faction that liberties were being taken by the inner circle.

Norman Glaister was instrumental in the setting up of the Grith Fyrd camp at Greenwood in Sandy Balls, as a work camp for unemployed men. A Pathé news team recorded the whippet-lean men in action, and writers Aldous Huxley and J. B. Priestley also paid a visit. The aim of Grith Fyrd was laudable: to take young unemployed men out of the cities and relocate them at Sandy Balls, where they would be taught to live communally and self-sufficiently, and in doing so, restore their pride and sense of self. As with the Forest School, camping was educational. For the depressed, malnourished men, it was proposed as a cure for uselessness; like the consumptive camps of the Adirondacks, the men would return to society after six months energized and fit to find a new place in society. When self-sufficiency did not meet all their needs, funds were pooled through the men's dole money, as Aubrey Westlake and Norman Glaister had successfully lobbied for the men to effectively sign on at Grith Fyrd rather than return to their home towns to do so. The camp was more spiritual than political. It was a place where men volunteered to work at their own salvation, and for their own freedom.

The Grith Fyrd began at Greenwood in March 1932 and was considered by its originators as a serious experiment in a new method of life. The initial intake of six men was faced immediately with the challenge of fashioning living quarters for themselves and setting up basic amenities. Co-operation was necessary for survival. Everyone was needed, a powerful message for the human scrapheap of the Depression.

The plan was advertised in the national press and unemployed men drifted to Sandy Balls. The first six men built a bunk hut and broke ground for an allotment. Gradually they established a measure of self-sufficiency. For leisure, there were singsongs and morris dancing, a deliberate attempt to revive Merrie England. The notion of national revival guided the long camping hikes of the summer, some of which lasted eight weeks and covered 500 miles as the men learned about both the beautiful and the ugly aspects of the country.

The numbers at Grith Fyrd reached the optimum level of fifty. The men wove their own clothes on home-made looms, milked goats and bathed in the Avon. They ate together in a dining house they had made. Nothing was sold. The men used their dole money to purchase the goods they could not supply for themselves. A second camp was established at Shining Cliff in Derbyshire. Norman Glaister devised a system of exchange so that the two communities could trade without money. Money was a way of making people do work they did not want to do. The Quaker ideal of 'service', the religious foundation for Ernest Westlake's chivalry, preached that work be joyful and fulfilling and its own reward. The avoidance of money was a spiritual rather than purely political gesture.

By 1934, Sandy Balls held the Forest School, the Grith Fyrd encampments for unemployed men, regular camps by the Order of Woodcraft Chivalry and twelve furnished camping huts for holidaymakers. The mortgage on Sandy Balls was onerous, and the site would require further commercial development if it was to continue to support its idealistic projects. As Aubrey Westlake was the inheritor of his father's land, the financial situation weighed upon him but was of no concern to the other leading lights such as Norman Glaister. Meanwhile the membership rolls of the Order were falling and for the first time, adults outnumbered children.

The decline in membership and the imperative to take control of the economic side of Sandy Balls no doubt contributed to Aubrey Westlake's plan to assert total control over the movement, to oust Norman Glaister, reject the resistive-sensitive scheme and consolidate power around himself and three others. But only partly. Norman Glaister warned that there was a dark force emerging within the movement: the temptation of dictatorship. The conflict culminated in a ferocious folk moot in 1934.

That June, a rally of Oswald Mosley's fascist supporters broke out into brawling at Olympia. In July, the Nazi party undertook the Röhm-Putsch, the Night of the Long Knives, which executed critics and enemies of Hitler. Prominent leaders of the German youth movement were included in that purge, including Eber-hard Köbel, better known as Tusk, a renowned leader of the Bünde group dj.1.11 (the Deutsche Jungenschaft vom 1.11), a youth group founded by Köbel on 1 November 1929. Tusk was a legend. Inspired by John Hargrave and H. G. Wells's idea of the Samurai, the youth movement as creator of a social elite, Tusk introduced punishing military drills into the dj.1.11, as well as Zen teachings, communist ardour, and the infiltration and subversion of the Hitler Youth. He pioneered the use of the Laplanders' black tent, the kohte, which is still used today. Tusk was arrested by the Gestapo and only escaped by slitting his wrists and then leaping out of a hospital window. Most of the German youth movements co-operated with Hitler. The British youth move-ments, through their contact with their counterparts in Germany, lost friends and acquaintances during the purge; some, like the woodcraft leader Leslie Paul, issued prescient warnings about the inevitable consequences of Hitler's regime. Others took longer to realize the dangers, and some were too late to salvage their reputations.

One man in particular, Rolf Gardiner, whom we encountered briefly earlier as the go-between for the Kibbo Kift and the Ger-man youth movements, was a link between the youth of the two nations. Gardiner is a problematic figure who flits in and out of the various movements at the time, and was a regular visitor to Sandy Balls. He exulted in extreme morris dancing; with his group the Travelling Morrice, he performed rituals of potency and sword play. Gardiner was involved in introducing work camps to Britain. He attended the working camps held by the Deutsche Freischar every Easter, and instituted the same in Cleveland in the North-East in 1932. Each camp converted a bit of moorland into a garden. The men were mostly unemployed miners; they told stories of their lives and of the history of the region. He saw the work camps as a medium, a place where the various interests of the area – the farmers and squires, miners and teachers – could fuse into a movement of regional influence and self-determination.

Rolf Gardiner's abiding passion was the revival of the agricultural tradition and of local governance. He held a series of educational camps in Gore Farm to establish a model rural estate that could rejuvenate Wessex. He dismissed the Kibbo Kift as a sect, and felt that the Bünde offered the better example:

> The Bund is an elite. It is a soil, ever being self-raked, re-dug, remanured, in which strong natures can grow. It is a container of experiences. It is not a spearhead like a Fascist body; it is rather a ferment which fructifies dead material, which impregnates all that it comes in contact with, with fertilising energy. It is finally discipline, form, an organism.

It is no coincidence, when one considers such compost-inspired rhetoric, that Gardiner went on to be a co-founder of the Soil Association and prove instrumental in the organic food movement.

Gardiner was very wrong about the Nazi project. He envisaged the Third Reich as a kind of Holy Grail, ever to be sought after, never to be achieved. He conducted a running argument about the nature of the Hitler Youth with Leslie Paul in the pages of the *Adelphi* journal; Paul typified Hitler's promise of regeneration as a bait to trap the youth movements. 'German Youth, for all its desires, is free no longer, save to work for a pittance and to die for the Fatherland, when the hour strikes.' Gardiner argued that Hitler did not betray the youth movements, rather that National Socialism was the culmination of their ambition, a successful revival of a spirit across 'thirty years' rediscovery of German soil'. The quasi-mystical properties Gardiner saw in soil blinded him to the human tragedy Nazism entailed.

His eyes were opened at the end of the decade. On a German youth camp in 1937, Gardiner discerned 'a hard emptiness and mechanical enthusiasm' that did not marry with his ideals. Observing a speech by Göring at the Bauerntag Congress, he was witness to the disturbing mass mind of the Nazi meeting:

> A current of mass fervour surged through the vast room, over-powering and effacing every individual, swamping all personal thought and reflection. It was for me a terrifying experience. For I felt that blind, irresistible forces were being let loose. There was in this fervour no restraint, no self-criticism, no kindliness, no humanity. It was inwardly wild and elemental, impersonal and demonic. History and Fate swept over men in this hour like the wings of a vast Genii; and they bore with them reckless power but not a trace of patience, nor of forbearance, nor of love.

This realization came too late for Gardiner to be entirely exoner-ated from his ideological errors. His insistence upon the link between blood and soil was at the heart of the Nazi ideology. Some of his more obscure essays in the early 1930s are anti-Semitic and, as former associate Stephen Bone noted, 'even Auschwitz had no effect on your opinion.'

The great schism in the Order took place early in the sum-mer of 1934. Simply put, Aubrey Westlake attempted to seize control of the movement, he was rejected and so he withdrew from participation, and took Sandy Balls with him. During his power bid, Aubrey made a comment about the importance of recognizing the positive element in Hitlerism and considering how this could energize the movement, simplifying the organ-ization and concentrating its direction into a group that could act together and be of one mind. He proposed dissolving the constitution and made a commitment to force: 'We shall not hesitate to use force if the circumstances require it, regarding it as an integral part of life, as a good and beautiful thing, if used wisely and with responsibility.' How could a movement founded in 1916 as a reaction against the authoritarian behaviour of the

Boy Scouts reach the point of casting admiring glances at Hitler in 1934?

The pervasive sense of crisis contributed to the call for a big chief, an action man. Aubrey's proposition was rejected by the Order, and to his credit he accepted their decision. On taking control as the new chieftain, George Parsons committed the Order to the cause of world peace and took a moment to contemplate the mood for a Führer. 'Have we been through a "Führer" period, or are the troubles of the past three years due to our being afraid of such an experience? Whatever be the case, I am sure we are not prepared for a "Führer" now.'

Aubrey Westlake did not regard his actions as dictatorial. He genuinely felt he was acting in the best interests of all. He foresaw the importance of making Sandy Balls a going concern, and that would involve changes incompatible with the psychosocial experiments of Norman Glaister. The split was traumatic for all involved, and perhaps it would have been nothing more than an argument over money, except that the historical backdrop, and Aubrey's unfortunate mentioning of Hitler, meant that for an evening the terrible shadow of the times passed over a wooded glade at Sandy Balls. Later that year, Nazi youth representatives, under the aegis of Rolf Gardiner, visited the Grith Fyrd camp. Aubrey did not meet with them.

Having broken with the Order, Aubrey wanted the Grith Fyrd off his land, and they eventually moved on to their Derbyshire camp. Two hundred men had passed through the scheme. The Second World War would take care of mass unemployment. Norman Glaister would go on to found Braziers Park School of Integrative Social Research in Oxfordshire, its management committee also consisting of Glynn Faithfull and Dorothy Revel. Rolf Gardiner continued to run work camps at his farm in Springhead throughout the Second World War, even taking in German prisoners-of-war. Today the farmhouse is a centre for creative and sustainable living. The Forest School was wound down in 1937, by which time it had only sixteen pupils. A group of teachers and former pupils formed a company, Forest School Camps, which continues to practise the ideas of Ernest Westlake and others.

In 1937, Aubrey Westlake's partner in his practice at Bermondsey, Alfred Salter, was killed in a car crash. On hearing the news, Aubrey, in a flash of inspiration, decided that London was not a safe place for his wife and five children, and the family should relocate to Sandy Balls full time. The campsite would be their Noah's Ark. Alternative medicine and organic farming would be Aubrey Westlake's concerns, along with resisting some of the commercial initiatives undertaken in the further development of Sandy Balls. He would be reconciled with the Order of Woodcraft Chivalry and honoured as grand chieftain towards the end of his life. He died in October 1985, the Order's shield emblem rendered in flowers and laid at the foot of the coffin. He was buried on a cold autumnal Saturday upon Good Friday Hill. The Order of Woodcraft Chivalry continues to camp every year at the Greenwood in Sandy Balls. It now numbers fewer than fifty.

As a footnote to this exploration of the relationship between the German and British youth movements, it is worth noting the courting of Baden-Powell's Scouts by the Hitler Youth. In 1937, the Tamworth Scouts visited the Hitler Youth camp at Cuxhaven, north-west of Hamburg on the coast of the North Sea. The Scouts, aged thirteen, joined in with the Heil Hitler salutes during a torch-lit memorial parade, an experience the boys found both stirring and disturbing.

There were various camping trips by the Hitler Youth to Britain. On 30 July 1937, a cycling party of Hitler Youth landed at Spalding in Lincolnshire, met with the Rotary Club, dined on sausage and mash, then camped at Fulney Park. Twenty of them posed for a photograph for the local *Boston and Spalding Free Press*. On 8 August, twenty-two members of the Heidelberg Hitler

Youth were met on the platform at Liverpool Street Station by the Scoutmaster of the 1st Attleboro group in Norfolk. They travelled by Underground to Euston and then on to Liverpool, where they were met by another Scoutmaster and taken on a camping tour of Wales. In Hull, a party of Hitler Youth cyclists camped for five days at the Duke of York's holiday camp in Baslow in Derbyshire. The leaders of these bands always took photographs, which was much resented by the local population, and there was suspicion that camping was being used as cover for spying.

That November, Hartmann Lauterbacher, a high area leader of the Hitler Youth, met with Lord Baden-Powell to discuss closer links between the two organizations. The interview was considered a success, with Baden-Powell securing an agreement to overturn a ban on English Scouts wearing their uniforms when visiting Germany. While Scout leaders Lord Somers and Hubert Martin sought advice from the British government on how best to respond to these overtures, Baden-Powell responded with a letter to the German ambassador:

> I am grateful for the kind conversation you accorded me which opened my eyes to the feeling of your country towards Britain which I may say reciprocates exactly the feeling which I have for Germany. I sincerely hope that we shall be able, in the near future, to give expression to it through the youth on both sides.

The German ambassador took Baden-Powell aside and insisted that true peace between Britain and Germany depended upon the youth being brought up on friendly terms together. He promised Baden-Powell a meeting with Hitler to discuss this plan further. Baden-Powell insisted that he was fully in favour of any action that could foster better understanding between the nations. The proposed meeting with Hitler never took place.

6
The Perfect Campsite

'Why do we camp so much? What are we looking for?' I am sitting beside the campfire on the high meadow field of Comrie Croft near Crieff in Perthshire, watching clouds graze upon low, dark hills.

'What do you mean, why do we camp?' Cath's expression is not quite impatience, nor is it entirely exasperation; often the first thing out of my mouth is the last thing she expects. She is delicately, deliberately, cracking eggs into neat cradles of silver foil.

'This is our twelfth camping trip of the year.' I have counted them up; thirty-six nights under canvas. A parallel life. I prod the campfire with my boot. Looking after the fire is my task, but the fire is doing most of the work.

'What are we looking for with all this camping? Are we looking for a place where we belong?'

Cath and I were both born and raised in Liverpool, then spent over a decade in London before decamping to Sussex. Our migration is entirely typical. You can't go home again.

'I don't think it is about belonging,' says Cath. 'When we started camping a lot, you used to always stand in a field and ask me, "Could we live here?" Sometimes it would be a lighthouse on the Isle of Skye, or a cottage in Ireland, and I would . . . I don't know . . . I would not listen. For me, camping is about doing.'

Cath is very keen on doing. We are coming out of the relentless phase of parenthood; our two youngest children were born barely twelve months apart soon after we moved into a new town. There hasn't been the time to take stock or settle down. When friends ask me what it is like having a baby, and it's always an expectant dad who asks this question, I put my arm on their shoulder and remind them that they are standing on the platform holding a ticket, waiting for an express train roaring down the track. If they show any sign of quailing at the prospect, Cath will lean over and whisper to them, 'You'll have to man up.' 'Man up' means take your medicine with silent dignity, it means 'be quietly grateful that you are not the woman, and do what you have to do to make parenthood work for everyone'. 'Man up' means that when you are sitting around a campfire, complaining at some length about a split toenail, remember that your audience of glinting-eyed mothers lost, between them, a bathtub of blood in the delivery suite. Three years of continuous, heavy-duty mothering has made Cath fierce. Gone is the lotus-eating middle manager, the shy and diffident consumer. There are tasks to be done and now is the time to do them. Camping is a verb.

I make myself useful; I take the silver parcels containing the quivering eggs and lay them gently upon the grill dangling over the fire.

'Do you think there is such a thing as a perfect campsite?'

'Could you make one from all the sites we have visited?'

My perfect campsite has a river running through it. There are woods, just like at Comrie Croft. There is a dawn chorus. Bird-song makes us feel good because it is the sound of safety. Birds stop singing when there is danger. My peak camping moments come back to me, hot spots of memory, moments seared into the fabric: lying awake at dawn in Edale listening to the stream perco-late through the pebbles; sitting upon a large flat stone at the edge of Doulus Bay in the Ring of Kerry. I want animals on my perfect campsite, like the chickens which have just laid our break-fast, or the brown and white Meuse Rhine Issel cattle on Plaw Hatch Farm with their bovine soap opera; from behind a fence, the bull moaned soul music and the lady cows scampered and tittered at the prospect. For hygiene on our perfect campsite, let us take the wood-panelled solar-heated showers from South Pen-quite Farm on Bodmin Moor and the rough earth closets from the woods of Abbey Home Farm in Gloucestershire. In our quest for perfection, let us not forget the weather. On my perfect site the weather is varied, so I can study each of its manifestations, watch the rain shower approach along the valley and thrill in the rainbow afterwards. I'll even take a strong wind at night to give me the satisfaction of fixing my guy ropes.

Campsites have a centre and a periphery. The centre is invari-ably the reception office and the little shop. Or it can be the woodpile. Or a bonfire. My perfect campsite is an organization that spreads out from the centre, improvised, provisional, but good enough. No allocated and numbered pitches. A ramshackle order emerges from the individual desires and talents of the campers. From a few simple principles – that we pitch a discreet distance from our neighbour yet near enough to facilities – a pat-tern will emerge. This is our preferred method for achieving order, a self-organizing, bottom-up system. It is the opposite of the top-down military camp as perfected by the Romans. The centre of the Roman camp was the praetorium, or general's quarters, which rose above all others. The surrounding camp was marked out, levelled, a perfect quadrangle of broad, straight roads enclosed by a rampart twelve feet high and defended by an equally deep ditch. According to Gibbon, the Roman legions camped along the banks of the great rivers, the Rhine and the Danube, or along the frontiers of the barbarians. They perfected the order of the military camp, the mobile fortified city. I am no expert in classical history, but I am guessing that a Roman legion did not require permission from the landowner before erecting camp. If I could pitch my tent anywhere in Britain, the search for the perfect campsite would entail a logistic calculation that would not differ substantially from that made by the legion, even down to the proximity of barbarians. A campsite must have water and wood, level ground and good drainage, which is determined by the soil; impermeable clay soils are particularly cold at night, and any latrines dug in such earth will take a while to empty. Rock and slate will not take a peg, but chalk drains easily, and perhaps the best ground would be the sandy machair of the Western Isles, a light layer of grass draped over sand and kept trim by grazing sheep.

Once suitable ground has been located, there are logistical questions of access, privacy and supplies to consider. The site must be easily reached but not so accessible as to be overlooked by a road or a footpath. In the quest for privacy, do not be tempted to go deep into the woods; the sun rarely shines there and the camp will be damp. Never pitch under a tree. There is the danger of dead branches, 'widowmakers', falling upon you and your tent, with elm trees being particularly susceptible to losing their limbs without warning. After rainfall, water will run along the branches and drip steadily upon a spot of your tent for half an hour or more, compromising the waterproofing. Trees habitually shuck off various flecks of flora, all of which will adhere and stain the tent.

Then we must consider the prevailing wind; a campsite half-way up a hill will receive a stiff breeze that will blow away midges and minor insects, but not be so strong as to compromise the tents. Valley floors are not ideal places to camp as they are liable to flash floods and develop a particular chill at nightfall, when the cold air rolls down the hillside and forms a mist that slicks back your hair.

The perfect campsite does not require an exceptional landscape. A high meadow with a copse to its back and a hill leading down to a stream or river could accommodate a party of a hundred campers. The direction of the wind determines the layout of camp. A prevailing south-easterly wind puts the latrines and the cooking fire to the east of camp. Obviously these should be at opposite poles, latrines to the north-east end of the camp, near that copse and at least 200 yards away from the water supply, and the cooking fire at the south-east, near to the river and so with ready access to water. The cooking fire requires a grease pit and a refuse pit dug nearby. With the wind at their back, pitch the tents in a three-quarter circle, gazing down towards the stream or river. Then add people.

In a letter to the *New York Times* on 20 May 1900, a correspondent notes that 'There are many ideal camps but it takes ideal people to make them.' Who are the ideal people? Not us. The sides of our tent quake with family noise: toddlers screaming at dawn, Dad snoring deep into the night. I should put cones around the tent, and police incident tape. How do you make an ideal camp out of people like us? You must balance individual freedom against group necessity. Striking that balance requires rules.

How campsites love their rules! There are always rules. Rules on noise and strict times for lights out. Rules on the size of the tent and where to put the recycling, use of the games room and swimming pool, time of arrival and time of departure. Barbecues must not touch the grass. Ball games are not permitted. The ground rules are laid down immediately upon arrival. Tie this to your tent so that we know you have paid. Give us your passport and we will keep it in the safe.

Here is my rule: if there is a sign warning against the placing of dog baskets in the washing machine, then the site has too many rules.

Most adults abide by the unspoken consensus of the campsite. Dogs and children need everything spelt out in little signs that inform them where they may or may not go and by what time they must leave. Dogs must be supervised by an adult at all times. Children should not be let off the leash. I remember on childhood holidays in France a special enclosure for children, or fun club. Parents had to pay extra to have their children stamped and sectioned in the fun club. My parents never paid extra for anything, so I mooched against the cross-hatched wire fence and watched sophisticated Italian boys and girls turn somersaults upon the trampoline.

Campsite rules are required because a campsite brings together disparate ages, nationalities, ethnicities and social groups who do not share a consensus on the behaviour of children or, to use an equally divisive example, the role of radios and dogs at camp (a correspondent to the Camping Club once suggested that sites be divided between radios-and-dogs and no-radios-and-no-dogs). There is a general camping code, but if, like myself, you do not belong to a camping organization, such as the Camping Club or Scouts, then your first few trips will be spent in blissful ignorance of how annoying you are to other people. As a young man, I was a diabolically inconsiderate camper who not only played ball games on the grass but did so at two o'clock in the morning while swigging from a can of lager. If I had known that other people found this behaviour offensive, I would have been mortified. But it was so dark I couldn't read the little signs.

One of the earliest known British holiday camps was the Cunningham Young Men's Camp, established on the Isle of Man in 1894. The first rule of Cunningham Camp was 'Only youths and men of good moral character are eligible for admission to this Holiday Camp, and should anyone unfortunately prove, by word or deed, to be otherwise, he will be liable to instant expulsion.'

Cunningham Camp, named after its founder Joseph Cunningham, started out in 1887 as an annual summer camp for the boys of Toxteth in Liverpool. It travelled to Great Orme's Head near Llandudno and then moved to the Isle of Man, first at Laxey and then, in 1894, to a site at Howstrake, two miles from Douglas.

At Cunningham Camp, serried ranks of candle-lit bell tents awaited the male campers. At the turn of the century, 600 men visited the site every week. The self-styled 'Finest Holiday on Earth' held considerable albeit temperate attraction when compared to the more restrictive and expensive offerings of the Blackpool boarding house and its tyrannical lower-middle-class landlady.

After a storm in the summer of 1903, when sixty-five of his tents were shredded, Joseph Cunningham found a new site on the island, Little Switzerland, which covered five acres, was ranged around a turreted pavilion and hosted 1,500 tents, including a 100-foot dining marquee. Each tent was pitched upon a wooden floor, with eight spring beds. A forerunner to the holiday camps of Billy Butlin, the tents and bungalows were fitted with electric light and there were set dinner times and mass catering for thousands of guests. In the early days of Cunningham Camp, local residents aired their suspicions at town-hall meetings about illegal goings-on with young women. All campers had to wear a badge with an insignia of a bell tent and golden Legs-of-Man so that they could be easily identified. During the Great War, the Howstrake site was requisitioned as an internment camp. The holiday camps were easily repurposed for martial law, a lick of paint transforming the peremptory regime of desire into military efficiency. Redcoats are the sergeant majors of fun. Hedonism and internment both entail a suspension of the usual laws governing behaviour; camp is a place where the individual or the state can behave badly and get away with it.

The word 'camp' derives from *campus*, Latin for 'field'; the university campus is invariably set on the periphery of towns and cities because the acquisition of knowledge, in the monastic tradition, is a contemplation and partaking of the eternal, so the activity must be sited as far from the distracting heresies of secular life as is practical. Different rules apply at camp, out there on the threshold. In his *Means Without End*, the philosopher Giorgio Agamben asks 'What is Camp?'; his answer, writing in the shadow of the Holocaust, is that 'The camp is the place in which the most absolute conditio inhumana ever to appear on Earth was realized.' The concentration camp originated either in the *campos de concentración* created in 1896 by the Spaniards in Cuba, or the concentration camps the British established for the Boers (not long after Baden-Powell left the battlefield). Agamben declares, 'The camp is the space that opens up when the state of exception starts to become the rule.' Arising out of martial law and the accompanying suspension of legal rights, the camp is the embodiment of that extra-legal status in space. Guantánamo Bay, the Camp X-Ray. The camps for asylum seekers, people slipping between systems.

The campsite owner makes the rules. Some disperse commandments throughout the site to correct various errors made by campers over the years; a rare few keep the restrictions to a minimum, testing the notion that the more freedom people are granted, the more responsibility they will display. Progressive movements are attracted to camping because it promises autonomy from the rules of society. Anarchist philosopher Hakim Bey writes about Temporary Autonomous Zones, brief fugitive uprisings of communal activity, a camp where people come together to realize mutual desires, 'a bit of land ruled only by freedom'. The freedom to impose your own rules.

Camp is the instrument to inculcate values in subjects: the army training camp, the university campus, the various summer camps of American childhood. Camp can be a site of training, of belonging and play, or, in its evil reverse, a site of quarantine and forced work, where the protection of the law is revoked.

The political promise of the camp is explored in a slim volume, *Why Not Socialism?*, by the philosopher G. A. Cohen. He uses the example of life in camp to demonstrate how naturally and easily the tenets of capitalism fall away. Cohen imagines a camping trip in which the campers are all equal and anticipating a good time. They all bring individual equipment and share it readily and easily. This reciprocity stems from a mutual understanding that camp is a place where things are shared; those who excel at cooking do so on the understanding that others will wash up. A camper leaving the site will often distribute their remaining perishable food among the campers who are staying behind. Their generosity is not given in expectation of receiving something directly in return. After all, they are about to leave. Rather, handing over a pint of milk or a few eggs to your neighbouring tent is an easy way of encouraging a circulation of goodwill that extends not just to this camp but to other camps in the future. For Cohen, although he professes no love of camping himself, the socialist model is self-evidently a better way of organizing a camping trip than a capitalist one; if campers attempted to set up market exchange for their mutual aid rather than giving it generously in anticipation of reciprocal behaviour from their fellow campers, then the camp would quickly dissolve. Community and equality are the inherent qualities of the campsite. The perfect campsite is a level playing field.

I decided to put some of these ideas to a campsite owner. Cath and I returned to Wapsbourne Farm to speak to Paul and Jean Cragg, proprietors of the campsite known as Wowo. Wowo is very popular, and deservedly so. It fulfils many of my criteria for the perfect campsite, particularly in its minimal signage.

'A sign is pollution,' explains Paul Cragg. We are sitting in his office in an outbuilding beside his Tudor farmhouse. 'A sign is a degradation of the physical, mental and emotional environment.'

'How do you let people know what the rules are?' I ask.

'Rules stem from a general principle of respect that people intuitively sign up to. We hope to attract people with loving values.'

Wowo attracts a lot of people, and the trick, for Paul and Jean, is to spread their visitors across their fifty pitches for as much of the camping season as possible. 'The camping season lasts eight months,' says Paul. 'It is made up of four months' high season, and two months either side of that, what we call shoulder seasons. Everyone wants to stay on the summer bank holidays. They are the first to go. The next hot period is the weekends between May and August. Then the weekends either side of that. Next, you want to sell capacity in the midweek school holidays across July and August. We sold all of that this summer. Next year, we hope to sell all our midweek capacity in May and June. Our midweek capacity in March and April and late October is mostly unsold. You are looking to attract a different demographic at those times. Families don't like to camp when it is cold, and it is much colder in spring than in autumn. You are looking for survival types, bushwhackers, the people who really like to get nature in their face.'

Wowo has far more enquiries than they have spaces for, and we discuss ways in which he could use the Internet to measure the potential market. Paul is thinking about a membership scheme that would give participating campers priority when it came to bagging a pitch, with unsold capacity being available for non-members. Membership would, I suspect, be a pivotal step in fulfilling the ambitions he had when he first came to the farm in 1979. His father, a potato farmer, had bought the house and the land with the profits he made during the drought of 1976. Mr Cragg's potatoes were planted on a clay soil that retained water better than the land of rival growers, and this gave him pricing power; on such factors are fortunes made or lost in farming.

Paul was kicked out of school for smoking pot. He hitchhiked around Europe when he was fourteen, and again when he was fifteen.

'I was a seeker,' he says.

'Of what?'

'I was searching for a way back to an experience of expanded consciousness that I had when I was younger.'

Paul met Jean, who is Canadian, at a Cree Indian community. He was seventeen. From there, Paul became interested in transcendental meditation and attended the TM university in San Francisco for three years. When he rocked up at Wapsbourne Farm in 1979, he was intent upon becoming an organic farmer. His father gave him a tractor and Paul quickly ran up an overdraft. There wasn't much of a market for organic produce in the late 1970s. The Craggs had three children in the early to mid 1980s, 'and then somehow my life goes off in a different direction, and I end up being a large-scale monoculture industrial farmer for supermarkets'. The Craggs profitably grew strawberries as part of a large, farmer-owned co-operative until they were broken up by the supermarkets in the early 1990s. Debt followed. Enormous, crippling debt. The farm and the manor house were very nearly sold. A decade of punishing financial crisis management ensued. They diversified the business, but by 2005 those businesses too started to contract. It looked like the For Sale boards were going to have to go up again.

'I was fiftyish, and of sufficiently old age to be wondering why I had achieved so little of what I had set out to do, which was to set up a spiritual intentional community apart from industrial consumer culture. But I had made no meaningful progress. Then Jean came up with this idea of camping. It couldn't have been a dafter idea really. I thought it would pay the electricity bill if we were lucky. She pestered me and so I bought a big mower for the back of the tractor and landscaped and tidied up a field for camping. She got a listing on one of the big aggregators on the Internet. The number of visitors grew exponentially. It was then that I realized that London offered a practically infinite market of campers, and there was a shortage of supply of the type of campsite we were proposing to offer. It was a wonderful blessing.'

There is no shortage of campsites in Britain, but there is a shortage of the right kind of campsite. What is the right kind of campsite?

A campsite that permits fires. 'We could have done almost everything else wrong, but just the ability to have a fire means that people will put up with a huge amount.' On Friday and Saturday night, Paul walks through the campsite checking that no one is too intoxicated or antisocial. He feels the anticipation in the campers, as they finish off their evening meal, pour a couple of glasses of wine or beer and settle down for the main event. 'The whole campsite is mesmerized by campfires,' he says. 'They are all undergoing fire therapy.' In a year, 300 tons of wood are burned at Wowo's campfires.

Wowo is the Craggs' home, and they want to ensure that their home is shared with the right people. A membership scheme would allow them to refine and cultivate values for campers, rather than rules. 'Fundamentally social values,' explains Paul, 'respect for other people and their property. As a campsite owner, you get the experience of seeing the transformation in people's emotional energy, from being angry, negative and in your face when they arrive, stressed out by the journey, and then, after two days of listening to the dawn chorus and two nights of fire therapy, they leave transformed. It's like Jekyll and Hyde.' We talk some more about his lifelong quest for esoteric knowledge and some of his unorthodox ideas about fire elementals, and then we join Jean and Cath, my children and a collection of Wowo people in the rustic kitchen of the manor house for garlic soup. Anecdotes are shared about some of the more demanding campers, particularly those who stay in the yurts and tipis, where the expectation of service is higher. One lad told of the time that a camper complained to him that the hot-water bottle he had been issued with was too hot.

It had never occurred to me that campsite owners were in the hospitality business. I don't hold the owner responsible for my happiness. I bring my happiness with me.

I also bring my anger. I am the camper who arrives as Mr Hyde and departs as Dr Jekyll. A central theme in this history of camping is the potential of campsites for transformation. That potential was realized by the woodcrafters through the adoption of different names and costumes. The emotional changes observed by Paul Cragg are indications of a more common and contemporary transformation, a switching between selves, from angry, impatient, petulant consumer to calm human being. Innumerable palliatives are sold for stress, from herbal essences to sudoku; camping, that combination of light physical activity, simple tasks, plenty of daylight, relaxing, ambient sounds of birdsong and running water, and the purgative fire, could be the cure, if only the packing and travelling to the campsite were not so stressful.

The first time I drove on a bank holiday, I got a taste of just how angry England can be: long arguments of traffic and in those cars, grievances and recrimination. The caravans don't help. Caravans turned over on roundabouts. Caravans coned off on the hard shoulder. As any actuary knows, the first bank holiday of the year is lethal for men in early middle age. They are the ones who own motorbikes but tend not to ride them during the cold winter. At the first sign of sun, and at the prospect of a razz around the countryside, they get the bike out but are a bit rusty and a bit fat after the break, and make the mistake of weaving through the traffic jam. And that is that, a dead man coned off on the hard shoulder, and on we drive to our bank holiday.

The Bank Holidays Act was passed in 1871. To take advantage of this new leisure time, workers' organizations helped their members to save for group holidays, mainly excursions to the seaside resorts. Other young working-class men and women, intent on self-improvement, spent the bank holiday engaged in life-enhancing camping, rambling and hiking. These young urban people in hobnailed boots joined the loose fellowships that sprang up around the *Clarion* newspaper and its columnist Robert Blatchford.

The *Clarion* was advertised as 'an illustrated weekly journal of Literature, Politics, Fiction, Philosophy, Theatricals, Pastimes, Criticism, and everything else'. In other words, perfect reading for the working-class man or woman educated at the elementary schools who wanted to elevate themselves. The broad remit reflected the vagueness of the founders' conception of the paper; their main criteria were that it should earn enough money to keep the founders and their families, and that star writer Robert Blatchford be free to write whatever he wished. Even the name of the paper was an accident; co-founder Alexander Thompson suggested it should be called the *Champion*, and he was misheard. On 12 December 1891, the first copy of the weekly appeared on the streets of Manchester, a belching, filthy, industrial city that was, in the words of William Morris, 'a vestibule of hell'. The newspaper quickly became a phenomenon.

A former fusilier, Blatchford already had a following for his columns on soldiering. A convert to socialism, he wrote a polemic, *Merrie England*, advocating a natural life removed from the oppression of the factory and the squalor of the slums. He preached improvement through education supported by temperance and physical fitness. He wrote, 'My ideal is frugality of body and opulence of mind.' Groups of *Clarion* Scouts were formed to sell the penny edition of *Merrie England*, and *Clarion* cyclists rode out to the remote villages to spread the word. The *Clarion* clubs were for plain living and high thinking, offering sociable socialism in the open air. Blatchford never read Karl Marx, and perhaps this was why his tracts were so popular.

The young *Clarion* cyclists raced around the rural north, distributing *Merrie England*, and then settling down to camp before the next day's ride. Camping was a way to distribute propaganda, and it was a training in socialism. The contrast between the countryside of the Pennines and the squalor of the towns and cities hardened their resolve to smash the system. The first Manchester *Clarion* camp was pitched at Tabley Brook, Cheshire, in August 1895 and consisted of four bell tents, a square kitchen tent and a marquee. *Clarion* camps in the Peak District attracted over 400 camping cyclists. Charlie Reekie, a Mancunian railway clerk, commemorated the *Clarion* camp in verse:

> Where thrushes sing and busy bee hums,
> Far from the stinking, stifling slums,
> We'll pitch our tents by a troutlet stream,
> Sink all sorrow, nor think of the morrow,
> But look on life as a happy dream.

Socialism in this era developed in two directions. In the words of George Bernard Shaw, one branch was out 'to organize the docks' while the other wanted to 'sit among the dandelions'. Blatchford was in the dandelion camp. He did not want to reform industrialism but to sweep it away. He was another believer in Albion; as evoked by William Morris and William Blake, Richard Jefferies and, most recently, Peter Doherty, Albion is a shadow nation, England's very own Eden, a romantic vision of a rural England under common ownership.

The *Clarion* clubs sold over a million copies of *Merrie England*. Robert Blatchford was declared the greatest living danger to the existing social system, a power that he threw away with his support of the Great War. Blatchford was never a traditional socialist. An old soldier, his politics were that of the Little Englander, or Britain for the British, as the title of another of his books insists. He was against the expansion of empire because it required the industrial North to power it; he thought a leisured working class preferable to colonies. His obsession with the threat of Germany led to his advocacy of universal military training. The *Clarion* fellowship, a host of organizations dedicated to doing something to improve the world, the *Clarion* Scouts and cyclists, *Clarion* Choirs, *Clarion* Handicraft Guilds and *Clarion* Holiday Camps, loose and informal, were at odds with his strident vision of national service. With the war, circulation of the *Clarion* dropped from 90,000 to 10,000.

John Fletcher Dodd was a *Clarion* cyclist. He camped with his two sons a mile from the village of Caister in Norfolk. In 1906, having scouted out the location, he took ten friends from the East End and they camped in tents by the shore. Sitting around the campfire, the sound of the waves breaking clear in the night air, they decided that this would be the perfect location for a socialist campsite. Soon a thousand people were camping at Caister Camp, waking to the call of 'Good morning, comrades!' Many of these early campers were trade unionists, and they organized both dances and debates. A camp garden was planted; the men tended and harvested the vegetables, which the women cooked. Leading lights of the Labour party visited, including George Bernard Shaw and Keir Hardie. Fletcher Dodd was temperate and strict in his enforcement of the campsite rules. There was to be no alcohol, no gambling, no improper language, no children under two years old and no noise after 11 p.m. Such restrictions ensured that most of the clientele were white-collar workers, with the working class taking their pleasure elsewhere in the more commercial resorts. As ever, the rules of camp determine who feels welcome and who feels excluded.

As Caister Camp grew, so chalets appeared among the tents, hardening the site into a holiday camp. As part of a basic package, bell tents remained at Caister Camp well into the 1930s, perhaps because of their association with freedom. In contrast to the paramilitary pleasuredomes of Billy Butlin, Caister Camp was advertised with the promise that 'You can do just as you please. There is no regimentation at Caister.' The Norfolk Holiday

Camps Express train was thronged with holidaymakers carrying ukuleles and drums and trumpets, striking up impromptu bands. John Fletcher Dodd ran Caister Holiday Park well into the 1950s. It continues today under the ownership of Haven, an operator of UK family holiday parks that has recently added a camping field to the site, an acknowledgement of the resurgent popularity of camping.

The different socialist camping groups shared political values and a keen sense of self-improvement. With their origins in the temperance movements, they were not everyone's idea of a good time, but for the aspirational working class, camping was a way out of industrial squalor.

Cyril Joad is standing at a microphone at a meeting in Winnats Pass, Derbyshire. It is June 1932. Joad is forty years old, with cropped grey hair, short bristly beard and a shabby suit. The hillside is flanked with ramblers and campers, the verge strewn with cycles. A van from the *Daily Express* is parked up, and speakers placed upon its roof broadcast Joad's speech to the gathering, the 10,000 ramblers assembled to demand the passage of the Access to Mountains Bill. Some have come on horses, some on donkeys and in carts, most on foot and a few in the hated motor car. The bill has a long history as a progressive cause, dating back to 1884.

Joad surveys the sea of bare knees and brown faces, the islands of rucksacks and camping kit, then explains the proposals contained in the Access to Mountains:

> The bill provides that walkers and artists should be given access to waste places and to wild places. These include all land over a certain height, moorland, and other land which it can be shown is not required for the purposes of cultivation or of pasture. The walker – and the name may stand for the artist, the field naturalist, and the lounger, the seeker after solitude, the poet and the mystical

wooer of Nature – is more important in this crowded island than the landowner, the sportsman, or even the farmer!

He pauses to study the effect of his words. The ramblers are so very young, and the rapt attention of the bare-legged girls makes this old libertine smile. He is a great believer in freedom, beauty and sexual reform. He exults in the vigour of the northern heath, the virgin freshness of the wild place, the psychic charge that emanates from secret places. If Nature is ravished by too many lovers, as in the leafy lanes of Hampstead Heath, then she loses the power to console and renew.

Joad is a southerner. The crowd are northerners. 'Those of us who live in the south have little conception of the hold which the rambling movement has upon the young people of the north. You have turned your backs upon the cities that your fathers made. Your army makes sorties at any and every opportunity into the countryside. You are the living witnesses of a revolution.' The crowd applauds. He gazes up at the towering limestone peaks and is reminded of the raw plateau of Kinder Scout, further north, where, that Easter, ramblers confronted gamekeepers. The seed of defiance was planted at a camp in Rowarth. The ramblers had intended to walk to Bleaklow but were stopped by a group of gamekeepers, who abused and threatened them. Humiliated and frustrated, the ramblers returned to camp. In the words of Benny Rothman, the lead organizer of the trespass, 'It was agreed that if enough ramblers had been there, no body of keepers could have kept them off the moorland. We decided to organize a Mass Trespass to prove our point.'

Joad's address to the crowd at Winnats Pass echoed Benny Rothman's inspiring and impromptu address on the morning of the trespass. Rothman climbed on to a rock outcrop in a quarry and looked down over hundreds of young men and women dressed in idiosyncratic rambling gear, shorts of every length and colour, army packs and outsize rucksacks, and, unrehearsed, he sketched out the history of injustice and theft of the land, from the enclosures of common land to the landowners lobbying in Parliament against the Access to Mountains Bill.

The mountain country between Manchester and Sheffield was protected by gamekeepers with sticks and guns. For twelve days a year, Kinder Scout was used for the shooting of game. The walkers wanted a path they could use the rest of the year. Kinder Scout was encircled by paths but not a single public footpath crossed it. In his *Charter for Ramblers*, Cyril Joad describes the scene:

> All the approaches to Kinder Scout, the high plateau which raising its ugly head to a height of some two thousand feet commands the district, are guarded by keepers, and the footpath itself is keeper-engirt. A walker only has to stray for a hundred yards or so for a keeper to appear. And the walkers, being law-abiding, do not stray, with the result that, restricted to the path itself, they form, on a fine Sunday, an almost continuous line stretching its entire length. The congestion, indeed, is hardly less than that of a motor road! And on each side, stretching away to the horizon, are the vast empty spaces of the moor, wasted and empty – empty, that is, save for keepers.

Eight gamekeepers waited for the trespassers of Kinder Scout on the slopes below Sandy Heys. Young men and women marched towards confrontation, their faces conflicted between resolve and trepidation, and out of the pack came yells of disobedience, verses of 'The Red Flag' and the Internationale. The women dropped back. The men went on, forty in number, removing their belts. There was a scuffle. The keepers used their sticks, and one of their number, Edward Beever, was knocked unconscious. It was nothing serious. The ramblers gained Kinder Scout and then returned to Hayfield where they met a strong force of police. Benny Rothman was one of five men arrested and would spend four months in prison for trespassing.

The Kinder Scout Trespass is a key moment in the battle for access to the British countryside. It was inspired by the disbelief that so few men could wield such dominion over the wild places, especially when so many needed access to the wild in order to make their lives bearable. There were three cheap things that were available to the young unemployed of Manchester and Sheffield: cycling, camping and rambling. The camping was home-made and wild. The writer Tom Waghorn remembers using a rucksack his mother had sewn together from the material of a silver barrage balloon. His tent had no door. For a ground-sheet, he used newspapers and a towel, and his hobnail boots were his pillow. The tents were barely more than a bivouac bag, meals were cooked over campfires with 'dixies' (a large metal pot or kettle) or with a Primus stove. But it represented freedom. The folk music figurehead Ewan MacColl acted as press officer for the Kinder Trespass, and each verse of his song 'The Manchester Rambler' emphasizes the importance of the cause. It was almost a religion. Sunday was for hiking. The moors replaced church, the congregation wore hobnail boots, and Benny Rothman and Cyril Joad were their preachers. They had faith that salvation lay in 'the enhanced self-consciousness which attends the enjoyment of solitude in Nature'.

The action at Kinder Scout was part of wider campaign for access to the British countryside. After his speech, Cyril Joad returned to London where he was busy gathering together the individuals and societies of the progressive movement under one banner, the Federation of Progressive Societies and Individuals, or the FPSI. Their manifesto included an essay by Clough Williams-Ellis setting out proposals for national parks, the passing of the Access to Mountains Bill and slum clearance, all progressive measures to improve the British environment. Williams-Ellis saw the national park in the same terms as the areas of wilderness set aside in America: 'A National Park is a place for the quiet study of Nature in all her manifestations, a place for walking, climbing and exploration, a place for camping, a paradise for pedestrians, a sanctuary for scenery, and a townsman's refuge from the grinding hurly-burly of his everyday life.'

Aldous Huxley, affiliated to the FPSI, attended their education group of 1935. They were the acceptable face of the crank, actively interested in sex education, nudism, or gymnosophy, and the healing power of the sun. Huxley's short story 'The Claxtons', published in 1930, is an acid satire on the hypocrisy of the cranks, the progressive types with their virtuous self-denial and disastrously passive methods of child-rearing. In 'The Claxtons', the rucksack is a badge of spirituality. 'For the modern high-thinking, pure-hearted Teuton or Anglo-Saxon the scandal of the rucksack is what the scandal of the cross was to the Franciscans.' Affecting a windswept beard and knickerbockers, Herbert Claxton always sports his rucksack, even when shopping in Oxford Street. Huxley gives this pitiful figure a few spirited lines that acknowledged the author's own ambivalence towards the crank: 'And yet, if it hadn't been for the cranks . . . where would you be now, what would you be doing? You'd be beating children and torturing animals and hanging people for stealing a shilling, and doing all the other horrible things they did in the good old days.' 'The Claxtons' appears in Huxley's collection of short stories *Brief Candles*, which contains withering depictions of the progressive idealism of the age and is not above insinuations as to the sexual motivation underlying some of the interest of middle-aged men in camping: 'He was fifty. It's the age when clergymen first begin to be preoccupied with the underclothing of little schoolgirls in trains, the age when eminent archaeologists start taking a really passionate interest in the Scout movement.'

A dyspeptic attack on the cranky side of socialism also appears in George Orwell's *The Road to Wigan Pier*. This passage from Orwell is so vituperative it marks a clean break between the two strains within socialism, that of the docks and that of the dandelions:

There is the horrible – the really disquieting – prevalence of cranks wherever Socialists are gathered together. One sometimes gets the impression that the mere words 'Socialism' and 'Communism' draw towards them with magnetic force every fruit-juice drinker, nudist, sandal-wearer, sex-maniac, Quaker, 'Nature Cure' quack, pacifist and feminist in England.

Orwell is particularly affronted by the sight of pistachio-coloured shirts and broad backsides in khaki shorts; in a word, campers. Justified or not, Orwell's scathing dismissal of the progressive camping fraternity anticipated the shift the left wing would take after the Second World War, turning away from the concerns of the countryside and focusing upon urban renewal.

The socialist camping youth movement the Woodcraft Folk was formed by Leslie Paul after leaving the cranky Kibbo Kift with an initial membership of seventy people. Contributing to *Comradeship and the Wheatsheaf* magazine, Leslie Paul emphasized the role of camping, woodcraft and health in the class struggle: 'Nature unadorned gives us the vital health and philosophy to fight against capitalism.' There was to be none of that 'below-stairs servant girl' theosophy that infected the Kindred. The Kibbo Kift was a debacle, and beyond the pale. Woodcraft Folk ceremonies were to be short, dignified and to the point. Paul's rhetorical style owed much to the romantic reactionaries of the Wandervogel; he was defiant in the face of mass society, a punk to John Hargrave's hippy:

> The sort of person who reads the *News of the World* gets a trifle perturbed when he sees us hiking down the street; he feels we don't fit in with the *Daily Mail*, a cup of tea and a Bath bun, and church on Sunday morning. So he calls us mad. And mad we are; for man is most sane when he takes no thought of sanity. We laugh and sing and grow sunburnt. We hike and we camp and we snap our fingers at the rain. We defy the word of the mob. We

violate unwritten law. We are not bound by convention. We hate your factories, your clothes and your mental and moral standards; we hate your muddy streets, your garish hoardings, your 'truth in advertising'. We hate your houses, your furniture, your wall-paper and your 'safety first' minds. It's all rot. It's all pretence . . . It's dope, dope, dope, and bayonets and machine guns if the dope isn't strong enough.

Woodcraft camp began with a simple ceremony of seizing the earth, a sod of turf cut out by the keeper of the council fire. Then the latrines were dug, the fire lit, the tents pitched. Woodcraft was an educational training camp. The camp timetable varied slightly over the years but the basic routine remained the same. A wake-up call was at half past seven in the morning, then ten minutes to half an hour of exercise, followed by the Wapenshaw or 'weapon show' in which folk would take their belongings out of the tent to check nothing had been lost and to air the tent. After a quarter of an hour of council, activities ensued: sunbathing, running, jumping, nature lore, tests of silence, supple limb and keen eye. The midday meal was digested over an hour's rest. The early afternoon saw debate, pow-wows on war and peace, capitalism and socialism. Free time was enjoyed from half past four until tea at five. At eight o'clock, everyone assembled for the fire-lighting. A spokesman from each fellowship brought to the assembled folk a message, and then placed a branch on the fire. Songs and funny stories followed until a quarter to nine or ten o'clock, when the assembly broke up with the 'Ceremony of Leave Taking' and the singing of the campfire carol. The older youths, the pioneers, could stay up an extra half-hour. The elders were expected to retire at eleven.

The location of the camps continued the Kibbo Kift's interest in the archaic sites of Albion. The Woodcraft Folk camp at Steyning in 1928 was almost under the shadow of Chanctonbury Ring. The perfect campsite required vestiges of Albion. In 1933, the

Woodcraft Folk camped for three weeks at Huntsham Court Farm, at Symonds Yat; a meadow of fifty-six acres beside the River Wye. The site included the Queen Stone, a Bronze Age stone standing six and a half feet tall with another seven and a half feet of it buried in the ground. The ancient camps marking the border between England and Wales were also nearby, as were the grand ruins of Tintern Abbey.

Around 500 folk attended the camp at Huntsham Court Farm, somewhat fewer than the 800 who were anticipated. The Queen Stone was the subject of a lecture by the visiting Alfred Watkins, the discoverer (or inventor) of ley lines. Watkins had studied Britain's early camps and decided they were sited at a nexus of these ley lines, or lines of sight. Ley lines appealed to the progressive movement as they suggested a way of organizing the land that pre-dated enclosure: the national grid of Albion. Watkins saw, in the grooves scoured in the Queen Stone, proof of his theory that this was a sacred site. The grooves were, he maintained, for the insertion of 'withies', which would in turn have supported a large wicker cage containing a human sacrifice. For the purpose of the lecture, the folk constructed just such a cage and placed one of their own inside it.

Leslie Paul did not attend the camp; he was ill and sent his apologies, along with a note urging the camp to consider peace above all other issues. The note employed the threat of Nazi Germany to encourage participation in the Woodcraft Folk. Paul cited the racial mystique and fabrications in Nazi school textbooks and the songs of the Hitler Youth as evidence that war was inevitable. 'London could be bombed and gassed out of existence two hours after the declaration of war,' he warned.

In 1937, the Woodcraft Folk participated in an International Children's Camp on Beacon Hill in the South Downs. Ten nations were represented at the camp, including France, Czechoslovakia, Switzerland and Belgium. The banners and flags of the socialist youth movement the Red Falcons flew over the South Downs.

Like the Wandervogel, the Red Falcons abhorred smoking and drinking, and instructions given to the Woodcraft elders stressed the importance of discretion when nipping out for a crafty fag. The presence of so much socialism on the English landscape attracted disapproval from the nearby communities of Rottingdean and Ovingdean. It was alleged the camp was run by Jews. The *Brighton Evening Argus* ran an interview with a local resident, one Dr Greene, that related a plot to cut down the tents. In the event, only a few flags were stolen. The camp was impressive, masses of bell tents pitched on the sprightly overlook of the English coast, a coming together of international youth under the gathering storm. In 1946, they would camp together again.

Thomas Hiram Holding died in 1930. The founder of the Camping Club passed away at the same time as an increase in the use of local by-laws to restrict camping. The Central Committee for Camping Legislation was established in 1928 to lobby against any anti-camping proposals. It included representatives from the Scouts, the Guides, the Camping Club and the Order of Woodcraft Chivalry. Their victory was a clause introduced into a restrictive bill put forward by Surrey County Council that exempted national organizations that undertook responsibility for members while in camp.

The summer of 1933 was one of glorious weather. At the same time as the Woodcraft Folk attended to their wicker man, there was a camping frenzy across the south of England. At Birling Gap near Eastbourne, hundreds pitched up in informal camps. Cyril Joad described amateur camps as being rowdy, messy, destructive and invariably ending in an evening game of football illuminated by car headlights. The spectre of the Moveable Dwellings and Encampments Bill was revived; back in 1922, John Hargrave had threatened to break the law to oppose the Moveable Dwellings Bill, a threat that contributed to the break-up of the Kibbo Kift. The Moveable Dwellings Bill owed its origins to the nineteenth-century philanthropy of George Smith. His contact with the hardship of the poor living on barges or in caravans inspired his lobbying of Parliament for legislation of vagrants and therefore improved conditions. But the bill was never ratified. It was first presented to the House of Lords on 18 February 1908, only to be withdrawn. An amended bill failed to pass both Houses in the run-up to the Great War. It included an impractical clause demanding the registration of all moveable dwellings, including every tarpaulin stretched over stakes and the home-made tents of weekend campers. The bill was designed to limit the wanderings of Romany and non-Romany travellers, to protect a sedentary society discomfited by the proximity of nomadic camps. The lobbying by the Camping Club and other organized groups was intended to separate them in the eyes of the law from 'undesirables', whether it was the thoughtless townies tearing up the farmer's gate for firewood, or the Other-within of the Gypsy. In December 1933, 200 campers braved the snow to assemble on the Yorkshire moors and gather signatures to petition the Minister of Health. Their petition succeeded, but at a price.

The Public Health Act of 1936 contained the first national measures for the control of camping. Tents were not to be pitched within twenty feet of a hedge. No bread, milk or butter could be sold on-site. Only one moveable dwelling was permitted per acre. Not only did the campsite require a licence but so did the campers, who had to apply for permission to camp from the local authority. The Camping Club negotiated an exemption certificate that permitted their members to stay on any site where camping was a sideline rather than a business. If you wanted to camp, you had to become a member of a club and submit to their regulation.

To ensure compliance with the law, the Camping Club undertook inspections of sanitary arrangements at their sites, inaugurating an obsession with toilet facilities that continues to this day. Campsite reviews on the Web detail how often and how thoroughly the toilets and showers are cleaned, an unappealing cranky trait.

Cyril Joad was not a great advocate of camping, but he recognized that the legal restrictions would hamper its appeal; campers would be 'confined to the margins of the highways and to scheduled camping sites, in order that they may be regulated and controlled; in order, that is to say, that a kind government may insist that the latrines are "just so", and that nobody may blow his nose after 10.30.' Campers would be herded into 'commercialized concentration camps' (Joad was writing in 1934, before the Nazis would render such hyperbole unacceptable). A more accurate observation of his was that camping on a regulated site would be like camping in a town. Or, more specifically, a dormitory suburb, a place without work where people go to sleep and eat. To retain its licence, the site would enforce rules and expected standards of behaviour. Joad hoped that there could be another, less restrictive way of establishing order, and his advice ought to be a guiding rule for any owner who wants to create the perfect campsite: 'The plain lesson of the past,' he writes, 'is that the only way to create good taste and good manners is to provide occasions for their exercise and to persist in providing them in spite of their being abused.' In the perfect campsite, the balance between group necessity and individual freedom rests on this lesson, if we are to avoid the pollution of rules.

In 1938, the Paid Holidays Act was passed. Prior to this legislation, workers had negotiated for either paid or unpaid breaks with their employers. Now the holiday was a right, albeit a right that would not be fully implemented until after the Second World War. The Camps Act of 1939 favoured the building of youth hostels, campsites and holidays camps to cater for the new holidaymakers. These permanent camps were used during the war to accommodate the women and children evacuated from the cities. The Land Army set up serried ranks of bell tents in Barwick to help with the flax harvest, and bombed-out families retreated to popular Camping Club sites such as Chertsey. Despite the difficulties in travelling, camping continued throughout the Second World War, albeit in camouflaged tents and with a very strict lights-out policy. After Dunkirk, no camping was allowed within ten miles of the South and East coast.

When it became clear that there would be victory in Europe for the Allies, thoughts returned to the renewal of Britain after the devastation of war. A review of countryside issues was undertaken, and included the vexing question of how the British countryside could accommodate mass camping. The Camping Club submitted a memorandum to the Post-War Reconstruction Committee recommending plenty of small campsites, no larger than twelve acres, set on farms and national parks, on Forestry Commission and National Trust land. The memorandum was ignored. In 1945, Cyril Joad published *The Untutored Townsman's Invasion of the Country*. He predicted a flood of fighting men, back from the war, taking their wives and girlfriends out to the countryside; without proper protection, 'much of the loveliest and most isolated country in the south of England will be ruined within the next two decades by riders in cars who parked their metal boxes on the ridges of the Downs for the express purpose of listening to Fat Stock Prices announced by radio.' The publication of Joad's tract coincided with a white paper on the proposal for national parks that was part of the new Labour government's plan for reconstruction. Legislation was passed in 1949, and the first designated national park was the Peak District, in tacit acknowledgement of the Kinder Scout Trespass.

In 1946, an advisory committee on camping was convened for the Ministry of Education. More than thirty of His Majesty's inspectors were sent camping, and there was an exploratory course undertaken in the Quantocks in Somerset. Their findings were collated in a pamphlet, 'Organized Camping', a guide for 'those responsible for introducing young people to camp life, and to give some idea of what constitutes "good camping"'. On the question of camp rules, the committee determined that although 'Some rules must govern the life of every community ... Camp regulations should be as few as possible but firm and consistent.' The greatest danger was the underestimation of the abilities of the children, and so the pamphlet recommended an intensive programme of activities. In the aftermath of the Second World War, there were frequent exchanges between the children of European nations, and this pamphlet is part of that recognition that camping had a role to play in the regeneration of society from the child upwards. The pamphlet was published in 1951, the year of the Festival of Britain. Two and a half thousand boys and girls from thirteen nations convened for an international youth camp. The festival and the camp were two ways for new energies to be unlocked for social renewal. Camps 'should always offer a new way of life in which the individual feels his significance and his responsibility; and the way of life must be attuned to the surroundings of the camp'.

By the end of the 1940s, 91 per cent of British workers enjoyed two weeks' paid holiday a year. The Camping Club declared 1949 to be its best year in its history, with 12,000 members and an unprecedented number of membership renewals. The conditions were in place for camping to be taken up by the masses, no longer the preserve of cranks, youths or Scouts. At midnight on 26 May 1950, on the eve of the Whitsuntide bank holiday, petrol came off the ration. The decision was swift and unexpected. Motorists hurried to use up their remaining fuel coupons. Traffic queues of ten miles stretched out of London. In Britain, the age of mass car camping had begun.

7

Car Camping

'The less there is between you and the environment, the more you appreciate that environment . . . the bigger and more efficient your means of transportation, the further you become divorced from the reality through which you are travelling.'

Colin Fletcher's Law of Inverse Appreciation, *The Complete Walker* (1968)

Of my childhood camping holidays, it is the drives that I remember most clearly, an annual 2,000-mile round trip from Liverpool to the South of France wedged between my older brother and sister in the middle of the back seat. The beige Cortina Estate was loaded with an icebox and a gas cooker, bedding and pots, catering quantities of rice and four kilos of TVP (textured vegetable protein). My mother plugged gaps in this heaving wall of stuff with jars of sandwich paste, tins of Spam, cans of pilchards and so on. Not for us the goat cheeses of the Pyrenees or the smoked wild boar of Limousin, for we had squeezy tubes of Primula and a horseshoe of sheathed Mattessons sausage. Sylvia packed for nuclear war, not for three weeks in the fertile lands of Provence.

Eddie and Sylvia owned a large green frame tent in the French style, with patio and kitchen area, thick transparent plastic windows and dainty orange curtains. A big frame tent weighs between forty and fifty kilos, over twice as heavy as the family tent I lug around today. A furious feat of strength was required to get the packed tent on to the roof rack, then strap it into place with elasticated spider cords. And the fury did not end there; it was only the beginning of the angry Dad-silence of the long drive. In the months beforehand, my father had spent his evenings consulting maps of Europe. In a book bound with brown faux-crocodile skin, he wrote meticulous directions for Sylvia to read out during the journey, as she couldn't decipher a map, or rather, she was so easily flustered and prone to daydreaming that she could never say with any certainty where we were.

The grey, hardback AA atlas was a sacred text in an otherwise secular house. I loved to trace my fingers along the orange autobahns and autoroutes and motorways of Europe. How easy it seemed to get from here to there, to cross frontiers and expand our repertoire of European countries. The atlas contained a key to the self-adhesive oval badges used to declare a car's nation of origin, codes for such unknown territories as Andorra, Lichtenstein and Luxembourg – how I longed to visit Luxembourg! Sticking our own badge, GB, to the rear of the Cortina and putting a yellow refractor on the headlights completed our preparation; the car was ready to go abroad.

It was imperative that we did not miss the ferry. We were always booked on the cheapest available crossing, setting sail at dawn on non-transferable tickets. Eddie, being an organized man and perhaps over-cautious in matters of punctuality, left wiggle room for eventualities, sometimes as much as twelve hours. I remember all those eventualities: the gasket head blowing outside Dover, the radiator giving up in Liverpool, the time we turned back at Warrington because my mother thought she had forgotten the plugs for the air beds. (The plugs were in her purse, of course.) The journeys were studded with landmarks of parental stress. First, there was the leaving of Liverpool itself, and the fret over travellers' cheques, passports, currency and ferry tickets. Then Birmingham and Spaghetti Junction with its reputation for concrete chaos. Once we were free of the Midlands, London loomed. My mother turned the map this way and that, but, prior to the M25, London could not be avoided. We stopped to ask for directions – for the Dartford Tunnel. London was strange and exotic. The cockney accent was impenetrable to my little Scouse ears. Only my worldly father understood their tongue. From London, Eddie drove us down through Kent and we held our breath in anticipation that the next hill crest would fall away to reveal the English Channel and that steep road down into Dover.

We slept in the car on the seafront. At dawn, my mother allocated a single wet wipe to each child, and then we boarded the ferry, directed into the car deck by boiler-suited operatives, my first glimpse of the surly French bottom lip. The gilded ferry interior with its threadbare carpet, second-hand smoke and naval affectations was an ersatz replica of how the other half lived. On the upper decks, display cabinets of dead posh things, glass Pierrots and porcelain tigers and jade cigarette lighters, the dreck the rich leave behind on their migration to new continents of taste. In the duty-free shop, I lost my innocence concerning money. The outsized luxuries indicated another class of people, a wealthy elite who could afford to impulse-buy a Toblerone the size of a rocket launcher. The shop was a glimmering wonderland of gluttonous portions of luxury, glass diving bells of Chanel

No 5 and lighthouses of whisky. Into our basket went a carton of Senior Service, which we bought on the way out and on the way back for Auntie Brenda, her fiver in my mother's purse, the only smoker in the family. Neither of my mother's sisters travelled out of the Wirral; Auntie Brenda and Auntie Sheila shared a dread of the Mersey Tunnel that kept them bunkered down – their refusal even to leave Liverpool threw a flattering light upon the relative adventurousness of my mother.

The klaxon sounded at the approach of Calais and we trooped down the decks to the car. My parents were grim with fear that the Cortina would break down and make them the ones, the idiots, who snarled up the disembarkation of all the other holidaymakers. We sat there in dark, tense silence waiting for the crack of light and the lowering of the ramp. Sylvia, who knew she should remain silent, was unable to stop herself from saying it, just in case Eddie had forgotten. What if she didn't say it and something terrible happened, then it would be her fault? So she said it:

'Don't forget to drive on the right.'

Eddie looked at her as if she had reminded him to drive on the ground.

After the first contrawise roundabout of panic, we relaxed into France. By St Omer, the dread of the Parisian *périphérique* and Sylvia's recurring nightmare of driving down the Champs-Elysées spread from the front seats to the back. 'Let's push on,' said Eddie. We pushed on. Just because we had been driving for two days was no reason to stop. With Paris behind us, we tapered south for the next leg of the journey, three or so hours to a campsite outside Chinon in the Loire. At Chinon, Eddie, exhausted by the drive and coming off two weeks of police night shifts, marshalled a bad-tempered construction of the frame tent and then slept for two days. We did not disturb him as he regained his strength for the next big push to some enormous campsite in the Dordogne, Grasse or St Raphael.

Because of these journeys I didn't learn to drive until I was thirty-seven. Only when it became apparent that carless camping with three children would result in me keeling over on a train platform with a rucksack the size of a fridge – the cause of death: humiliation – did I take the driving test. Now I assume the front seat of Dad-silence, doling out the lessons I learned thirty years earlier on the back seat of the Cortina Estate.

'I don't like the way we behave in the car,' says Cath, 'and I don't like the way the children behave either.'

They don't behave well. But then they are strapped down in a way that we never were. Driving to camp, I make furious, paradoxical demands for calm. Driver and passenger do not share eye contact. That makes bad behaviour easier, for both parties; sandwich crusts and pen tops rebound off the back of my indignant head, tossed by the disgruntled groundlings imprisoned in their seats for the duration of my driving performance. I lose myself in some tirade against their begging for food and threaten to turn back; gone is the man of reason at the head of the table replaced by the deranged driver.

Not all of Dad's threats were hollow. I remember the afternoon my father abandoned us in Avignon. We were on our way back from a month's holiday, long enough for cracks in the family amity to become crevasses. My older brother, fifteen years old, in all his zitted, surly pomp, was crammed into the seat behind Eddie like a mantis in a matchbox. The Cortina had no air conditioning, and winding down the windows only exposed us to the meteorological hairdryer of the mistral; it was over 100 degrees Fahrenheit, rotting leftovers were hidden somewhere in the packing, and a spatula was required to loosen the bond between my thighs and the vinyl seating. Nevertheless, my father wanted to stop and visit the Palais des Papes. We did not want to stop. He left us by a fountain and went off into the narrow alleyways of the city. This was a time before mobile phones, or my mother's driving licence. Without Eddie, we were marooned, and there were no directions written out in a book bound in brown faux-crocodile skin telling us where to go next. Those instructions we had to infer.

When I asked my father why he felt impelled to drive 2,000 miles on his annual holiday he told me that it was because camping in the South of France would expand his children's knowledge. We would know and experience more than just Liverpool. A visit to the continent was also a sign that the family was doing well. The French Riviera from Cannes to Monaco to Monte Carlo represented social advancement. The long car trip was a journey into the middle classes, if only for three weeks.

The advent of the cross-Channel car ferry made car camping to the continent accessible to the aspirational working class. It had been possible to take a car from Dover to Calais as early as 1928, when a collier ship adapted by Captain Townsend took fifteen cars at a time across the Channel. The cars had to be loaded on to the ship by crane. In 1950, just as petrol came off the ration, Townsend customized a former naval frigate into the first drive-on vessel, the *Halladale*. He gave the port of Calais a car ramp adapted from a military bridge so that his passengers could drive straight off the boat and into their holiday. Townsend pursued the ideal of the roll-on, roll-off ferry, recognizing the practical advantages in terms of loading time and its aptness: hoisting a car into the air and dropping it on the top deck violently broke the logic of the car journey. A roll-on, roll-off ferry meant the car stayed on the ground and so kept the logic of driving intact.

In his book *Abroad* (1980), Paul Fussell declares 1939 to be the end of the age of travel; after the war, there would be only tourism. The index of social position provided by foreign travel became available to the lower orders, who added to it their own snobberies and sense of differentiation. Real travellers reviled the tourist for his or her passivity, their crass delight in mementos and enthusiastic engagement with the simulation and the replica. Travel required authenticity and an engagement with the real

France, an undiscovered beach, or that little patisserie with the hot rolls. The image of the empty beach pandered to the tourist's belief in their own discernment. Holidays designed for the working class promoted the crowded beach with its revelry and sexual possibilities. Avoiding the crowd was a mark of middle-class status. For us, camping on an enormous campsite in the South of France in the 1970s was to mingle with a better class of crowd.

Being working class and holidaying in France was to be anxious about two tiers of snobbery, that of the French and that of the English middle class pretending to be French. These anxieties focused upon the bidet, an object of obscure purpose located for maximum social embarrassment in the toilet. My father washed his feet in it. On the campsite, subtle class differences existed between those who brought their own tents and those who were staying in the Eurocamp tents. Founded in 1975 in the wake of the oil shock and the recessionary 1970s, Eurocamp was aimed at the type of people who would not normally go on a camping holiday. Eurocamp promised a self-drive camping experience for the middle-class professional who arrived to a pitched tent equipped with a cooker, a fridge, electric lights and a local courier to help out. Camp itself was no longer the priority. The pre-pitched tents of Eurocamp were a cheap way to enjoy the French Riviera. With a Michelin guide to hand, the family could drive out from the campsite and sightsee and conscientiously explore the region, returning at the end of the day to eat and sleep. Camping, which had always promised an encounter with the real, submitted to the artifice of the tourist.

France, for us, was a shelf of Michelin Green Guides. A nation divided into regions – the Dordogne, Alsace, Brittany, the Vendée, Provence and so on – with each summer holiday dedicated to the exploration of that region. My family camped across France for a decade, piece by piece, year by year, guide by guide.

The first Michelin guide was published in 1926, a catalogue of the historical sites and local colour of Bretagne. The Green

Guide – as opposed to the more famous red Michelin restaurant guide – parcelled up verdant country for the discerning driver. The marketing benefit to Michelin, a tyre manufacturer, was that it positioned their tyres as steeped in Gallic tradition and as the choice of the sophisticate. This marketing cultivated the higher qualities of discernment and freedom above and beyond the merely functional promise of grip. In the early days of motoring, the tyre, oil and petrol companies gave away maps and guides, promoting the day trip, the tour and the country drive, to educate motorists into using their cars more. Mankind does not have an instinct to drive aimlessly along country lanes on a Sunday afternoon; that pattern of behaviour was created to sell more petrol. The clichés of car advertising, the executive saloon speeding through a mountain pass, the muddy 4x4 conquering the wild, owe much to the fusing of the promises of driving and camping in the early days of mass motoring.

Almost immediately after Henry Ford's Model T went on sale in 1908, people started to customize these affordable family cars so that they could go camping, inaugurating a fashion for what was known at the time as motor gypsying, autocamping or vagabonding. The growth of autocamping matched the improvement in America's roads; in 1916, President Woodrow Wilson signed the Federal Aid Road Act, providing federal funding for rural post roads. This implementation of the Act was impeded by America's involvement in the Great War. Subsequently the Federal Aid Highway Act of 1921 provided more than 75 million dollars of funds for states to build and improve roads. Accordingly, train travel in America peaked in 1920 when 1.2 billion passengers purchased tickets; the 1920s would see the popularity and availability of cars entice people off the trains.

The most famous autocamper of the era was Henry Ford himself. Ford undertook a series of camping tours with his mentor, Thomas Edison, the bringer of electric light, and Harvey Firestone, of Firestone Tire and Rubber Company. The fourth member of the party was the antithesis of the modern industrial-ist, the ageing writer John Burroughs, disciple of Walt Whitman, friend of Theodore Roosevelt and the man who had accused Ernest Thompson Seton of nature fakery. Burroughs was a critic of the era of mass production, of which Ford's cars and Edison's light bulbs were potent symbols, but he had been courted by Ford, and his presence on the trips was a symbol of two Ameri-can centuries conversing around the campfire.

Henry Ford was a farm boy who couldn't read a blueprint. He was nervous and energetic, emotionally immature, and puritan in matters of intoxication. A genius with his hands rather than his head, he did not read many books, but he did enjoy the works of John Burroughs, due to a shared interest in birdspotting. In December 1912, Ford wrote to Burroughs telling him that few persons in the world had given him as much pleasure as he had. In return, he wanted to do something for Burroughs. He wanted to give him a car. He assured Burroughs that it was not a publi-city stunt, and the car could be there by January.

Burroughs had misgivings. He was seventy-five years old, an advanced age for a learner driver. Friends persuaded him to accept the gift and the old man spent the winter attempting to master it, with comically haphazard results. Behind the wheel, he was easily distracted by rare birds or plants, and would take his eyes off the road to follow them, his white bushy head rattling as the car bumped over the farm track. Driving scared him. He was not the master of the car. This technology was an unbroken horse.

In June, Burroughs travelled to Detroit to visit Henry Ford. The two men got on. After a tour of the factory, Burroughs described the manufacturing process with the eyes of a nature writer; it was a 'wilderness of men and machinery covering over forty acres. The Ford cars grow before your eyes, and every day a thousand of them issue from the rear.' After returning home to Roxbury, Burroughs went to park his car in the barn but 'it run wild', bursting through the side of the building and rattling on to a drop of fifteen feet. The forward axle went out over the edge but the wheels caught enough purchase to prevent the car landing at the foot of the steep hill. The old man regarded the accident with shame.

Ford's courting of Burroughs continued. In September, Henry Ford undertook a pilgrimage in Burroughs's company to Concord to visit Thoreau's pond at Walden and the house of Ralph Waldo Emerson, the central figure of the Philosophers' Camp of 1858. The camping trips that Ford, Burroughs, Thomas Edison and Harvey Firestone undertook echoed the transcendentalist gathering. Only at camp, removed from the demands and pressures of daily life, could great men discern the greater good.

Ford and Burroughs visited Thomas Edison's home in Fort Meyer in Florida. Edison was a decade younger than Burroughs, and sixteen years older than Ford, or as Burroughs put it, 'Mr Edison and Mr Ford are as young as I am, but no younger.' The public images of all three men relied upon their physical vigour. Burroughs was uncommonly fit for a man in his seventies. When dallying at a cliff edge, it was suggested to him that he show caution and step back. In defiance, the old man sprang on to his hands, his feet in the air, to prove there was no danger. In his early fifties, Henry Ford could run like a deer, and prided himself upon his high kicks and leaps. Edison was famous for his pronouncements concerning diet and sleep, claiming that he subsisted on four or five hours' rest a night and ate a sparing diet of toast and hot milk. Their camping trips saw a relaxing of Edison's frugal regime; as Burroughs's diary of his first visit to Florida relates, 'We begin the day so late here . . . Edison sleeps ten to twelve hours in the twenty-four; says he can store up enough sleep to last him two years.' Edison suggested that the men and their wives should take a break from Fort Meyer and go down to the Everglades and revert back to nature. 'We will get away from fictitious civilization,' said Edison to a reporter, 'and we expect to be happy and learn much.' In early March, the party slipped away for two days' camping, with two guides and a cook. The trip was a success. More ambitious camping trips were to follow, billed by the *Washington Times* as 'Edison and Ford to go back to nature'.

Edison spent several weeks studying maps of the Adirondacks, drawing up a route that was scenic and avoided popular towns and roads. He then wrote to his esteemed friends informing them of the plan. Then, another letter would arrive, informing them of the changes to the plan. During the autocamp, he would generally improvise an entirely different route, sat up front beside the driver, holding his compass. When he felt that the convoy had gone far enough, he would decide to camp.

The night before the trip, Edison checked that everything had been packed satisfactorily in his big motor truck, then went to bed early with the intention of setting off at seven in the morning. On 29 August 1916, he met Harvey Firestone at the Edison Factory and they were waved off by all 6,500 employees. It was Firestone's job to take along the cook and provisions, at least to begin with. At their first camp, a farmer confronted them and had to be bought off for the sum of five dollars. From there, on a wet and cold morning, they drove to Burroughs's Woodchuck Lodge in Roxbury and camped in his orchard under old apple trees. On a high hillside overlooking the Delaware Valley, four large tents and a dining tent were pitched and illuminated by Edison's electric lights. An English chef prepared an elaborate meal but Edison confined himself to toast and hot milk, an ostentatious display of frugality. After dinner, the men sat in deckchairs around the campfire and talked of the war in Europe, a subject that weighed heavily upon the thoughts of John Burroughs. The conversation turned lighter, to old men's memories of boyhood and then, inspired by the fire, speculations on the life of primitive man. It was a cold night, but Edison would not be coddled. The great inventor and self-publicist had built his reputation on a seemingly superhuman capacity for self-discipline; camping was a continuation of his personal mythology. Also, it suited him more than high society and luxury; he was naturally scruffy and played the vagabond with ease, sleeping in his clothes and napping under a tree after lunch, then rising to replenish the campfire. He basked in nature's 'primal sanities', in the words of Walt Whitman (when Burroughs was twenty-six years old, Whitman compared his face to a field of wheat).

The press were informed that the men intended to rough it in the wilderness, although they were – in modern parlance – glamping; the camping party consisted of two big Packard cars, two Fords, two trucks and a crew of seven men, 'the Waldorf-Astoria on wheels' as Burroughs described it. The dining tent contained a nine-foot-long collapsible table with a lazy Susan, a revolving section in the centre. Their army tents measured ten foot by ten foot and were set up by helpers.

The party moved on from Burroughs's back garden. The purpose of these autocamping trips was to explore, not to settle; the party drove from Roxbury to Ten Eyck via the Catskills, Edison's ascetic route ensuring Burroughs's bony backside was rattled by every mile of the trip. Edison ruled that there must be no shaving in camp, an edict broken on a particularly cold night when it was decided that John Burroughs should sleep indoors. Harvey Firestone took him to a local hotel, and there he shaved and bathed, a weakness for which Edison mocked him upon his return; 'You're a tenderfoot,' he laughed. 'Soon you'll be dressing up like a dude.' When two girls driving a big car down a wet, slippery street suddenly skidded and turned about, leaving the amazed girls looking up the street instead of down, Edison remarked, 'Organized matter sometimes behaves in a very strange manner.' Edison had a particular wit.

Henry Ford did not show up on this first camping trip, claiming his son's wedding as an excuse. America's entry into the Great War precluded any camping trips in 1917, but Ford was at the forefront of a more ambitious camping tour of the South in 1918, the trip

that Firestone declared to be the best of them all. The four vagabonds were joined by Edward Hurley, chairman of the shipping
board and connected to the Wilson administration and the war.
The plan was to drive from Pennsylvania through West Virginia to
Tennessee, then swing over to North Carolina, Virginia and Maryland. Their camping tour was not merely an encounter with
nature, it was also a survey of the state of the nation and a meet-
and-greet with American folk. And the folk came in droves to
observe the great men. Sometimes John Burroughs was the most
popular: one Pennsylvanian mountaineer refused them permission to camp on his land, denied all knowledge of Ford and Edison
and only relented upon the mention of John Burroughs. Mostly
they came for Henry Ford. A journalist in Philadelphia captured
the mood of goodwill that accompanied this roaming 'picnic':

> Everybody hopes they are having a good time . . . There are per-
> haps greater scientists in the country than Mr Edison, greater
> mechanics than Mr Ford and more accomplished naturalists than
> Mr Burroughs. But on the way to eminence they have lost some-
> thing that Ford, Edison and Burroughs jealously retain. That is a
> fellowship with the common man and a governing concern for
> the little man's interests and welfare. All three were once poor.
> When poverty left them they retained the best gifts that poverty
> carries in her thin hands for those who have eyes to see. They
> achieved kindliness, a sense of humor and tempered hearts.

A more cynical perspective is that the camping tours were publicity stunts by two great self-promoters. Charlie Sorensen, in his
book *My Forty Years with Ford* (1956), portrayed the trips as examples of Ford's inability or refusal to maintain close friends in
the way he turned this annual meet into a media jamboree:

> With squads of newswriters and platoons of cameramen to report
> and film the posed nature studies of the four eminent campers,

these well-equipped excursions into readily accessible solitudes were as private and secluded as a Hollywood opening, and Ford appreciated the publicity. He admired Edison . . . but aside from this annual camp get-together and an occasional Edison visit to Detroit and Dearborn they seldom saw each other.

Their exploits were front-page news, particularly when a reporter collared Ford or Edison after a few days' seclusion and sought out their opinion on the matter of the day. When camping, the men became a chorus commenting on the daily drama of America. But if their camping was purely a public relations exercise, why did their convoy include two large Packard cars? The press always enjoyed catching Henry Ford in a vehicle that his company did not manufacture. 'I'm on vacation,' he explained, 'we are in no hurry. We don't care when we get home. That's why I'm not in a Ford.'

On the road outside Pittsburgh, a convoy of army trucks rolled past on their way to the fight in Europe. The difficulty the American army convoys experienced in driving across the country made subsequent development of the highway system a matter of national security. 'We live in an age of iron,' noted Burroughs, passing through a cloud of dirt and dust thrown up by the army trucks and the stink of Pittsburgh's industries. 'It's all we can do to keep the iron from entering our souls.' Burroughs's role, public and private, was to instruct Edison and Ford in the American countryside; whenever the cars stopped, Edison would collect a handful of flowers from the roadside and request that he name them. Burroughs was the living embodiment of the values the industrialists wanted to retain in themselves, their personal mythology, their bulwark against the iron. The public conversion of Burroughs to autocamping connected driving to transcendentalism, bridging the two centuries so that the values of freedom and self-reliance espoused by the transcendentalists were transferred to the American automobile. Prior to their acquaintance, Henry Ford said that Burroughs:

> ... detested money and especially he detested the power which money gives to vulgar people to despoil the lovely countryside. He grew to dislike the industry out of which money is made ... He criticized industrial progress, and he declared the automobile was going to kill the appreciation of nature ... So I sent him an automobile with the request that he try it out and discover for himself whether or not it would help him to know nature better. The automobile ... completely changed his point of view. He found that it helped him to see more, and from the time of getting it, he made nearly all of his bird-hunting expeditions behind the steering wheel ... the whole countryside was open to him.

Before the car and the improved roads, America was obscure to itself. Autocamping was a fad for national self-discovery.

The large travelling party rarely covered more than fifty miles a day, mostly camping whenever night overtook them. After a camp thirty miles south-east of Pittsburgh, at Greensburg, they slept indoors at Uniontown in Pennsylvania, compromising their stated aim of roughing it. By late August, they were dawdling in West Virginia, exultant with the drive across mountain ranges and along roadsides of purple eupatorium and ironweed. On the banks of a clear creek near Horseshoe Run, the men posed for a press photograph upon a waterwheel. Next they camped in the grounds of the Cheat Mountain Club to a rousing reception from the clubhouse. They reached Bolar Springs on 23 August. The spring was a perfect camp, level and beside sugar-maple woods with copious amounts of fresh water that gathered in a bathing pool. The next day, they were at Wolf Creek, watching fish jump in the water. Here no one knew who they were. In fact, the area was so remote that when a car went past, Burroughs heard a woman cry, 'What in hell is that?'

Burroughs could be difficult in camp, a curmudgeon who asked that his tent be pitched apart from the others, and was given to grumbling about the lateness of dinner. His wife, Ursula, had died the previous year. Of his nine brothers and sisters, only a brother was still living and he was to die in 1919. His journals and letters from this period are an unrelenting itinerary of death notices and funerals. For all his complaints, the camps provided him with renewal, a 'shaking up' of his morbid condition. He had just the one child, a son. In Virginia, a large Southern family of thirteen reminded him both of the large family that he came from, and the family he did not produce: 'Every branch the tree puts out lays it open more to the storms and tempests of life; it lays it open also to the light and the sunshine, and to the singing and mating of birds. A childless life is a tree without branches.'

As Burroughs grouched and brooded, Edison and Ford relished adversarial banter around the campfire. One evening, Ford was working on the design for a tractor, but he couldn't crack the steering mechanism. He insisted Edison have a go. Edison produced a sketch, Ford rejected it and tried again, and pressed Edison to respond; this was how the two men worked, trial and error, fumbling their way to understanding. Ford sketched a mechanism that he believed would work; Edison dismissed it as the worst idea yet – wrongly, for that was the design that would go into production. On another campfire session, Ford tasked Edison with devising a new monetary system that was simple, scientific and outside of the control of the bankers. This challenge led to three months of concerted effort from Edison to solve the problem of money. Unfortunately, he failed.

The candour of campfire conversation drew the men together. It had personal and symbolic value; for all their wealth and power, the ill-educated Henry Ford and cranky Edison (all that obsessing over food and sleep) regarded themselves as outsiders to the establishment. Edison relished the slovenly informality of camp, bathing in creeks, sleeping in his clothes and carelessly spitting out tainted tobacco juice. He detested formal society. Camp was a chance for him to meditate, investigate plant life, observe nature with an engineer's practical curiosity – and to hold forth. Erudite and witty, he was the leader of the campfire conversation. Henry Ford was alienated and monstrously wealthy. In 1915, at the personal cost of half a million pounds, Ford led a boat of 163 pacifists, cranks, suffragettes, prohibitionists and scornful journalists on a peace mission to Europe to broker an end to the Great War. At the dock, onlookers mocked Ford and his cranks mercilessly. In return, he threw them roses. Edison and Burroughs waved him off. Ignorant of European history and politics but naively insistent that something must be done to arrest the slaughter, Ford's peace mission was a grotesque failure; the boat, the *Oscar II*, was confined at Kirkwall in the Orkneys for three days by the British authorities and then arrived in Norway. Abandoned by Ford, the squabbling, impassioned delegation travelled down through Stockholm and Copenhagen and headed for The Hague. When America entered the war, patriotic fervour ensured that the reputations of many who sailed on the *Oscar II* were ruined. Henry Ford manufactured munitions for the war effort.

In the wake of a disastrous peace mission, the autocamping trips can be seen as Ford's way of reconnecting to the American heartland. A campfire is a heart – consequently, we think of the conversations taking place around it as being close to the heart. For powerful men, to sit around the campfire was a demonstration that they could talk plainly and honestly. Campfire conversation is the opposite of the sophisticated badinage of the urban establishment; whenever an American leader camps, it is a disavowal of the kind of speech that Washington demands. Pitching tents, meeting the various folk of the nation, being at ease in the pastoral: this symbolic role of the rural camp in American leadership continues in the presidential retreat of Camp David. Camp David is a secure naval establishment and bears no resemblance to a campsite – nevertheless, the meaning of 'camp' hangs over it.

Camp David is associated with negotiation after the Egyptian–Israeli peace accord brokered by Jimmy Carter. It is, in the public imagination, a place without distraction where candid conversations can be had and the wider picture addressed. George W. Bush spent 487 days of his two terms as president at Camp David. He also spent 490 days at his Crawford ranch. He must have thought the White House was bad for his image. Barack Obama has complained that economic crises kept him in Washington more than he would have liked. His relatively infrequent visits to Camp David perhaps contribute to the perception of him as a passionless establishment technocrat. Frankly, Obama needs to camp.

The four vagabonds autocamped around New England in the summer of 1919, taking in the Adirondacks and the Green and White Mountains. The convoy included a Cadillac touring car with a covered body and special compartments to carry the equipment, and a Ford fitted out like a grocery store with a kitchen utilized by Sato, Ford's butler, who acted as chef and major-domo. On this later trip, the men's idiosyncrasies were more evident: the tender, broken, bedtime prayer-song of John Burroughs; Thomas Edison's bizarre theory of monoids, tiny beings which he maintained were responsible for the regulation of his mind; the anti-Semitism of Henry Ford, *Protocols-of-Zion*-inspired howling tirades against Jewish capitalists, which greatly offended Burroughs.

Thomas Edison's eating and sleeping habits, so contrary to his public pronouncements, irked and amused Burroughs. In his journal he notes:

Ten AM. Edison not up yet – the man of little sleep! He inveighs against cane-sugar, yet puts two heaping teaspoonfuls in each cup of coffee, and he takes three or four cups a day! He smokes three or four cigars each day. He eats more than I do, yet calls me a gourmand. He eats pie by the yard, if he can get it, and he bolts his food. O Consistency, thy name is not Edison!

Their campfire discussions on the high cost of living made the front page of the *Washington Times*. The reporter describes a ghost-like tented village somewhere in the Adirondack Mountains: eight tents of oiled silk, 'almost transparent with the incandescent lamps inside them . . . like so many jewels against the velvet blackness of the forest on all sides. In the centre of the tiny village a camp fire burned . . . fifty miles off the main line of any railroad.' Around the campfire, Henry Ford played the provocateur, advocating that farmers should eliminate horses, cows and pigs from their land, and that America do without meat: 'The world would be better off without meat. It's seventy per cent ashes anyway. Milk can be manufactured chemically. Every animal used on the farm these days is a waste of time.' Waste in production was his obsession; he regarded the war as a terrible if necessary waste, and he could barely glance at a mountain stream without fulminating at the energy that could be harnessed from its waters and used to power machinery. With a stroke of his long grey beard, Burroughs skewered Ford's vision of the ultra-efficient farm. He told a story about a man who invented a hog fattener. The man took his invention to a farmer, claiming that it would make hogs fat in short order. The farmer laughed, and insisted that the old method of feeding them grain was better. 'But,' said the salesman, 'it's such a waste of time.' The farmer replied, 'What's time to a hog?' The joke cuts to the heart of it: does technological improvement constitute human progress? Or is the wisdom of the old ways superior to the ceaseless novelty of the modernist?

'They say I have a lot of queer ideas,' ruminated Ford to a reporter two days later, while breaking camp near Plattsburgh, beside Lake Champlain, north-east of the Adirondack Park. He defined the solution to the problem of the high cost of living as lying in a combination of three arts, 'manufacturing, agriculture, and transportation'. On the question of strikes, he insisted, 'My men never strike. Nature never strikes.'

Their opinions dispensed, the campers disappeared again into the mountains on a pilgrimage that 'doesn't know where it is going. And cares less.' The men relished the excitement caused by the impromptu arrival of their convoy. Stopping in Springfield, Massachusetts, for half an hour, they attracted a crowd. Edison, deeply tanned, lolled back in the enormous touring car, reading the newspaper and ignoring the people. Henry Ford sent a personal telegram at the Western Union, then called in at the Worthy Hotel barber shop for a shave. When it was time to pay, Ford pulled out a wad of notes, peeled off a five-dollar bill, accepted his change and then handed over a tip. What a contrast he made to John Burroughs on the sunlit streets: Henry Ford, hatless, in a dark brown mohair suit with pinched back, and Burroughs with his grey hair spilling out from under a shabby cap and his hermit's clothes, pockets crammed with the odds and sods required at camp.

The following year there was no summer camp. Instead the men met at Yama Farm in November, where they engaged in a public tree-felling contest, with Burroughs beating Ford to the chop by four minutes. Then, at two in the morning on 29 March 1921, John Burroughs died mid-conversation with Clara Barrus, the late love of his life. He was buried at his home in Roxbury. Henry Ford secured the deed to the land so that his resting place would never be disturbed. Ford described him as a 'natural man' and a 'fine campmate', and recalled their time philosophizing together. 'Well, he used to wonder what it was like beyond,' said Ford, 'and I suppose he will begin philosophizing as soon as he gets his bearings. There will be birds where John Burroughs is – birds and great trees.' Edison described his campmate as 'one of the highest types yet evolved in the advance of men to a higher stage'. Edison sketched their roles. 'I was the geologist of the party. Burroughs was the botanist . . . Ford was a bit of an authority on birds. We had intended to meet again this summer for a journey into the wilds.'

The summer camp went ahead as planned, with Burroughs's place taken, for one evening, by President Harding. The election of the Republican Harding as president had inspired Burroughs to write in his journal that he was ashamed to call himself an American; the Harding presidency is regarded as one of the least successful and was curtailed by Harding's death from cardiac arrest.

Harvey Firestone was old friends with the president. He, Ford and Edison left camp and went out to Funkstown to meet him on 21 July 1921. The president was a fast driver, and, with a secret-service man, drove himself to the meeting. After arriving in a cloud of dust, he joined the vagabonds in their car for the trip to camp, the secret-service agent displacing Edison from his usual front seat. Offered a cigar by the president, Edison refused, saying he did not smoke (films show Edison puffing away on a cigar beside the campfire). 'I don't smoke, I chew,' said Edison. 'With that,' remembers Firestone, 'the President pulled a big plug of chewing tobacco out of his hip pocket. Mr Edison grinned and took a hefty chew. Later he announced, "Harding is all right. Any man who chews tobacco is all right."'

The camp was in a green meadow beside Licking Creek, shaded by oaks and sycamores and surrounded by gentle, sloping hills. The appearance of the president confirmed both the symbolic importance of camping to a leader, and that any genuine spirit of enquiry behind the camping trips had passed. Arriving at the camp at one in the afternoon, Harding turned the camp into a photo opportunity; for the press, he chopped wood unenthusiastically, drank water from a long-handled dipper, then after dinner retired to his tent, pausing at the entrance so that eleven cameramen could capture the moment. Around the campfire, the men talked of a conference on the limitation of arms, and Edison and the president argued about tarpon fishing, the tarpon being a great game fish found off the coast of Florida. The president spent a single night under canvas. The next day, he rode upon one of Harvey Firestone's horses. At this point, the camp had grown to twenty tents and a fleet of trucks, and included Mrs Edison, Mrs Ford, Mrs Firestone, Edsel Ford and his wife, Harvey Firestone Jnr and his wife, the second Firestone lad, Russell, and the Bishop and Mrs William P. Anderson. The catering truck included a hundred chickens killed and dressed especially for the trip by Harvey's Aunt Nannie and the Ladies' Aid Society. After the president left, the convoy went on to Cumberland, Maryland, then to Fairmount and, on 3 August, back to Uniontown, where it broke up.

Then, in 1924, Edison quit the camps, describing them as a travelling circus. In his autobiography, the unfortunately titled *Men and Rubber*, Firestone states that:

> The publicity which the trips began to gather around them elim-
> inated their object and charm. We were never free. Instead of a
> simple, gipsy-like fortnight we found ourselves in the midst of
> motion-picture operators, reporters, and curiosity seekers.

So says the man who took six horses and two grooms on his 'simple, gipsy-like fortnight'. In 1921, the convoy was so large and the camp so lavish that the original stated aim of entering nature's laboratory and exposing themselves to its raw sanities was lost. The final trip in 1924 used the Wayside Inn as its headquarters and visited President Coolidge at his father's home in Plymouth, Vermont. Camping was off the agenda.

The publicity surrounding the trips elevated autocamping in the national psyche. Inspired by Edison, Ford, Burroughs and Firestone, millions of Americans took to the road, loaded up with canvas tents, collapsible baby cots and stoves. Campers customized their vehicles, adding food boxes to the running boards and spring-supported car cribs. The roll-a-bed tent was attached directly to the running board at the side of the car and when erected incorporated the driver's side door. Campers customized trailers and used them as trailer tents.

The first autocampers did not book ahead; as with Edison's improvised routes, they took pleasure in pitching wherever they happened to park up at nightfall. The trend for autocamping inspired towns to set up free municipal camps to attract the mostly middle-class campers. By the mid 1920s, there were 5,000 of these camps across the country. As the roads improved, car journeys became faster and less attentive of the surroundings. More people jumped on to the car-camping bandwagon. The 'real thing' was to camp every night in a different place and cover lots of miles every day. The tents were physically attached to the cars, suggesting that driving was more important than the camping. Over the course of the decade, car camping went from a fit pursuit for a president to the down-at-heel holiday of the impoverished. Campsites started to charge fees of fifty cents a car. The municipal camps and cabins that appeared on the roadside to accommodate car travellers solidified into motels, and the characteristic American roadside developed from there.

If we are to regard the camping trips of Thomas Edison, Henry Ford, Harvey Firestone and John Burroughs as publicity stunts promoting the potential of the car, then the conversion of Burroughs by Henry Ford was an act of instinctive genius. Sanctioned by the bearded sage, the car became individualistic and rebellious. The prescriptive journeys of the railroads represented mainstream capitalism. Tootling off the beaten path according to Edison's improvisations of map and compass, along the 'poor undernourished routes which the dull, imitative rabble shun', car camping was as rugged and romantic as backpacking. It was 'Thoreau at 29 cents a gallon'. Ford's publicity coup fills the tank for the transcendental road trips to come, of Jack Kerouac and Neal Cassidy, the rock 'n' roll mythology of Route 66, the rebel yawp of the Harley Davidson.

Burroughs was enthusiastic about the camping trips, relishing the shaking up they gave him, and he confessed he had scarcely enjoyed himself so much for forty years. There was laughter around the campfire, which Burroughs attributed to camping giving the men a sideways perspective of normality. In Ford and Edison, he saw men unconsciously seeking out discomfort, to escape – if only temporarily – the gilded cage of greatness, 'just to touch naked reality once more'. As concerns the car, Burroughs wrote in a letter that he felt it put him in a false relation to the surrounding landscape. In a car, 'I am puffed up. I am a traveler. I am in sympathy with nothing around me; but on foot I am part of the country, and I get it into my blood.'

8

The Basics

Food

In the days before we go camping, Cath stocks up on her chosen tins and jars. She grinds pepper and mixes spices. A chicken pie is baked, as are flapjacks, for our Just-Pitched Dinner. The art of camp cookery requires preparation, siphoning off supplies from your kitchen and planning ahead so that you do not carry more than is required, nor leave undone the kind of jobs that are easy to do at home but difficult in a field. Various Tupperware containers are loaded with cereal, marinades and pieces of smoky bacon, their rinded fat reminding me of the camp cookery of the great American backwoodsmen Nessmuk and Horace Kephart, for whom pork fat was the essential ingredient.

Camp cooking is a gentle adventure. All the camping handbooks of the last hundred years note how life outdoors increases the appetite, as if fresh air were a delicious sauce. Every keen camper has their own recipes and cooking methods. Thomas Hiram Holding is particular about frying bacon: 'First, there is a right and wrong way of cooking bacon, as there is of choosing a wife, making out a lawyer's bill, or cleaning a ditch.' He liked his bacon rashers to be, at most, four inches long, and he always nicked the fat twice so that they did not curl up when hot. The first rashers to be cooked were to be moved around slowly so that their fat thoroughly greased the pan.

Camping triggers our instinctive fret about exactly where the next meal is coming from. People who are diffident about their food at home become more animated around the cooking fire. The mood becomes intensely social, with campers sharing out their supplies and adding their own food to the communal feast. The atmosphere tightens when meat sizzles over the open fire. Heat up vegetarian curries for twenty people, and few will show the slightest interest in the content of the pans; roast a rack of ribs over hot coals, and you will soon be flanked by interested campers.

Meat was highly valued in hunter-gatherer societies. A man in possession of meat could barter it for political favours from men and sexual favours from women. Meat combined with fire repre-sents prehistoric power and status, a truth every man feels in his guts when he lights a barbecue. We hunted in packs, mutual aid being a more successful survival strategy than individual talent when it came to taking down big game. Around the campfire, I feel the excitement of the pack enjoying its spoils.

If you want to learn more about food in camp, a good place to start is *Camp Cookery* by Horace Kephart, the 'dean of American campers'. He was a small, intelligent and honest man with one deep brown eye, and one blue. His reputation rests on his com-pendium *Camping and Woodcraft* (1906), which contains all the knowledge an aspiring Robinson Crusoe requires. His legacy also includes his contribution to the formation of the National Park of the Great Smoky Mountains, for which he lobbied during his lifetime, and the Appalachian trails that he pioneered. But it is his talent as a camp chef that we are concerned with here. Kephart published *Camp Cookery* in 1910 and *Sporting Firearms* in 1912; he was a man who cooked what he killed, relishing the fresh meat of the mountainside over the refrigerated steak served in town. His cookbook includes five pages on how a camper can dress the carcass of a freshly killed deer (although you must never eat meat that still retains its animal warmth), as well as advice on skinning a bear, scaling trout, splitting birds and jointing a squirrel. His cookbook describes curing hams from deer or elk in camp, dissecting the meat into small pieces and rubbing them with allspice, pepper and salt, then hanging them from trees to dry in the wind. For a hunter and camper like Kephart, out in the wild for months at a time, techniques of meat preservation were as important as meal preparation.

Kephart was an epicure of the camp ground. He dismissed sweet condensed milk as 'an abomination' and rejected the masochist's rations of hardtack or ship's biscuit; he packed plain flour to make his own pancakes over the campfire, made stock in camp out of two pounds of venison, and snuck pressed sage into his kit to stuff game birds, along with half a pint of brandy for brandy sauce. Although he was, according to outdoors writer Jim Casada, America's most knowledgeable firearms authority in the first quarter of the twentieth century, locals who knew Kephart claimed that he was happier in camp finessing his dishes than out in the Smoky Mountains hunting the black bear.

Kephart's recipe for roast beaver tail (gelatinous, tasting somewhat like pork) and his lyrical delight in the meat of the possum reveal a rugged outdoorsman who took care and time over his camping meals. The most appealing of Kephart's recipes is his 'Planked Fish', no doubt cooked with the speckled trout of the Smoky Mountains:

Split and smooth a slab of sweet hardwood two or three inches thick, two feet long, and wider than the opened fish. Prop it in front of a bed of coals until it is sizzling hot. Split the fish down the back of its entire length but do not cut through the belly skin. Clean and wipe it quite dry. When the plank is hot, spread the fish out like an opened book, tack it, skin side down, to the plank and prop before the fire. Baste continuously with a bit of pork on a switch held above it. Reverse ends of plank from time to time. If the flesh is flaky when pierced with a fork, it is done. Sprinkle salt and pepper over the fish, moisten with drippings and serve on the hot plank. Plenty of butter improves it at table.

In Kephart's novel *Smoky Mountain Magic* (finally published in 2009), a housewife Marian comes across the backwoods kitchen of Tom, who lives a simple life in the wilderness much like the author. She notices his collection of tinned foods; on his shelves there are tins of boned chicken from Massachusetts, soups from Chicago and New Jersey, chilli from Texas, Swiss cheese from the Emmenthal, brown bread from Boston, beaten biscuits from Maryland, pumpernickel from Germany, fruits and nut butters from California, jams and jellies from York State, sauces from England and even a purée of foie gras which 'exalts the midday sandwich to something worshipful'.

Ingredients were important to Kephart. On his 'Heavy Ration' list for one man for one month, there is a note in brackets: 'Best of everything'. Along with essentials such as ten dozen fresh eggs and an egg carrier, he packed grated Parmesan cheese and olive oil, reminders of the time he tramped the Alps and lived in Florence. But he regarded fire as the real secret to outdoor cookery. In prolonged camps, Kephart set a separate cooking fire and built his own range of two stout forked stakes, each about four foot high, set five feet apart. Across the crotches or forks, he lay a broomstick-thick green log from which green sticks of varying lengths hung so that his kettle or pot could be adjusted at different heights over the fire. He packed a flat fire iron for frying, the handle of a pan being a perennial packing problem for a camper. When roasting a joint, Kephart put a reflector behind a high fire to throw the heat forwards. With this simple set-up he prepared dishes as exotic as porcupine cooked in clay or the 'Baked Deer's Head' ('Insert neck first into the ground . . .'), which sound otherworldly to palates raised on trimmed supermarket chicken breasts.

Inspired by Kephart, I set a keyhole campfire, which consists of one large blaze to warm the people sitting around it, and an adjacent bed of hot coals raked out of its companion. Keen to remove a bulky barbecue from my kit, I asked a local blacksmith to make me a cooking tripod. The classic iron tripod has a single hook and chain from which a pot or kettle is hung. After a chat with the smithy, he suggested a tripod with a central ring; from this ring, I could hang as many chains as I wanted over the fire. A week later the tripod was forged, three iron legs each about three feet in length attached to an iron ring, their gathered tops held in place by a horned cap. Folded flat, the tripod took up an insignificant amount of boot space. I bought a large circular grill, varying lengths of chain-link and the S-shaped metal hooks commonly used on pan racks. This additional kit would allow me to turn the tripod into a barbecue by dangling three chains from the central ring and hooking their ends to the grill. Over the summer, suspending the grill in this fashion proved trickier in practice than in theory, especially if the fire was already lit. The set-up did, however, allow the grill to be methodically raised or lowered one chain-link at a time according to the requirements of the meat, from the first ferocious sizzle to the long slow roast. (Kephart advises the camp cook to 'imprison in each dish, at the outset, its natural juice and characteristic flavour'.)

The tripod grill is spectacular and ostentatious with its two-foot diameter of swinging sizzling meat, but ultimately it requires too large a fire to be anything other than my idiosyncrasy. The time I cooked a dozen beefburgers using a single burning log and the grills salvaged from disposable barbecues is a sounder example of camp craft than my tripod. I have, however, mastered Kephart's small fires for the quick cooking of lunch, using an armful of sticks each about the size of a pencil. At the base of three of these sticks he advises carving a ballgown of shavings so that they kindle more keenly. With a delicate and intricately set fire, I spend a lot of time on my knees, a fat god blowing life into a miniature ecosystem until suddenly creation takes on a life of its own, and it is left to me to either throw more fuel upon it or administer a corrective kick.

Kephart's *Camp Cookery* contains vestiges of Indian practices; his method of cooking a deer in its own hide, for example, is similar to the description in Reginald and Gladys Laubin's *Indian Tipi* (1957) of the cooking of a stew in the paunch of a buffalo. It was also a method used by the Scottish Highlanders, whom Kephart researched in the writing of his novel about the Appalachian people. The paunch of the animal is suspended from a four-legged prop and filled with water. Stones are heated and then dropped into the water until it boils. Small chunks of meat are cast into the stew and, when they are done, eaten with skewers. The paunch itself can also be consumed, sparing the bother of washing-up.

In his book *The Wilderness Life* (1975), writer Calvin Rutstrum described dinner with an Indian family, noting the wisdom of cooking in such a way that washing-up was avoided. Chunks of goose were boiled in a kettle, and each family member used a pointed stick to take what they wanted – a kind of meat fondue. For a beverage, the goose broth was drunk in a tin cup. When the meat was eaten, the mother emptied the kettle, boiled some water and added wood ashes to make a lye solution and saponify the goose fat to make the cups easier to wash in the lake. Camp cookery is about minimizing the amount of water required, and limiting washing-up is sound practice. When attending an Indian feast, guests were expected to bring their own utensils, bowl and knife, and this sparing use of pots and pans continues in the camping cook's one-pot dinner.

Cath wrote me a note about the principles of one-pot camp cooking:

> One-pot meals need the carbohydrates, protein and vegetables to be in the pot together. Many cultures have their one-pot standby: minestrone in Italy, paella in Spain, scouse in Liverpool. What they have in common is there is no set list of ingredients, only that they must be both local and seasonal. When camping by the coast we have fish and seafood paella, and the vegetables in minestrone vary from season to season. One-pot meals are often cooked in stock for taste and to thicken the gravy. At home, I make my own chicken, fish and game stock and store it in the freezer. It would be crazy to do this when camping, so I take some with me or buy fresh stock from the supermarket. Other options would be to use concentrate or a stock cube, or alcohol; travelling in France we lived off vegetables and garlic sausage stewed in table wine, whereas in Britain you can always braise beef in a rich brown ale. If you cook with pulses, they add a sort of soupy stock themselves.

One camping standard that we are yet to revive is pemmican, a pressed cake of shredded dried meat mixed with berries and perfected by the Plains Indians. Pemmican was much sought after by soldiers during the Civil War in preference to their own iron rations. There are so many recipes for pemmican in the history of camping that we could broaden the definition of the dish to include any compact, nutrient-rich food that does not require cooking, keeps well and fits easily into lightweight kit.

Ernest Thompson Seton sent instructions for a new method of making pemmican derived from the techniques of Canadian Indians to the meatpacking firm of Armour and Company of Chicago. The Arctic explorer Sir John Richardson dried the meat for his pemmican in the malting equipment of a brewery and mixed one part with Zante currants and another with sugar to create separate sweet and savoury pemmicans. The Laubins describe the making of Indian pemmican. Jerky is roasted over coals until it turns the rich brown colour of seared meat. This jerky is then pounded until fine, along with dried chokecherries. Suet is poured over the mix, which is then patted into shape and stored in a bladder or rawhide. The Ojibwa Indians dug mortar holes in the ground, lined them with skins, pounded meat with a stone pestle and packed the blended pemmican in hide containers. These caches, secreted along the trail, remained in the earth for up to three years before spoiling. The Victorian explorer Francis Galton gives precise measurements for his preferred pemmican: 'a mixture of about five-ninths of pounded dry meat to four-ninths of melted or boiled grease; it is put into a skin bag or tin can whilst warm and soft . . . wild berries are sometimes added. The skin bags for the pemmican should be shaped like pillow cases for the convenience of packing on horseback.'

Arctic explorers relished pemmican, describing it as the only food they could stand eating three times a day, every day, for months on end. In 1853, Lieutenant Cresswell, the first officer to cover the Northwest Passage, describes his arctic camps thusly: 'We used to travel journeys of about ten hours, and then encamp, light our spirits-of-wine, put our kettle on it to thaw our snow-water, and after we had had our supper – just a piece of pemmican, and a glass of water – we were glad to smoke our pipes and turn into bed.'

Kephart the gourmand reassures us that campers do not need to suffer terrible food. We may have no need for the cached food-stuffs of nomadic Indians, or the deer eviscerated and served fresh at the camp, but that does not mean our camp cookery must be artless or lacking a taste of the locality. Beside my tent I have eaten as memorably as at any restaurant: a ratatouille of Provençal vegetables tumbling on the Trangia in Avignon; the wild garlic picked from a glade in East Sussex and rubbed into flatbreads baked over the campfire; the lamb shoulder impolitely roasted within olfactory range of its flock in the Cotswolds; spaghetti vongole with freshly landed clams cooked on a misty Cornish hillside; and brigand steak in the Highlands, the method copied directly from Clara Barrus's biography of John Burroughs:

> They selected, peeled, and sharpened a straight maple limb, six or eight feet long, which tapered to the size of a lead pencil . . . On this peeled end the Scout Master strung the pieces of steak, sliced very thin and cut in portions about one and one-half inches square, the folded slices of bacon, and the tender young onions, like beads on a string. Placing a big stone back of the fire on which to rest the tip of the long stick, they slowly turned the stick, thus roasting the meat and onions over the flame. And when all was done to a turn . . . and their appetites were whetted to distraction by the savory smell, the salt added, the string unstrung, the three boys of varying age and size, but each with a brigand's appetite, fell to, and made way with the feast.

Sleep

It is the middle of the night and I need to piss. The body expends heat warming a bladder full of urine. There is nothing to be gained by just lying there in the dark, gazing up at the low cotton vault of the inner tent, but I lie there anyway. On a cold night like this, only the hood of the mummy bag makes sleeping possible. My ankles are gathered together in the tapering end of the bag, my arms pressed in a variety of configurations against my torso. I am wearing hiking socks, a thermal vest and jumper. A silk liner is draped over me, and when it is particularly cold, I put this over my face and breathe through it. The air is not my enemy. The land is my enemy, the cold, cold ground that turns a standard air bed into a cold block. I don't use an air bed any more. I have reverted to the Therm-a-Rest, the thin mattress that is inflated by a few vigorous breaths. Underneath the Therm-a-Rest, a sheepskin rug provides vital insulation. My hands clasp one another over my heart. I am warm.

Must I leave all this behind to go for a piss?

The flanks of the tent shiver in the wind.

I unzip the inner tent, and the warmth of the vault is replaced by the loitering chill. I put on my cold jeans and boots and clamber out on to dewy meadow grass and into the night, the seething pitch silhouettes of winter trees, the ashen velveteen of a wheat field. The call of a screech owl from the woods. The night sky is an indifferent leviathan, heavy with stars and inhospitable astronomical fathoms. The tops of the pines thrash together. Even trees have moments of self-abandonment. I turn my back against the sky and piss in the woods. First light pulses in the east, while in the west the crescent moon and a clutch of stars hold court like the last drunks at a party. The birds assume their positions for the dawn chorus and await their cue. I shiver in anticipation of the sun rising to challenge the moon and her hangers-on. The valley stirs under grainy bands of blue. Nebulae overhead, indigo blades of grass below – to think I was reluctant to get out of bed! I should have set my alarm to catch this moment – the universe redressing the set between acts. In the towns and cities, the day is either on or off, like a screen, or a button; it's all binary thinking. The camper sees the vermilion subtleties, the in-between shades. I blow one last kiss to the canopy of stars, the tented heavens, and then return to my own tent, bringing the curtain down on a state of mind.

In the sleeping bag, my animal heat is quickly restored. The bag traps warm air in a thick layer around my body. A sleeping man generates between seventy-five and a hundred watts of heat; the exact amount of metabolic heat is dependent upon body fat, age and sex. I consider my wattage to be my most attractive feature.

The Arctic explorers of the 1850s made their beds out of a macintosh covering and a blanket in the form of a bag of coarse drugget covered with brown holland – drugget is a coarse cheap wool and brown holland a Dutch linen. The explorer Francis Fox Tuckett tested a prototype alpine sleeping bag in 1861 and declared it a disaster as the underside was a rubber-coated macintosh and so covered with condensation.

The principle of the sleeping bag has long been known, with bags of reindeer skin used in polar climates and desert folk weaving theirs from camel hair. In *The Art of Travel* (1855), Francis Galton notes the sheepskin sleeping bags used by the French douaniers, or customs officers, who watched the mountain passes of the Pyrenean frontier. Each bag came with five buckles so that it rolled and fastened into a knapsack. A letter to *The Times* on 12 February 1855 describes the sleeping sacks used by peasants in northern Germany, a strong linen sack made to draw at one end which was then stuffed with straw, hay and dry leaves. The peasants put their feet into it and drew the mouth of the bag up to their armpits. The most famous bespoke sleeping bag belonged to Robert Louis Stevenson. When he was a young, long-haired bohemian Stevenson wrote a comic account of a twelve-day hiking trip through the Cévennes Mountains of the South of France in the company of a recalcitrant ass called Modestine. For his adventure, a journey of self-discovery worthy of the Beats, Stevenson packed a spirit-lamp, a pan, two changes of clothes, chocolate, a railway rug, tins of Bologna sausage, a leg of cold mutton, a bottle of Beaujolais, an empty bottle for milk, an egg beater, black bread and white, a travelling suit of country velveteen, pilot-coat and knitted spencer – and a revolver. He considered a tent too conspicuous in the mountains and so designed for himself a large sleeping sack made out of waterproof cart cloth on the exterior and lined with blue sheep's wool. His 'sleeping sack' was six feet square, with two triangular flaps to serve as a pillow, and was so large it required a donkey to carry it – hence the recalcitrant ass. It was warm and dry and he could bury himself up to the neck in it, with a fur cap to cover his head.

Wool's thick fibres provide excellent insulation, especially when combined with an impermeable layer of sheepskin. Inside the front cover of Thomas Hiram Holding's *Camper's Handbook* there is an advert from Jaeger advocating the insulating properties of wool in its camping outfits 'to guard against the danger of sudden change from heat to cold, especially when extreme heat by day is followed by a great fall in temperature after sunset'. Jaeger, today a high-street brand, was then synonymous with Dr Gustav Jaeger, the crank's crank. Jaeger believed in keeping rough fabrics such as wool close to the skin at all times. He also believed he could smell the soul, and he drank tinctures made by soaking ladies' hairnets in water – as always, where there are bohemians, there are cranks, and where there are cranks and bohemians, there is camping. Holding describes in detail the sleeping arrangements in a camp with two of his fellows. Let his account put this matter to bed:

> After the pipe and the chat, we make up our pillows. After the pillows we each get into a sleeping bag, thick and warm, which buttons well up to the neck, and is fitted with a hood for the head. We feel as we are turning in that the air is getting crisper. Over the three campers a great red horse blanket with a 12-inch valance sewn around the edges is spread, and this is carefully tied down at the four corners and centre of each side, and boots and other things put on the valance at the foot – if we are too lazy to tie it there ... At 3 o'clock in the morning (when the air is coldest) though we are sleeping in our clothes, have on sleeping bags, and have over them a blanket, even that is not sufficient. The cold air will penetrate these. Therefore, we have a large 10-ft square gossamer sheet. It is simply a piece of macintosh with lanyards at the corners. This is hitched over the top of all, so that it cannot be

pulled off. It is this thing that keeps warmth in and cold out, and that in the coldest nights.

The Rain

Our camping tour of South-West England began at the Port Eliot festival, then moved on to South Penquite Farm atop Bodmin Moor for a couple of days before heading up along the coast and over Exmoor, descending steeply at Cloud Farm in Doone Valley. The tour took in the rich variety of rain the area has to offer. We did not miss a single drop. It rained in the morning when the children screamed for breakfast. It rained in the car when the children fought over pencils like old lags bickering over snout. It rained when I pitched camp and it rained when I struck camp.

I have three tips for camping in the rain:

1. Hide in the car.
2. Never go to the local museum.
3. Let the children get wet and muddy. And give them more biscuits than they require.

Camping with three small children in seven days and seven nights of rain is not an arrangement that springs to mind upon hearing the word 'holiday'. The Met Office promised a barbecue summer. We got the usual monsoon. The newspapers ran photographs of flooded campsites in the Lake District alongside stories of midnight evacuations. Campers muttered darkly to me about government conspiracies: was the weather forecast faked so that we holidayed at home to help the flatlining economy? Was the prime minister, in a headdress of turquoise feathers, leading the naked Cabinet through the ancient ritual of bringing down the rains to douse the spirits of the electorate lest sunlight distract us from our lot of hopeless, ill-rewarded, desperate, pointless, hated toil?

Seven days and seven nights of rain can strip a man of his reason. It's the noise of the rain against the tent: an unending ovation of sarcastic applause with the occasional catcall of children. There is no secret to surviving the misery of a wet day.

In the past I have been cavalier about rainy-day camping, based on my discredited conviction that it rarely rains every hour of the day. I maintained that there is the odd shower, an hour of downpour and then the clouds move on. In Thomas Hiram Holding's *Camper's Handbook*, he shares the delight of a walk he undertook during two wet days:

> I put on my waterproof and strolled onto a pulpit of lofty rock. Gazed across Loch Erne; saw the whirlwind gathering a column of water under the steep mountain opposite. This spiral pillar of water towered up, scattered and broke, and gathered again until it came and spent itself at a little point of rock five hundred yards away in the bay.

I envy Holding's solitary wet walk. He identifies one of the uses of camping as follows: 'It enables a man to get away from his family; or his family to get away from him for a spell.' Notice he does not write, 'It confines a man with his family, and prevents his family from gaining any respite from him.'

I devised the rule about local museums after taking refuge from the rain in the local attractions. Other families in steaming waterproofs formed a forbidding queue outside the dinosaur museum. I refused to queue in the rain for an experience I would – under normal conditions – have paid good money to avoid, so we ended up in a museum dedicated to the Chinese Terracotta Warriors. Here replicas of the statues created by 'museum and conservation technicians in China' were positioned behind velvet ropes and security devices. Dad-anger consumed me. I pledged to Cath that upon my return home I would visit the garden centre, buy replicas of Michelangelo's

David, stick them behind a velvet rope and charge the thick end of twenty quid so that families could experience the wonder of the Italian Renaissance.

Rain is a part of camping. Complaining about the rain when you are camping is like complaining about traffic in central London: what else did you expect? And if you take children camping, you must expect them to get wet and perhaps if you let them run around baptizing each other in the muddy waters, then they will learn for themselves the importance of protecting their gear from the rain. When we first went camping with the children, so many of our troubles stemmed from resisting their natural inclination to run around heedless of the weather.

We pitched and struck camp in the rain frequently on the holiday, working with silent efficiency. There is nothing to it. Pitch the outer tent first. Keep your groundsheet dry. At the entrance of the tent, fold back a yard of groundsheet so that – as you enter the tent – you step first on grass, which will absorb the water running off yourself. Take your boots off here and then step on to the groundsheet. If you fear flooding, and can't face striking camp, dig a trench around the tent. I've trenched tents at festivals, but campsite owners rarely approve of the practice. Tents will leak if anything touches the flysheet – the outer tent. So do not touch the sides. Be thankful for modern tents. Charles Dudley Warner, the neighbour of Mark Twain, described the roof of his camp shelter as a discriminating sieve, leaking upon certain members of his party, sparing others. Conquer the storm. Get out there and secure the guy ropes and take grim satisfaction in the hardiness of your kit. That is the only practical advice I have to offer for wet days at camp.

For consolation, I offer the thoughts of Jerome K. Jerome on the subject, from his *Three Men in a Boat*, so that we can be reassured that it was ever thus – with one exception: Jerome was spared the false hope peddled by the Met Office.

It is evening. You are wet through, and there is a good two inches of water in the boat, and all the things are damp. You find a place on the banks that is not quite so puddly as other places you have seen, and you land and lug out the tent, and two of you proceed to fix it.

It is soaked and heavy, and it flops about, and tumbles down on you, and clings around your head and makes you mad. The rain is pouring down steadily all the time. It is difficult enough to fix a tent in dry weather: in wet, the task becomes herculean. Instead of helping you, it seems to you that the other man is simply playing the fool. Just as you get your side beautifully fixed, he gives it a hoist from his end, and spoils it all.

Children and Character

Father and son lie down in long spears of meadow grass to watch a bee dutifully buzz between wild flowers. Alfred searches my face for clarification.

'Bee,' I say.

'Bee! Bee!' replies Alfred, as excited by his newly learned ability to name things as by the thing itself.

The queen is responsible for propagating the species. The unused sexual energy of the other bees is diverted into the activity of the hive. Honey, as sensual a substance as exists in nature, flirting between a solid and a liquid, is a product of the bee's sexual repression. The worker bee has no sex life. She is a dutiful middle manager in nature's office and tormented by her glamorous and sensual clients, the flowers. I explain to Alfred that this bee will make the honey that he drips into his morning porridge. He nods. He doesn't understand what I am talking about, but it's enough that I make the effort to explain and that he learns how to listen.

The bee and surrounding meadow are part of a biodynamic

farm; that is, a farm inspired by the cosmic philosophy of Rudolf Steiner. Biodynamic agriculture is a closed and self-sustaining system, a precursor to organic farming. The pollination of flowers by the bees plays a crucial role, hence the pair of beehives beside polytunnels of vegetables. Steiner regarded the imbibing of honey as an act of communion with the universe: 'Making this detour by way of the beehive, the entire cosmos can find its way into human beings and help to make them sound in mind and body.' Like Albert Einstein, Rudolf Steiner saw no future for mankind if the bee ever resigned its position.

Alfred laughs with astonishment at the flight of the bee, and looks across to check that I too am witnessing this marvel, a bee with a will of its own, going about its business. The bee is not a familiar DVD lobbied for and reluctantly put on, rather it provides the kind of accidental, free-range entertainment and education that only messing around outdoors can give. For contemporary children, camping replaces their highly structured day with a space where they can seek out the stimulation their development requires. We say that it builds character. But what is character, and why do we need it?

Since the mid nineteenth century, American children have been sent to summer camps in the belief that a period outdoors develops character. The American summer camp comes in a multitude of flavours, from fat camp to computer camp, but it is always organized. From its beginnings, life at the organized camp was, in the words of a pioneer of summer camps Ernest Balch, 'a rushing driving life, full to the brim'. Summer camps were founded to combat the idleness of July and August when boys would otherwise fall under the feminizing influence of mother. The earliest boys' camps took place in the first year of the American Civil War. In 1861, Frederick William Gunn took the students of his Gunnery School for Boys away for two weeks of hiking, boating and fishing in Mitford. The types of the Good Soldier and the Ideal Camper are related. Reminiscing about his time in a Civil War soldiers' camp, Benjamin Franklin Taylor writes that army camps are a capital place 'to get rid of notions; to settle loose joints into solid independence; to fall in love with mother earth and free air'. His fellow Union soldiers were highly skilled, making furniture for every encampment of Sibley and dog tents: 'they are tailors, they are tinkers, they are writers; fencing, boxing, cooking, eating, drilling – those who say that camp life is a lazy life know little about it.'

Pragmatic, self-reliant, active – these are the masculine virtues that pass from the Civil War camp into the summer camp for the moral instruction of generations of American boys. With camping and masculinity thus entwined, some commentators were appalled when families attempted to camp together; in 1872, a columnist in the *New York Times* railed against the fad for family camping, reporting that 'the sand-hills of New Jersey and the beaches of Long Island were speedily strewed with pitiable wrecks of disheveled and weeping women, squalling infants, and despairing and starving fathers.' Family camping is the disorganized alternative to the organized camp, and therein lies its virtue.

An early developer of organized camps for boys, Ernest Balch purchased Burnt Island in New Hampshire in 1881. Renamed Chocorua Island, he and his friends took five Christian boys to the island for an educational, spiritual and sporting programme of activities. Dressed in a uniform of grey flannel shirts and shorts, the boys were encouraged to be self-reliant and self-governing. In addition to the fishing and canoeing at Chocorua, Balch instructed the boys in capitalism. They were issued with an allowance of twenty-five cents a week. An in-camp labour market meant boys could either provide services such as washing dishes and clothes, or pay for the labour of others. A system of legal redress, organized and staffed by the boys, dealt with disputes arising from broken commercial contracts. At Chocorua camp, boys aspired and achieved, learned co-operation, decision-making and leadership. The island hosted camps for nine years until an outbreak of typhoid in the final season of 1889 condemned Balch to debt and obscurity. But his idea thrived. The summer camp was taken up with greater success by the muscular Christianity of movements such as the YMCA. By the 1920s, there were over a thousand summer camps in America. In 1922, Charles Eliot, president of Harvard University, expressed his conviction that a 'few weeks spent in a well-organized summer camp may be of more value educationally than a whole year of formal school work'.

Camp is a finishing school for the American citizen. Michael Eisner, the former CEO of Disney, put his camp experiences at the centre of his life story, writing a book about the lessons he learned at Keewaydin, a Vermont summer camp. As decided by the Keewaydin Council, the virtues of the ideal camper were honesty, loyalty, modesty, willingness to help, cleanliness, leadership, broad-mindedness, helpfulness and an ability to 'take his medicine when he deserves it'. The seven-year-old Eisner was taken to camp by his father, 'without a sister or a mother in sight'. On his first day, his father and the camp leader, Waboos, arranged a boxing bout between Michael and a nine-year-old boy. The bigger boy beat him up. Michael took his punishment like a man. His father was proud of him for being a 'stand-up boy'. This, suggests Eisner, was the making of him.

Camp's intensity ensures its lessons leave a deep mark. The child psychologist Fritz Redl was an advocate of therapeutic camping, being 'firmly convinced of the tremendous value of camping, educationally and as a means of therapy'. An arch realist accustomed to dealing with troubled children, Redl dismissed the Indian imagery and authenticity mongering at camp that, by the 1950s and 1960s, were 'dated daydreams', arguing that as our children have urban identities, undermining or belittling the urban was counterproductive. 'We are using camping on various levels to help youngsters grow up,' he wrote in 1966:

We use the camp for character training, for supportive mental hygiene, for the treatment of disturbed children, and to stimulate normal values. But just because camping is such a powerful drug, it also shares the properties of all other powerful drugs on the market. It is risky, if the wrong person swallows it, or if the right one swallows too much of it, or at the wrong time. In short, the camp itself is not only something through which children are supposed to adjust better, but also something to which they have to adjust.

Many adults have sour memories of their first Cub or Guide camp. I remember being chased through the woods by older boys. Cath recalls ganging up with the other Liverpudlian girls and hunting out 'woollybacks' – a pejorative Scouse term for anyone who shares an indecent amount of DNA with a sheep. I don't remember any camping at these camps; rather we bunked in dormitories and milled around the games room as the rain battered against the cross-hatched wire of the windows. The reality of the organized camp was, for me, a week of internment. Without leadership or guidance, the great outdoors was merely an arms cache for the arbitrary gang war of adolescence.

In lauding camping's benefits to children, we must be careful not to lapse into hypocrisy. As adults we embrace technology and are deeply invested, whether we like it or not, in a capitalist consumer culture that consumes the vast majority of our time and effort. Camping is the dream, and working life the reality; the countryside a place for the imagination, and the city the domain of the pragmatic. G. K. Chesterton, railing against the simple-life movement, argued that it is a historic fact that 'the artificial is, if anything, older than the natural,' and 'in the middle of the wildest fields the most rustic child is, ten to one, playing at steam engines.'

I do not subscribe to the simple life, to any camping manifesto, movement or order. I just want space and unallocated time. I want disorganized activity for my children. I want the timetable to be torn up. I want them to push through the boredom barrier and discover their own way. Being outdoors gives the children the space to explore. No matter how hard they try, they can't break nature, and although it contains dangers, as parents we have to steel ourselves and make reasonable judgements about risk. It's not easy. The sensation is like an invisible elastic band tied between my heart and the child, and as they go further away, the band tightens until the tension becomes unbearable. But the benefit to their character makes it worthwhile.

'Active, unstructured, outdoor play needs to be restored in children's lives,' insists a brief paper prepared for the American Medical Association by Hillary L. Burdette and Robert C. Whitaker. 'While playing outdoors a child is likely to encounter opportunities for decision making that stimulate problem solving and creative thinking because outdoor spaces are often more varied and less structured than indoor spaces.' We do not need to invest woodland with any spiritual properties to appreciate the developmental benefit accrued in crossing a rivulet, climbing over a fallen tree or finding your own way. Camping and character-building have always been linked because of the responsibility the child or adult is forced to take for their own well-being.

The nature trial is a rite of passage. In Edale, I came across a gaggle of waterproofed girls hemmed in by a cow in the corner of a field. The girls were undertaking the Duke of Edinburgh Award. To receive the Duke of Edinburgh Gold Award, a sixteen-year-old must hike and camp for three nights. The animal could not get purchase on a muddy bank and was pacing anxiously. After reassuring the girls that I would handle the cow situation, I charged at the cow, and in fear it found the strength to scale the bank and trot back to the herd. The girls thanked me and continued their hike. I wondered how and why the Duke of Edinburgh was associated with this rite of passage, one I would have loved to have undergone as a teenager if only I had known of its existence. (Instead, my rite of passage as a sixteen-year-old boy involved sleeping on the floor of a small caravan with four friends in Settle, Yorkshire; we shadowed local girls and, after failing to entice them back to the caravan, found collective solace in thirty cans of lager and two packs of Hamlets from the local off-licence, a boredom only alleviated by an aborted attempt to break into a paper factory – try making a Brat Pack movie out of that.)

The Duke of Edinburgh, Prince Philip of Greece, was educated at Gordonstoun School, founded by German educationalist Kurt Hahn. Hahn, under the patronage of the Germany's last imperial chancellor, established his reputation as a progressive educationalist with Salem School, a boarding school founded to prepare boys and girls for a life of moral and civic virtue, thereby liberating the children of the rich 'from the paralyzing awareness of their privilege'. With non-competitive physical activities and social co-operation – resembling Ernest Thompson Seton's formula of mutual aid and the awarding of coups – Salem prepared children for a life of service, of putting the common good ahead of individual ambition. The long camping hike was an important part of his ethos as it offered silent reflection and challenged the children to plan ahead. Like other outdoor movements of the 1920s, Hahn and the Salem School were concerned by the enervating influence of modernity and the dangers of extremism. Hahn, a German Jew, was a vociferous opponent of Hitler and sought to rally the school and alumni against him. When Hitler became chancellor of Germany, Hahn was imprisoned and only released after a plea by British prime minister Ramsay MacDonald. Emigrating to Britain, he was offered the position of headmaster at Eton. Instead, he founded Gordonstoun School in Moray, Scotland. As headmaster of an exclusive school, only the few benefited from his progressive educational ideas. So that other children could partake of the Gordonstoun spirit, he founded the Moray Badge earned by feats of skill, self-discipline and fitness. It was this badge that attracted the patronage of former pupil Prince Philip and so forms the basis of the Duke of Edinburgh Award.

The camping hike claims to be character-forming. It fosters comradeship, forward-planning, resourcefulness, responsibility and the ability to set an achievable and tangible goal. 'Character is expressed by loyalty and mutual commitment, or through the pursuit of long-term goals, or by the practice of delayed gratification for the sake of a future end,' writes Richard Sennett in his study of the enervating effects of capitalism upon character. 'Character concerns the personal traits which we value in ourselves and for which we seek to be valued by others.'

Charities and youth organizations have used the camping hike as a route to redemption for teenagers following the wrong trail, to correct bad character. The growth in camping among younger families can be seen as a desire to give their children a 'back-to-basics experience' that will form character. Neither school nor media teach character, what we describe as backbone – the ability to overcome adversity and take responsibility. Character is built on scarcity; that is, learning that you can't always get what you want, that you will have to work hard to achieve anything, and that you will need to navigate an unfair system and bad luck to abide with dignity. Character is imperilled by excess, by disposable goods and inconsequential actions; during the long, deranged boom, parents struggled to instil values of restraint, proper proportion and equality within a culture that glorified the opposite. The change in economic fortunes has been accompanied by a re-evaluation of cultural priorities, and a suspicion that our children may need to be tougher than us. And so families, in all their disorganized splendour, camp.

9
The Perfect Tent

The camping fields of the festival are covered with dome and tunnel tents, pop-up tents and low-slung mountain tents, their organic curves starkly contrasted by the lurid artificial colourings – purple and gold, aquamarine with an orange trim – of their polygonal panels. Gone are the tents of my childhood, the frame tents with their rigid skeletons. Here are domes with tunnels, and tunnels with domes. Pitched among them, a pair of canvas bell tents are defiant anachronisms, military tents that have become part of a trend for things organic and authentic, shelters against the future.

In the face of their ubiquity, it's difficult to recall the strangeness and unfamiliarity of the first dome tents. The dome tent was a paradigm shift from the military tent design, which remained, according to tent designer Bill Moss, unchanged since the American Civil War.

Here was a light tent with sufficient headroom that did not require the precision pitching of the alpine tent, and was stable even without guy ropes. You could pick the tent up and drop it somewhere else. My first dome tent was a small yellow and grey one that Cath and I lived in for a month outside Edinburgh, on a campsite between the Silverknowes golf course and Muirhouse housing estate. I had unpaid work writing reviews during the arts festival. Every morning, we awoke, washed and took the bus into town, where, over coffee, I would write sheaves of largely ignored copy, attend a day and night of shows, then trundle back on the last bus, through the forbidding ranks of Muirhouse, and into the miniature world of our cold little dome. The tent withstood the Scottish climate, although I did not; my sleeping bag was little better than a kilt (and by that I do not mean the feileadh mor, or great kilt, that the Scottish clansmen used as camouflaged groundsheet and sleeping bag. I would have traded in my press pass for a feileadh mor). I tried to buy a blanket, but no one seemed to sell blankets in Edinburgh, only duvets. In desperation I bought some little tartan dog blankets and draped them over my body.

The dome encloses the maximum amount of space with the minimum amount of material, an advantage for a tent as it results in greater volume for less weight. The dome has a circular footprint, and a circle is the most efficient use of materials to create a perimeter. Mankind has long exploited the aerodynamic superiority of rounded structures: the tipi is an asymmetrical cone, and the Mongolian yurt is a round house with a conical roof.

The tents of my childhood were not round. Frame tents, with their ninety-degree angles and rectangular vestibules, were first sighted on the Camping Club site of Polesden Lacey in 1954. With four perpendicular walls and roof section, the frame tent was a big Wendy house, all the way down to the polythene windows and dinky little curtains. A rectangular structure has high drag. On breezy campsites, the spectacle of a frame tent transformed into tumbleweed was a common one.

The strongest type of dome is the geodesic dome, in which the load is distributed in all directions throughout the entire structure, not just downward. A geodesic line is the shortest line between two points on a curved surface. Inscribe geodesic lines across a sphere and their intersections form equilateral triangles, and it is these triangles that disperse the load.

R. Buckminster Fuller is synonymous with the geodesic dome. He designed for a world fifty years ahead of his own, a world in which resources were scarce; his Dymaxion car of the 1930s claimed thirty miles to the gallon and could carry eleven passengers; it was completely at odds with an era in which petrol was a gallon a dime, and better suited to our current predicament. He did not build the first geodesic dome; that honour belongs to a German engineer, Walther Bauersfeld, who used it as the framework for the Zeiss planetarium. But as Bauersfeld did not use the principles of the geodesic dome again, nor seek a patent for it, Buckminster Fuller's understanding of the underlying mathematics of the dome ensured an American patent and deserved possession of the concept.

Buckminster Fuller's domes were as important for their symbolic implications as their practical ones. In a patent, he boasts of the frugality of his construction, claiming that 'a good index to the performance of any building frame is the structural weight required to shelter a square foot of floor from the weather. In conventional wall and roof designs the figure is often 50lbs per sq.ft. I have discovered how to do the job at around 0.78lb per sq.ft . . .' In the 1960s, the countercultural back-to-the-landers were receptive to Bucky's (as his friends called him) message of doing more with less. His vision was global: he was against conventional employment, materialism and received wisdom, and viewed his life as an experiment in discovering what an individual, starting with nothing, could do to benefit all humanity. He became an unlikely inspiration to a movement within the counterculture that was heading out into deserted America to form communes and outlying camps. (I maintain that the cultural import of Woodstock lay in the mind-expanding qualities of camping, and that the sex, drugs and rock 'n' roll were incidental.) The product of the meeting between Buckminster Fuller and pragmatically minded hippies was the dome tent. It was the shape of things to come.

Buckminster Fuller looked, in his own words, like 'a second-rate bank clerk'. He described himself as a comprehensive, anticipatory design scientist. With his closely cropped hair, characteristic round glasses and dark suit and tie, he was, outwardly, a square, an impression he cultivated so as not to undermine his unconventional ideas. He was a maniac for rationality. Buckminster Fuller formulated his own word-tools so that he could chisel out precise meanings. To hear him speak (or, nowadays, to watch recordings of his lectures) is to oscillate between mind expansion and the conviction that he is undergoing some kind of breakdown. These word-tools drew attention to the way figures of speech deceive us. We are taught that the wind blows, but in fact the wind sucks, the denser air drawn towards a low-pressure area. He disliked the words 'sunrise' and 'sunset', both of which are embedded in a pre-Copernican view of the solar system. To dismantle received wisdom required the breaking down and reassembly of language if he was to state his theories with any accuracy. In two volumes spanning 1,300 pages, he presented his discovery of Synergetics, a portmanteau concept combining the word 'synergy', which is defined as the performance of a whole far outstripping that of its component parts, with 'energetic geometry'; this was his new way of designating co-ordinates, which was more in accord with the universe than the conception of a flat earth that informed the x, y and z axes. The popular image of Bucky was of an inscrutable engineer-saint, 'a Leonardo da Vinci for our time' as a chat-show host introduced him. He was ignored by conventional scientists, as much for the company he kept as for the disruptive nature of his ideas. A film of him in conversation with the Maharishi, who had his own line in circular logic and repetition, is less like the promised meeting of countercultural gurus and more like an event at the windbag Olympics.

This disparity between studiously conventional exterior and radical mind-expanding wisdom made Bucky the guru-uncle of the pragmatic wing of the counterculture. It may come as a surprise to some readers to discover that the counterculture had a pragmatic wing, but it did: the back-to-the-land movement.

The bible of the back-to-the-landers was the *Whole Earth Catalog*, a compendium of useful information and tools that was described by *Time* magazine as the 'Boy Scout handbook of the counter-culture'. The first edition of the catalogue, published in San Francisco in 1968, set out a utilitarian approach to building new communities. An item was only listed in the catalogue if it was deemed to be:

1. Useful as a tool
2. Relevant to independent education
3. High quality or low cost
4. Not already common knowledge
5. Easily available by mail

There was to be 'No art, no religion, no politics'. The catalogue was upfront about money. Crucially, it was pro-technology. The editor, Stewart Brand, was inspired to create the catalogue by the insights of Buckminster Fuller, and the first few editions gleam with Fuller's can-do optimism about the future, the belief that 'man is about to become almost 100 percent successful as an occupant of Universe.' The introduction tells a fragment of Bucky's story. He was born in Milton, Massachusetts, on 12 July 1895, was twice expelled from Harvard, and served in the US Navy from 1917 to 1919, where he invented a winch that could save the lives of pilots of planes downed in water. He left the Navy in 1922 after the death of his first daughter from a disease that was caused, he felt, by his failure to provide healthy living conditions. From that tragic event onwards, he was obsessed with inventing better places to live. In 1926 he went into business with his father-in-law with a new method of producing concrete-reinforced buildings, only for the business to fail. Unemployed, bereaved and abject, Bucky stood on the edge of a lake and contemplated suicide. He was thirty-two years old.

In his book *Guinea Pig B*, Bucky explains why he did not kill himself. He realized that, judged by society's conventions of 'selfish, personal, family, corporate, or national advantage-gaining', he would always be a failure. But he also knew that his knowledge, the unique accumulation of his experiences, might prove to be of critical advantage to others, 'possibly to all others, possibly to Universe'. His suicide might rob the universe (or Universe as he insisted, always capitalizing it and never employing a definite or indefinite article) of a vital component in its evolution. So he killed his ego instead and set out to discover if his knowledge could benefit humanity. He became a living test subject, 'Guinea Pig B'. The *Whole Earth Catalog* takes his conversion, or nervous breakdown, as a freak-flag for other back-to-the-landers and quotes him in the first issue:

> In 1927 I gave up forever the general economic dictum of society, i.e. that every individual who wants to survive must earn a living . . . I sought for the tasks that needed to be done that no one else was doing or attempting to do, which if done would physically and economically advantage society and eliminate pain.

The title of the *Whole Earth Catalog* was inspired by Bucky's conception of the earth as a whole system. He believed that the outdated notion of a flat earth encouraged man to regard its resources as infinite, whereas a round earth was more like a spaceship with billions of astronauts. One day, in February 1966, 28-year-old Stewart Brand took acid and climbed up on to a roof overlooking San Francisco's North Beach. Shivering under a blanket, he remembered Buckminster Fuller's flat-earth theory and had a breakthrough: 'I'm looking at San Francisco from three hundred feet and one hundred micrograms up and thinking that I can see from here that the earth is curved. I had the idea that the higher you go the more you can see the earth as round.' There were no public photographs of the whole Earth at that time. If only mankind could see the Earth from space, then everything would change. When he came down, Brand distributed badges asking, 'Why haven't we seen a photograph of the whole Earth yet?'

The *Whole Earth Catalog* included a section on 'Nomadics', a compendium of hiking, camping, mountaineering and tipi knowledge edited by Jay Baldwin. Baldwin had attended a fourteen-hour lecture by Buckminster Fuller while studying design at the University of Michigan in 1952, and it had changed his view of the world. One day, returning to the university, Baldwin overheard a student discussing a 'dome-shaped tent'. Baldwin was intrigued, and sought out the tent's creator, Bill Moss, in his shop in Ann Arbor. The dome-shaped tent was the 'Pop-up tent', which Moss had filed a patent for with his colleague Henry Stribley on 19 July 1955, after eighteen months of trial and error. The Pop-up tent consisted of six flexible, lightweight, fibreglass poles or ribs that locked into a central hub at the apex of a tent of Egyptian cotton. The men envisaged their 'hemispherical shelter' being used by hunters, fishermen, campers, photographers or bathers on the beach. The patent was filed two years before Buckminster Fuller put in a patent for a 'Geodesic tent', and the two designs are vastly different. Bucky's is a spherical tent suspended within a geodesic frame by numerous conical supports – in other words, you are not taking it to Glastonbury. Moss's Pop-up tent worked like an umbrella, took minutes to erect and slept four people. There are two stories concerning its invention; one is told by Jay Baldwin, who says that Moss got the idea for the tent while he was out painting a portrait of a freshly caught trout. During a sudden downpour, he grabbed several fishing poles, punched them into the soft earth to make a circle, tied their tips together and then draped his poncho over them to form a dome. Another story, told by Moss to reporters, was that he first developed the concept when he was studying to be an artist. He was sculpting the canvas, which he warped into a 'giant inverted soup bowl'. Inside he painted abstract figures of fishermen, cut a door and added a chair. To move this art around, he designed it to be light-weight and collapsible. In Moss's version, the dome tent starts out as a work of fabric sculpture. 'Who wants to look at a painting when you can live inside one?' he said.

Moss brought his artistic sensibility to bear on all his tents. His Stargazer tent is in the Permanent Collection of New York's Museum of Modern Art; it is a six-pound backpacker's tent constructed out of two poles bent into hoops; where the hoops cross, there is an elliptical skylight through which the occupant can lose themselves in the night sky. Making a tent, he said, 'gives me the most amazing kind of satisfaction. I get the experience of making a piece of art. Then I go out in a field and see people making their lives better in these things. How many painters or sculptors can say that?'

Jay Baldwin worked as a prototype maker and designer for Bill Moss during the Pop-up tent era, from 1958 to 1962. Moss licensed the successful design to Thermos, and the company featured the tent in the background to their adverts for outdoor living gear. The Thermos Pop tent sold for 109 dollars. 'A sharp owner could erect a Pop tent in less than a minute, without pounding stakes, arranging ropes or structural members,' remembers Jay Baldwin. 'This was in great contrast to every other tent. The Pop tent had no real competitors, despite its price. The US Government gave the Pop tent credit for growing car camping very strongly; double every year for a while. The Pop tent was often featured in the Ford customer magazine. The Ford woodless station wagon even came with one. I once saw a thousand Pop tents erected in a minute at a Scout jamboree. There were many copies, but nothing like the original. The canvas of my 1959 original Pop tent finally gave out in 1977, after more than a 1,000 nights of use.'

The Pop-up tent was successful for a small operator like Bill Moss, but it was not taken up by a major tent retailer. Jay Baldwin attributes this failure of vision as a realization, on behalf of the buyer, that the paradigm shift that Moss's tent represented would render the rest of the stock worthless. The ground had shifted towards the dome tent, but the customer demand for it could still be resisted by vested interests.

Of itself, invention is not sufficient to change how we do things. It must fit into the spirit of the age. New ideas rarely belong to one man, they are the accretions of other inventions, and the dome tent is no exception. As previously noted, mankind has long known the advantage of curved structures for shedding wind and withstanding stresses. The Gypsy bender tent is fashioned from a dozen green and supple branches, each about ten feet in length, stuck into the ground in two rows of five and then bent and inserted into holes drilled into a central ridge pole. Over this tunnel structure, skins or cloth are thrown. The Mongolian yurt, known as the *ger* to the tribesmen, is a round house of latticed sections insulated with felt. The pleasure dome of Xanadu was no mere opium swoon on the part of Samuel Taylor Coleridge, it was a real structure inspired by the *ger*. Coleridge came across a description of Xanadu or Shangdu in *Hakluytus Posthumus*. This was based on Marco Polo's account of his visit to the Cane Palace at Shangdu, the summer capital of Kublai Khan's Yuan Dynasty. The palace had a domed roof of varnished cane supported by gilt and lacquered columns. It was designed in such a way that it could be taken down and moved elsewhere at the end of the summer season. Braced against the wind by more than 200 cords of silk, the Cane Palace combined nomadic and sedentary architecture to unite the peoples of Kublai Khan's dynasty, the nomadic Mongol and the elite of northern China.

Fast forward to the early twentieth century, and the dome tent crops up in accounts of polar exploration. Frank Herman Gotsche, inspired by the skin tents and igloos he saw at Point Barrow in Alaska, designed a tent that dispensed with ridge poles and uprights, using two semicircular arches to construct a proto-tunnel tent. His VXL tent was used by hunters and traders in the Arctic. In 1914, Ernest Shackleton and George Marston designed dome tents for their Imperial Trans-Antarctic Expedition: four differently sized, arched iron poles sewn into the canvas, which opened up like a concertina into a dome shape. Skip back to 1854, and Godfrey Rhodes, captain of Her Majesty's 94th Regiment, observed storms on the Crimean battlefields sweep away the British and Allied tents while the round tents of the Turk remained. In response, he designed his 'Guard tent' using semicircular and curvilinear arches to create a bosomy, parabolic frame with a canvas covering. Unlike the bell tent, it had no central pole, and was formed of stout ribs of ash or bamboo inserted into a head piece of wood or metal, with the base of the ribs secured by a band of double-twisted rope. The combination of head piece and bowed ribs is similar to the Pop-up tent. Unlike Bill Moss's invention, this tent weighed sixty-eight pounds and took eight soldiers working together to erect it.

The dome tent has pushed at the membrane between idea and reality throughout history. If an invention is a paradigm shift, it frequently has business-as-usual blocking it in the form of tradition or vested interest – a military reluctant to innovate, perhaps, or a supplier unwilling to undermine their stock. To overcome that reactionary force requires timing, a union of idea with opportunity that ensures the invention matches the temper of the people.

For the dome tent, that opportunity was a growing interest in leisure wilderness brought about by a febrile era of social change;

in other words, the 1960s. In 1964, Lyndon Johnson signed the Wilderness Act, the product of eight years of discussion in Congress and considerable public debate and consultation, which defined the wilderness as 'an area where the earth and community of life are untrammeled by man, where man himself is a visitor who does not remain'. The word 'untrammelled' is obscure, meaning 'not confined or limited'. Wilderness is a self-willed land, an area where evolution continues. Not all cultures have a concept of wilderness. Certainly the American Indian, prior to the arrival of European colonists, did not regard the landscape as a wilderness. Chief Luther Standing Bear writes, 'We did not think of the great open plains, the beautiful rolling hills, and winding streams with tangled growth, as "wild". Only to the white man was nature a "wilderness" and only to him was the land "infested" with "wild" animals and "savage" people. To us it was tame.' It is in the English colonies of America and Australia where the concept of wilderness is most prevalent, a projection of Puritan values upon the landscape. The Wilderness Act was a declaration that these areas needed to be protected from further development by industrial culture, while permitting 'outstanding opportunities for solitude or a primitive and unconfined type of recreation'. Protecting the wilderness while ensuring the access of campers and hikers was to prove challenging as the number of visitors increased.

The transcendental experience of camping in the wild, explored a century earlier in the Philosophers' Camp, was revived in the 1960s. In 1968, Colin Fletcher, the high priest of backpacking, published *The Man Who Walked Through Time*, relating the two months he spent walking on his own along the entire length of the Grand Canyon. In his early forties and coming off a few bad years, Fletcher overcame the devil of his midlife crisis in the wilderness.

Fletcher enjoyed a camping trip in the psychedelic sense of the word. He describes a growing awareness of the rhythm of the rock. He accepted the magnificence of the geological timespan, the terrifying eternity of time required to craft the landscape upon which he camped. Sprawled on the rocks beside the river, Fletcher's consciousness merged with the rock, and he apprehended the water, the fish, the sky, the whole pulsating interlocking web of life. Insights of an 'oceanic' nature, of the oneness of all things, and a unity between self and the environment, were very much of the time. Bucky Fuller's Whole System is a scientific metaphor that expresses the same insight. Fletcher discovered an inner and outer peace so profound that he was reluctant to light a campfire as 'for all its pulsating, dream-inducing fascination, [it] cuts you off from the reality of the night, and as the days passed I found myself becoming less and less tolerant of any barrier that came between me and the reality of the Canyon.' Then his becalmed oneness was shattered by two low-flying jet fighters roaring through the canyon. He expected to feel angry. But he was surprised at his own excitement, his awe at the magnificent technological achievement of the planes and the skill and bravery of the pilots. The jets represented a mishmash of 'careful intellect and crazy courage' that made mankind so admirable.

The aviator Charles Lindbergh also had a vision of aeroplanes in the wild. 'Airplanes combined the elements I loved,' he writes, 'bringing qualities of science and wilderness together without apparent conflict . . . I came to know the world's geography as man had never known it before: great bends of my Mississippi Valley; sweeps of western plains; Appalachian, Rocky and Sierra ridges dividing a continent . . . The human future depends on our ability to combine the knowledge of science with the wisdom of wildness.' Lindbergh's closing thought would fit perfectly in the opening pages of the *Whole Earth Catalog*, or as an epigraph to one of Buckminster Fuller's many tomes.

Stewart Brand was very clear on the importance of bringing nature and technology together. He incited his readership to

become New Indians, a new tribe of technologically savvy, outdoors, spiritual, pragmatic artist-nomads. Brand spent 'two
intense informal years (and five slack ones) hanging around Indians, reservations, anthropologists, and libraries . . . They gave
me more reliable information, and human warmth, than dope
and college put together.' The *Whole Earth Catalog* included re-
tailers of buckskin and beads. It was fashionable to wear
headbands, fringed jackets and moccasins, and name children
'Sunshine' or 'Moon' in a faux-Indian fashion, and yell 'Yi Yi Yi'
every time the joint completed a lap of the commune. The peyote
vision quest was co-opted as an excuse for the LSD trip; the long
hair of the hippy rejected the military buzz-cut and summoned
the brave. But the hippies who embraced the Indian as a way out
of capitalism were missing the point. Heading off to a hill on the
edge of town, setting up a couple of tipis and attempting to make
a living by selling Aleut soapstone carvings was not practical.

The tipi, a symbol of freedom and ancient traditional wisdom,
has a good claim to be the perfect tent. The tipi has been refined
over countless generations of American Indians, all the way back
to the ancestors who migrated from the tribes scattered around
the Arctic circle: the Lapps, the Yukaghir and the Caribou Eskimo.
Anthropologist Waldemar Bogoras studied the Chukchi tribe
while exiled in Siberia between 1890 and 1898. Like the tipi, the
tents of the Chukchi were built around three central poles. These
poles were sacred objects, and when a new house was pitched,
they received a separate sacrifice and blood offering. Visiting the
Chukchi fifty years earlier, nineteenth-century explorer William
Hooper describes them as using whale ribs for poles and walrus
skin for the covering 'so beautifully cured and prepared as to
retain its elasticity, and also to be semi-lucent'. Eighteen inches of
snow was heaped up against the walls to provide insulation.
Hooper's drawings of the tents resemble half-buried onions.

The nomads of the north migrated from Siberia to Alaska
across the Bering Strait, when the waters were locked in ice, and

travelled southwards across the continent of America hunting the big game, the mastodon, the mammoth and the giant buffalo. These nomads diversified into 500 nations, each of which adapted and developed shelter most suited to the environment in which they found themselves. Some tribes used a basic tripod to set up their tipi; some used four poles. Different woods would be employed, combining the desired virtues of lightness and strength depending on which trees were available. The wigwam is a structure associated with the Algonquin tribes and is a dome-shaped shelter made from bowed green saplings and lined with bark, thereby being both less portable and more adapted to the great wooded wilderness of Massachusetts. Tipi is a Sioux word, meaning to 'live in', and was used by the hunters of the Great Plains.

A true tipi is an asymmetrical cone pitched steeper on the windward side, and opening towards the sunrise. The smoke hole is managed by two flaps or ears, each attached to an external pole that can be used to manipulate the air flow over the vent. For all the innovations in tent design over the last forty years, no one has improved upon the tipi as a way of managing a campfire inside a tent. Once camp has been struck, the tipi poles form a cart upon which the tent materials are dragged. Do the poles of a modern tent turn into a roof rack? No, they do not. But the refined adaptations of the tipi to its environment make it unsuitable outside of that environment. Its long poles make a tipi difficult to transport by car along modern roads. I did wonder why no one had manufactured tipi poles out of aluminium sections, so that they could be folded up like the poles of a dome tent, until I realized that such poles, tied at their apex, would form an interlacing series of lightning conductors.

Reginald and Gladys Laubin lived in tipis for much of their lives. Their book *The Indian Tipi: Its History, Construction and Use*, first published in 1957, reveals the tipi to be a refined piece of wilderness technology. Consider the poles, shaved smooth so that rain runs directly along them and into the ground rather than striking an imperfection and dripping down into the interior. Consider the multi-purpose genius of the inner tent, providing insulation and privacy – it is the inner tent that prevents the shadows of inhabitants being visible to spies. The birch-bark tipi of the Cree Indians, pitched high above the snowline, also has an insulating outer cone filled with caribou moss. The moss is there to prevent the campfire from warming the exterior of the tipi, as that would melt the insulating layer of snow that builds up against it.

The tipi, like the yurt or *ger*, is a tent designed around a central fire. The problem with having a small campfire in a tent is the build-up of smoke. The tipi has a vent but it is no mere hole at the apex of the poles; that would be too large and let in too much rain. So how does the smoke hole work? I will let the Laubins explain:

> The Indians solved this problem by tilting the cone and extending the smoke hole down the long side, the front of the tent. The crossing of the poles is thus at the top end of the smoke hole instead of in the middle, so that it is possible to close the hole entirely by means of the projecting flap or ears. In a large tent, the order of placement of the poles is crucial for correct alignment of the smoke hole.

Sometimes the wind simply would not carry away the smoke. Wilderness writer Calvin Rutstrum recalls a stubborn layer of smoke in the birch-bark tipi of the Cree Indians. To clear it, he showed the Cree family a trick he had acquired from the Lapps, of digging a trench from outside of the tipi to come up underneath the campfire, with the mouth of the trench ending in flat stones. They covered the trench with birch bark held in place by branches. When the campfire was lit, air was drawn along the trench from outside, rising through the fire, making it burn brighter, and then forming a steady draught up to the vent, clearing the clouds of smoke. 'Joy came into the camp,' writes Rutstrum, 'the smoke curse would no longer lower the spirits of these Indians through the long northern winter.'

For the New Indians of the 1960s counterculture, there was no way back to the tipi, a symbol of what had been destroyed to make America possible. They had to accept the implications of technological mastery: that it made them in effect gods and so they may as well get good at it. A new portable structure became synonymous with the New Indians: the dome – and, as Jay Baldwin says, 'Domes were certainly NOT your father's house.'

Unfortunately, your father knew what he was talking about. Domes did not make great houses. Nearly all of them leaked, and they leaked geodesically. Dome dwellers enjoyed neither acoustic nor olfactory privacy. By the last *Whole Earth Catalog* in 1971, there were signs that communal living was wearing thin. 'One reason we promote communes is that there's no better place to make all your wishful mistakes, to get your nose rubbed in your fondest fantasies.' As the deficiencies in the commune way of life mounted, so the 'Nomadics' section seemed to expand. Faced with problems of dropping out full-time, Americans found the temporary escape of camping held more allure. Jay Baldwin is clear on the reason for the section's growth: '"Nomadics" expanded in the *Whole Earth Catalog* because there was a huge increase in car camping and trail hiking due to two things: firstly, cars were better and more trustworthy, and millions of Americans were taking to the road to look at the Western national parks; secondly, camping gear was very much better, led by Moss and other pioneers, such as the Eureka Draw-tite tents, and those by Jack Stephenson.' (Stephenson pioneered lightweight tunnel tents.)

Statistics of American wilderness visits vary but show a clear upward trend. Between 1960 and 1965, visits to the wilderness increased fivefold to 3.5 million visitor days per year. By 1975, recreational use of the wilderness totalled over 10 million visitor days. The growth in recreational use of the wilderness was skewed towards the Pacific coast region, where it grew 17 per cent annually between 1965 and 1974, compared to a national average of 9.4 per cent. This back-to-nature boom occurred in tandem with the growth of camping and hiking gear as a consumer product; taking your own dome tent into the wild was an act of environmental consideration compared to the woodcraft practices of Nessmuk and Horace Kephart. If the hatchet-wielding woodsman of the late nineteenth and early twentieth century had prided himself on his ability to fashion anything he required from the store cupboard of nature, the backpacker – as likely to be female as male – carried modern equipment that left only a faint footprint upon nature. As more people sought recreation in the wilderness, so technology and invention allowed them to do so with less environmental cost. When Colin Fletcher decided against setting a campfire, it was an expression of the backpacker's deeper sympathy with nature than the high bonfires of the great woodsman.

The backpacking boom expanded the market for lightweight, portable tents. The Pop tent's central hub made it too heavy for backpacking, and the doors zipped all the way up to the top, which meant that if you unzipped them during the rain, your bed would get wet. In 1972, self-professed hippy businessman Skip Yowell brought his own dome tent to market. Using an external pole system, Skip Yowell's 'Trail Dome' was a hit and put his company JanSport on the map. He envisaged the dome tent as being like an igloo, a place with plenty of room where people could sit around playing cards during a storm. With his cousin Murray Pletz, they tested material for the poles, selecting the aluminium poles with elastic shock cords developed by Easton. The walls were made of Dacron, a strong, lightweight polyester. 'We were so slammed with orders that we had to sell tents on an allocation basis for many years because we could never make enough,' remembers Yowell. Unfortunately, fulfilling those orders took precedence over filing for a patent. JanSport no longer makes tents.

The success of the Trail Dome inspired Mark Erickson at North Face to investigate the dome tent. In 1975, Bob Gillis, a dome-dwelling hippy from the Santa Cruz Mountains, arrived at North Face in a VW van to pitch the company on his designs for a geodesic dome tent. He and Erickson worked to refine the designs and the result was the 'OI', or Oval Intention tent. In form, the Oval Intention is unmistakably inspired by Bucky, the tent material suspended from an exoskeleton of interlacing hoops. The design proved so sturdy that North Face continues to sell a two-metre dome tent for mountain exploration. 'The North Face geodesic tents were a big success,' remembers Jay Baldwin, 'though relatively expensive to make. Bucky loved them, and North Face has some photos of him inside the big one.'

A tent embodies a world view, even a religion. Exodus contains detailed and daunting instructions for the Israelites to assemble the tabernacle, the tent of meeting in which God dwelled during their nomadic existence. The tipi is also a symbol of the universe, the floor representing the earth, the walls the sky, and the poles the binding between the earth and the Great Mystery. Within the tipi, a square of earth was set aside and consecrated to Mother Earth. A world view is also encoded in the geodesic dome. By dispensing with support pillars, and creating a structure in which stress is distributed evenly and outwardly throughout, the geodesic dome is analogous to the distributed networks of the Internet. The distributed network is a decentralized pattern of nodes in which knowledge flows in every direction, like the stresses along the geodesic nodes and struts. The values of the digital utopian, of flat hierarchies, of sharing and participation, were also attributed by the counterculture to their geodesic domes, and both the dome and the Internet can be scaled up to a great order of magnitude without significant loss of performance. In fact a geodesic dome gets stronger as it gets bigger. Likewise the usefulness of the Internet increases as more people are incorporated into the network.

Stewart Brand was an early advocate of the Internet, setting up an influential messageboard in 1985 called the WELL, or the Whole Earth 'Lectronic Link. Brand and his fellow Internet pioneers envisaged a cyber citizen who was nomadic and used portable digital technology to transcend the borders of nation states. The small-scale technologies of the San Francisco back-to-the-land movement cross-pollinated with Silicon Valley, infesting Cold War technology with countercultural notions of free speech and small-scale entrepreneurship. The computer became personal. With its 'user reviews' and vision of a peer-to-peer marketplace, the *Whole Earth Catalog* resembles a print mash-up between Wikipedia and eBay; readers would try the gear recommended in 'Nomadics' and then feed back their responses, which were included in future editions. Kevin Kelly, the founder editor of *Wired*, the publication that fed digital utopianism into the culture in the 1990s, also edited the quarterly *Whole Earth Review*. The utopian vision of the dome-dwelling communards became the intellectual and philosophical underlay of the Internet. The early archetype of the 'web surfer' is a direct descendant from Brand's nomadic, technology-loving New Indians.

So what happened to the domed utopia? Let us return to Glastonbury. Dome tents and a new generation of pop-up tents spread across the field like polyester fungi. Pennant flags, startled by the breeze, swing over last night's crash site; tipped over beer cans, fag butts stubbed out in the giant ashtray of nature, and a leg extruding from the tent entrance. Festivals are not the place to see a well-pitched tent; after a spot of rain and a gust of wind, most of the tents have a slack-jawed slump. The festival tent is so cheap it has become disposable; it lives only for the weekend, suggesting that as a form of human habitation the dome tent has adapted too well to its hedonistic environment. Eleven tonnes' worth of tent were dumped at Glastonbury in 2009, some of which, prior to being abandoned, were used by their owners as a toilet. Consumerism has turned the dome tent into pollution. As for the tipi, it costs over 800 pounds to hire one for the duration of the festival. I do not belong to the counterculture of the 1960s nor carry a flag for it, but I recognize a historical irony when I see it.

The final act of any camping trip is striking camp, when the camper packs up their gear and clears the land of any trace of their presence. On the final day of the festival, wandering past torn and shit-strewn dome tents, I experience a devil's epiphany: must our best intentions, when plugged into the matrix of consumerism, inevitably emerge in this gross and distorted form? The cashpoint at the heart of Glastonbury reminds me of the money changers who followed the 10,000-strong armies of the Civil War. Wherever tents have been pitched en masse, marketplaces, food stalls and small traders have appeared beside ad hoc thoroughfares. Commerce has always tagged along after nomadic encampments.

I wonder what campers throughout history would make of Glastonbury? The Kindred of the Kibbo Kift or the Order of Woodcraft Chivalry would enjoy the part of the festival known as the Green Fields, which hosts purveyors of alternative therapies: masseurs in tipis; the brokers of healing crystals and soul boards; self-published literature on trestle tables, carved Buddhas and incense sticks – a car-boot sale of the flotsam and jetsam left behind from the breaking of the hippy wave. The Green Fields promise an island of well-being. The actuality is a bazaar. I can't afford its health-giving virtues. I pass straight through the Green Fields and stop off in the beer tent for a pint. Thomas Hiram Holding would disapprove. The festival on its final day is proof of Holding's wisdom in keeping a temperate camp. The night before, the hay bales of the beer tent were soaked with the spillages of the fucked-up. Someone else had to clean up the vomit. The disengaged entitlement of the consumer is at odds with camping's egalitarian mucking-in. We want it all, the retox and the detox in the same afternoon. Vice and virtue co-exist at Glastonbury, an intertwining of the folk tradition of the carnival-esque with the nineteenth-century romantic primitivism of the camper.

A band takes the stage. A crowd thickens. The dairy farm in Somerset falls away and we could be anywhere, on a disused air-strip outside Reading or in a car loading bay in Shoreditch. Amplified music obliterates the ambient sounds of nature. Glastonbury covers over the countryside to stage the spectacle of the city. I wonder if a festival will be devised that dramatizes collaboration between the land and music, acoustic performances shrouded in valley mist and lit by sunset, in which birdsong and stream-babble mix with the human voice. The Kibbo Kift created their own music, their own art and theatre. Remove the stages and speakers from Glastonbury, and then you might really be on to something. Camping's ability to use technology to bring man closer to nature is sidelined by the imperative to get fucked up and expect others to clean up after you. What is truly twenty-first century about Glastonbury is the waste. All the campers in this history, from Thoreau to Nessmuk, from Buckminster Fuller to Henry Ford, would unite in horror at the waste.

Striking Camp

I tread deliberately around the flattened square of grass where, a minute earlier, my tent had stood. I pick up litter and pat the square of turf dug out for the fire pit back into position. Then I take a deep breath and prepare for the next stage of striking camp. The trip into the festival was hellish. For the return to the car park, I will go alone with the gear, then return empty-handed for the children. My rucksack is fully packed and my fisherman's trolley is loaded down with the tent and sleeping bags. In-between these two hikes across the festival site, I will earn my ticket by compèring three hours of talks and readings, my T-shirt hooped with salt rings of perspiration.

The noon sun is a hammer upon the anvil of 100,000 hang-overs. Sheets of newly forged light, reflected by the high metal perimeter fence, slice through the air. It is Sunday. Yes, we are

leaving early, rather than risk the five-hour jams of the Glastonbury car park on a Monday morning. We have three children
with us, and so I have a father's anticipatory mindset, all forethought and with no time for living in the present.

In a perfect world I would just bring our eldest child, Alice, to
the festival. She has the sensible heart of a firstborn, and is fascinated by adults behaving badly in this land of do-as-you-please.
At the House of Fairy Tales, she met the lad who is also Doctor
Who. He wandered the site with a tattoo of the time vortex on
his arm. Doctor Who posed for a photograph with her, then, at
sunset, she ran around outside the House of Fairy Tales with her
arms strapped to long purple wings.

Looking after the toddlers is more difficult. On our way into
the festival, I calculated that we could cover the mile from the car
park to the camp with all our gear so long as Alfred, my three-
year-old son, walked. He dawdled for ten yards then lay down on
the corrugated walkway with tired legs. Florence, our two-year-
old, slept in Cath's backpack, her lips drooling into her mother's
ear, her sweaty curls lolling around with every step. I was so
intent upon cajoling Alfred that we took a wrong turning and
ended up further away than from where we'd started. My family
sat down beside the corrugated steel path and bemoaned their
fate. I recalled one of Dorothy Revel's virtues of camping, that it
gave the family a rare opportunity to be together outside of the
routines of domestic and work life. I wondered, out loud, if it
was possible for a man to spend too much time with his family.

'You are not helping,' said Cath.

The first lesson of parenthood is that the buck stops with you.
There is no higher authority to come and bail you out when you
have miscalculated. And the same is true of camping. I slung
Alfred over my shoulder and pressed on. I was also carrying a
seventy-five-litre backpack and pulling a trolley loaded with
twenty kilograms of tent. The sun's pitiless gaze exposed every
sweating inch of my indignity.

The teenagers in the dome tents beside the walkway called me snail man.

I couldn't spare the breath for a rejoinder.

I did not come to Glastonbury to get off my face. I came knowing that, at best, I would see one band and spend the rest of my time parenting. I would not sit in the stone circle at dawn. I came to the festival because I was asked, and because I like camping with friends, particularly at sundown, when they all return to report on the day's adventures before heading out to lose themselves in the evening. A group camp with friends and their children at a festival, all of us working for our tickets, is the finest holiday I can conceive of.

Saturday night, on a hill overlooking a vale of lights and music, four of us sat around a campfire and laughed so hard it was purgative. Luke foraged for wooden stakes for fuel and lay them flat upon the long grass, their tips aflame in the fire pit. It was not the safest of campfires: the edges of the pit smouldered as the fire spread along the stake. But he knew what he was doing. For the weekend, he was the keeper of the flame.

The conversation turned to meat. Rupert had been to St John's Market in Liverpool where he had seen a man auction bags of 'assorted meats'. There was no indication of the contents, just meats, a variety thereof. Five quid a bag. Ten quid for a bigger bag. Laughing, Cath reminisced about the tongue and tripe stall at the same market.

On his camping trip with Thomas Edison and Henry Ford, John Burroughs attributed their laughter around the campfire to the way that camping situated them apart from the everyday, throwing the habitual absurdities of normal life into relief. Also, each camp is a new configuration of people. We laugh instinctively and readily to forge the bond of this group. Luke remembered a grill steaks advert that made a grand claim of a 'pocket of juice'. Other patties of reconstituted beef lacked this pouch of indeterminate fluid, and so they were – according to the advertising – inferior. The design flaw of high fat content was sold as a point of differentiation. I laughed at all the meetings and money that must have gone into marketing the advantage of a 'pocket of juice'.

There was a bottle of brandy, and then the bottle was empty. More people arrived to sit around the campfire and tell tales of their adventures in the festival below. A bottle of Jägermeister was produced, medicinal and tacky. I spoke of the women's clothing shop in my hometown where the clothes are made entirely of felt: stiff, brightly coloured felt dresses, felt blouses, felt shoes. Hooded felt capes accessorized with a dream catcher and a large amulet.

'What's the shop called?' asked Luke.

'Felt Up,' I replied.

The morning after, I wake with the lightness of well-being that comes after a swim or a long walk. Then I strike camp methodically, deflating and rolling up the thin thermal mats and putting them in their individual bags. The art of striking camp requires that you always keep track of the bags. The sleeping bags are pressed back into their bags, and then the clothes are loaded into their bags and then into the big bag of the rucksack. Bags within bags within bags, all the time reducing and compressing, so that the gear fits snugly inside itself. Using elasticated cords with hooked ends, I strap the tent and sleeping gear to the trolley. They are the same cords that my father used to tie plastic sheeting over the camping gear on the car roof rack, and they bind me to a continuum of camping dads. My grandfather Thomas Bateman used to take his five children camping in Wales. A fitter who worked the gasometers of Bootle, he had a next-door neighbour who owned an old army tent in which their families would camp. Thomas had a motorbike and a home-made sidecar. His two eldest sons also had motorbikes. In the sidecar went his wife Florence, a spaniel called Bonnie and my mother, the youngest child. Her two elder sisters rode pillion. In this formation they rode to camp, their gear lashed together with elasticated cords with hooked ends.

Cleaning a camp prior to departure is sound military practice. In *Scouting for Boys*, Baden-Powell writes, 'if you go away to another place, and leave an untidy ground behind you, it gives so much important information to enemy scouts.' Thomas Hiram Holding set down the principle of striking camp in his 1908 *Camper's Handbook*:

> I conceived early in the sport of Camping a habit of never leaving behind, on a site I had used or rented, any removable mark of a tent having been pitched there. When the tent is down, and the kit is packed up, the last act should be to remove every scrap of refuse, every loose stone that you may have used for, say, holding down your pegs, and all other evidence of having camped there.

Glastonbury pleads with the festival-goers to 'Leave No Trace'; in the 1980s, the federally sponsored Leave No Trace programme in America was a response to the pressure of the camping and back-packing boom upon the wilderness. It forbids campfires, or at least any fire that touches the ground and leaves a scar. Campers are encouraged to travel light, to pack in and pack out all their gear. This represents a shift away from the woodcraft of Ness-muk and Horace Kephart and its practice of hewing shelters and cooking ranges out of the materials of the forest. The woodsman knew nature intimately, and used the woods like a supermarket. As a result, their camps wreaked temporary devastation upon the land. 'The stricken camp is a melancholy sight,' wrote Charles Dudley Warner:

> The woods have been despoiled; the stumps are ugly; the bushes are scorched; the pine-leaf-strewn earth is trodden into mire; the landing looks like a cattle-ford; the ground is littered with all the unsightly debris of a hand-to-hand life; the dismantled shanty is a

shabby object; the charred and blackened logs, where the fire blazed, suggest the extinction of family life. Man has wrought his usual wrong upon Nature, and he can save his self-respect only by moving to virgin forests.

This way of camping is extinct. Innovations in lightweight, re-usable gear, from portable stoves to the dome tent, promise a light camping footprint. Unfortunately, the gear has become so cheap that it either breaks or we decide it is beneath us to pack it up and take it home. After the Glastonbury festival of 2009, 5,572 tents were left behind, as were 6,538 sleeping bags, 2,220 chairs, 3,321 air beds and 400 gazebos. With tents as cheap as a tenner, many people did not bother to strike camp. I have seen people dump beer and food in the car park on the way into Glastonbury rather than carry it; I want to grip them by the shoulders and ask them how far they thought they were going to get in the blazing heat with half a dozen plastic Tesco bags full of Pringles and beer. Is forethought really this unfashionable?

The litter is picked up and sorted into recyclables by the hundreds of volunteers who stay behind after the festival. That is how they earn their ticket. I confess, with the rucksack on my back and my blood pressure up, my thoughts turn sour. I wonder if the ticket price is so high because otherwise the volunteer army would not consider it worthwhile to take part in the clean-up, and it is only by printing its own money – the ticket – that Glastonbury can pay for the huge amount of labour required to clear the site. The more expensive the ticket becomes, the greater the sense of entitlement assumed by the festival-goer, consequently the more rubbish that is produced and the more volunteers required to restore the farm afterwards. I hypothesize a feedback loop of ever-increasing ticket prices and tonnage of waste. The organizers of Glastonbury are working to increase recycling and reduce dumping, encouraging people not to abandon their cheap gear and to take the time to put their litter in recycling bins on site. Such efforts push against the consumer mindset – in which the customer is never held accountable – and are inimical to the hedonistic spirit of the weekend, in which we are all teenagers (in our hearts) and nature is the house of somebody's holidaying parents. There is also a commercial imperative behind trash; bottled water, a needless waste, is lucrative for the concession stands. Already, on the Sunday, the bins are overflowing with cans, plastic bottles and paper cups, and mounds of bagged rubbish moulder in the sun. I look around the ziggurats of ketchup-stained polystyrene, votive offerings to the gods of getting fucked up, and realize that this is what happens when you give people a flush toilet and a sewer system; we are toilet-trained not to take responsibility for our own shit. Civilization, as Brian Aldiss observed, is the distance man has placed between himself and his excreta. I turn angrily into the crowd.

The wheel falls off my trolley, and my tent and gear spill everywhere. A dad nightmare. On my hands and knees, I snatch sleeping bags and bedding from under the passing multitude of trainers and sandals. People step over me. Briefly, I am litter.

I retrieve my gear and sit down beside the path, in the muddy gutter. The metal doors of the latrines slam incessantly and the air is rank. The pin securing the wheel to the trolley axle has fallen out. For about twenty seconds, I sit in a zone of silent, disbelieving despair as the crowd troops by. A kindly woman stops to ask me if I am all right. I consider asking her to carry twenty kilos of tent a mile up the road. No, the buck stops here. I venture a battered smile and she rejoins the migration.

'Is this the best Glasto ever?' asks a tattered page of the festival newspaper.

Back on my hands and knees, I scrabble around in the pissy ground and find discarded matchsticks. With my knife, I whittle one into a sharp point and use it in place of the missing metal pin. The trolley is a piece of shit, but now it is a repaired piece of shit. I push on.

The crowd trudges towards a distant field where an enormous screen is showing England's World Cup game. The match seemed so important before the festival, less so now. There is no excitement or anticipation in the crowd, merely a sense of duty. I lost my appetite for football at the same time as I started camping with my own family. I grew bored with proxy victories and defeats, and wanted victories of my own. I don't want my children to be spectators, drifting through life insubstantial and unfinished, believing that only up there, on the big screen, are events and lives of consequence. Camping snaps us out of passivity. It inspires action. After hiking along the Grand Canyon for two months, Colin Fletcher wrote a note to himself: 'The time has passed for contemplation. I must get out and do. For doing is what counts. The contemplation is only for that.' Camping is not easy; it is not leisure. Providing the basic human needs – food, warmth, shelter, a working trolley – may be menial work, but it is satisfying. After striking camp, the camper returns to his or her life inspired to get their hands dirty.

The commentator's lament echoes over the hot, dusty track. The match is not going well. There will be England sun hats burning in the campfires tonight. I step into the ditch to allow a quad bike to pass. It is pulling a trolley containing three lazing hipsters in sunglasses. My own trolley wobbles with jealousy. I kneel down and insert some more matchsticks into the axle. The tyre tread is filled with the famous Glastonbury mud, mud that has slathered naked hippies for over forty years, mud that liquefies into a sucking maw, mud that has been invested with English mysticism long before the advent of Christianity; alternative historian John Michell attributed the timeless religiosity of Glastonbury Tor and the surrounding land to a decree from nature, the intense, mystical quality of the light imbuing the land with an otherworldly feel. A faux-Druidic monument was added to the festival site in 1990 as a focus for mystical rumours of Albion and King Arthur, and to entice people away from the gatherings at the restricted site of Stonehenge. Sid Rawle, an influential figure in the counterculture history of the free festivals and Glastonbury, had a vision of Albion: land seized from landowners and returned to the common man. The rhythms and freedoms of pre-industrial rural life restored. A green community living sustainably in Britain once again. He died on the last day of a festival of his own devising, just before striking camp.

Festival-goers undertake a quest, journeying forth from the camping fields to lose themselves in the revelry, then passing through trials of the darkest hour, looming, gurning faces in Trash City. Eventually they stumble across the grail of the Green Fields, where sunrise promises absolution and acceptance. The layout of Glastonbury juxtaposes the sacred and the profane. A simple narrative of self-destruction followed by rebirth. Or an even more rudimentary drug story of high, then low, then the restoration of normality. No wonder the mud gets so churned up as thousands of people, physically, philosophically and pharmacologically, tread over the same old ground.

The sacred and profane laid out in a camp ground reminds me of the religious camp meetings of the nineteenth century. American Methodists used large camps to convert followers and strengthen ties between existing congregations. In the same way that Glastonbury has various areas hosting different experiences, the Methodist camps also had numerous stages, with three or four renowned preachers plying their visions of heaven and hell throughout the camp. Under the trees, there were small gatherings of musical parties and, just as at Glastonbury, the crowd was as much youthful and single as it was middle-aged and married. The same camp ground was used every year, so nearby hotels and boarding houses expanded to accommodate the festival rush. Even advocates of the Methodist camp meetings had to admit that much wickedness was committed at them.

Architect Benjamin Latrobe gives an account of a camp meeting he attended on 8 August 1809, four miles out from Georgetown, Virginia. He notes how well chosen the site of the camp is, being placed on the descent of a narrow ridge, a small stream at its foot with numerous springs. The rock-star preacher fascinates and appals him with his repetitive oratory of hell and temperance, a message of moderation in all things delivered immoderately. The preacher shakes violently and throws out his arms so that they quiver with astonishing velocity. Conversion itself is accompanied by shrieks and groans of sensual transportation. Among the trees, people loiter, religion the last thing on their minds. When the preaching and converting cease, campfires fill the night woods with enchantments. A turnabout dance begins, well-dressed black people and ill-dressed white people. The mixture of sex and God is heady. 'Young beaux and belles find the camping ground an admirable trysting place for summer long flirtation.'

Barlow Weed Gorham, evangelist, songwriter, and author of a manual and defence of the Methodist camp meeting, justified camp for familiar reasons: that camping removes people from their worldly business and is a time for greater spiritual contemplation, that it strengthens the bonds between them, and that it introduces new ideas. Camps are places of innovation and conversion. So I ask myself, as I haul my trolley on the long walk out of the festival, to what cause does Glastonbury festival convert me? To the bands, those modern preachers, so that I become a fan? To the brands and the sponsors? To the charities who benefit from the money raised at the festival? To the New Age values and spiritual bric-a-brac? 'The truth is, human life needs to be dotted over with occasions of stirring interest,' preaches Barlow Weed Gorham. 'Our nature requires the recurrence now and then, of some event of special interest; something that shall peer up from the dead level of existence – an object for hope to rest upon in the future.' Hope! The poet Simon Armitage describes Glastonbury as a celebration of 'some aspect of our otherness'. That otherness is youth, the aspect of ourselves that hopes for and is capable of change. John Michell believed the spiritual aura of Glastonbury made it a site of new forms and new ways of thought. Did

I fail to experience Glastonbury fully because I did not want my otherness to take over, because I stubbornly remained a parent throughout? Or is hedonism not enough for me any more, the music and the intoxication insufficient for the kind of change I am seeking? The annual Burning Man festival in Black Rock Desert promises radical self-reliance and no commercialism. Is that what I am looking for? Could I drag the tent and kids across a desert in 107 degrees of heat? Burning Man operates a strict Leave No Trace policy that includes participants taking their grey waste water and rubbish home, no campfires and not so much as a fag butt left behind on the playa; such a rigorously struck camp represents a new way of life.

The waste at Glastonbury shows how far we are from being able to strike camp properly. Minimizing the footprint of a camp requires more than diligent picking-up afterwards; it begins at preparation. Food must be stripped of its packaging, siphoned into the correct portions and put into reusable containers. Water flasks are packed in lieu of bottled water. What I need from camping, what I am looking for, is greater freedom. The camp-sites that offer that freedom will not pick up after me – upon striking camp, I drive my rubbish of mainly nappies out to the local dump and dispose of it there. The toilets are earth closets in the woods. If you want freedom, you have to strike camp responsibly.

The ultimate freedom is wild camping. Wild camping is legal in Scotland but largely forbidden in England. Is there a benefit to camping in the wild whenever the mood takes us, without first seeking permission? A report on Wilderness Management compiled in 1978 by the Forest Service of the US Department of Agriculture describes the wilderness as 'an intangible which has altered the American consciousness'. It is part of the national 'geography of hope'. How would sanctioned wild camping in the Lake District, the Peak District, Snowdonia, the New Forest and the Sussex Downs alter the consciousness of the English and the

Welsh? The national state of mind could do with a geography of hope. The victories of the rambling movement in securing access to the land was half the job. We need to camp there too, exercise the freedom to find our own camping places, and take responsibility for striking camp afterwards. Does Glastonbury prove that we cannot be trusted to pick up after ourselves? Or is it evidence that we are in dire need of the lessons of a wild camp? Hauling my gear through the crowds of Glastonbury, I feel as solitary and as savage as I do on Oxford Street, whereas wild camping in Scotland makes me feel civilized; in the Highlands, I fantasize about the restoration of civic society, of mindfulness about the consequences of our actions, beginning with sound camping practice.

Camping is profitable traffic between town and country, actuality and hope, between where we are and where we want to be next. And when we return home, we bring with us some of the insight gained at camp. Camping also renews our appreciation of running water on tap, duvets and central heating – of all that sedentary civilization has given us. This was a truth acknowledged at the beginning of leisurely camping. Ralph Waldo Emerson wrote that, for all the pleasure of the Philosophers' Camp, he would not give over the benefits of civilization for the ways of the Indian. Duty called, and he was better prepared for those duties after camping:

> The holidays were fruitful, but must end;
> One August evening had a cooler breath;
> Into each mind intruding duties crept;
> Under the cinders burned the fires of home;
> Nay, letters found us in our paradise:
> So in the gladness of the new event
> We struck our camp and left the happy hills.

Striking camp asserts that all camps are temporary, and that is the way it should be. And when the rucksack and tent and trolley are stowed in the car, and the children fetched and loaded, who does not look forward to the return home, the hot shower and the abundant bed? You must always go home. Then, within a day or so of domestic life, idly flicking through maps, wondering about all the places yet to visit, the planning begins; if there is one thing a camper loves more than camping, it is dreaming about the next trip.

Appendix: Cath's Packing List

Camping shops sell a wide range of items, only a few of which are essential. We pack as light as possible because it makes pitching and striking camp easier and quicker: maximum utility, minimum weight. If you are packing camping carpet, ask yourself if you have the right hobby.

Tent

Before rushing out to buy the biggest tent in the shop, bear in mind that some of the more interesting campsites are quite small and will refuse entry or charge more for an enormo-tent. At festivals, a big tent can be a problem, as it will be far too heavy to lug from the car park and you won't necessarily have a large enough pitch for it. Nearly all the family tents on sale play to the delusion that you are buying a house, in which square footage is important and weight irrelevant. You are not buying a house. You are camping because you want to be outdoors, not because you want to cover the outdoors in a giant bag. A well-designed family tent should have headroom in the living area, but low ceilings in the bedrooms to trap heat.

Tarp

You shouldn't cook inside a tent. A sheet of tarpaulin strung from a tree provides shelter for the chef in drizzly weather and breezy shade when it is a scorcher.

Waterproofs

It will rain, don't pretend to yourself that it won't. For children, pack waterproof suits, salopettes and waterproof booties. Adults need one stout waterproof jacket and, if waterproof trousers are beyond the pale, a pair of shorts for fair and foul weather. Wellies or walking boots for everyone and welly socks. I recently camped with an infamous writer, media personality and virgin camper who had neglected to bring sufficient welly socks and was dragging around a child who was clearly suffering from chafed calves. Something as simple as a longer sock would have made both their evenings more pleasant: an adult can overcome minor discomfort, whereas a child will make it the focus of their entire being.

Picnic rug

If you don't want to bother with a table and chairs, take a plastic-backed picnic rug.

Table and chairs

The only problem with using a rug is that after five years of eating off the ground, Matthew's longing for a chair was so intense I was concerned that he would resort to theft. I found flat pieces of reinforced plastic that slid unobtrusively into my rucksack and could be folded into small stools about six inches high, but the spectacle of him squatting on them only added to his indignity and sense of failure as a man. Once we switched to camping with a car, he bought himself the biggest chair in the shop.

Small child transport

With one baby and one toddler, one of my big problems was how to lug the kids around while we were out and about. The buggy takes up most of our boot space and can be a pain at Glastonbury or other festivals, with the mud and the crowds. So we carried the two crawlers around in backpacks, one each, which are more flexible when it comes to rural walks and take up less space in the car. Before we had the car, the buggy doubled up as transport for the cool bag and other supplies; in fact the buggies used to take so much punishment, the axle on one of them snapped in Cornwall.

Cooking matches

Long matches to light fires, stoves and barbecues. A cigarette lighter is not always suitable.

Ordnance Survey map of the area

Matthew is a great believer in the importance of orientating ourselves upon this earth. His maps don't take up significant space.

Clothes

Don't forget to take a big warm jumper; whatever the season, it gets cold at night. At bedtime, stuff the jumper into a pillowcase and rest your head upon it. If it's particularly cold, wear long-legged and long-armed thermal underwear under your jeans and jumper when sitting out in the evening, and under your pyjamas when you go to bed.

Grill

If your campsite allows campfires, then the fire is the heart of your kitchen. We have ditched the barbecue and instead use a grill, propped up with some bricks over the fire or hung on a chain from a tripod. A campfire is also a ravenous bin, burning up cardboard packaging.

Trangia

This methylated-spirit stove packs down small and comes with saucepans, a frying pan and a tiny kettle. But it can only cook one thing at a time. A two-ring propane stove lets you extend your culinary options, but will take up more space. Incidentally, if you are going to a festival, avoid cooking your own food if you can afford it. There is nowhere to wash up and you will miss all the fun while you are frying bacon.

Crockery and cutlery

Because you can't always use your fingers. And pack a wooden spoon or two for stirring, a nylon sieve and a fish slice. And tongs, for turning hot meat.

Kettle

A whistling kettle with a handle that folds flat.

Corkscrew and can opener

Not just the old rusty ones in the kitchen drawer, but ones that actually work.

Skewers

Wooden or metal ones for kebabs.

Meat thermometer

For cooking a joint of meat or a bird over a campfire. Because you are not using a domestic oven, with its reliable temperature, a thermometer spares the campfire cook all that uncertain prodding and poking.

Paring knife

Look for a very sharp paring knife with a protective cover. A bread knife, wrapped in a tea towel to protect the serrated blade, is also required; if someone could invent a camping bread knife with a cover, I'd be very grateful.

Opinel knife

A sharp knife is always useful. A sharp knife that folds back into its handle is essential. Hence the design classic that is the French Opinel knife. Used for cutting vegetables, whittling kindling, removing things from bike chains, opening packets, etc.

Potato peeler and vegetable brush

For scrubbing and peeling spuds. I have an abrasive glove that I use to clean my spuds.

Serving and mixing bowl

You can eat salad while camping, it is allowed.

Plates, small bowls, melamine mugs and a chopping board

We experimented with folding plastic mugs and plates, which I was adept at assembling but which completely defeated Matthew. I replaced them with melamine equivalents that should last us until the end of time.

Lock & Lock containers

Any sealable plastic containers are useful for storing leftovers.

Tinfoil

To cook a large joint of meat on the campfire, you will have to wrap it in tinfoil once it has been browned.

Cool bag or box

Boxes take up space, but keep food safe from wildlife and leaks. A cool bag will fold flat and is easier to pack when striking camp. Many sites let you chill ice blocks in their freezers, sometimes for free, sometimes at a price.

Prepared food

Prepare at least one meal for when you arrive, something you can easily heat up once you've pitched the tent.

Basic cooking ingredients

Olive oil, salt and pepper, butter. Amounts really depend on what you have to store it all in. Tea bags, coffee, sugar, of course.

Carbs and protein

I pack plenty of pasta, rice, couscous and even my campfire bread mix. Then some easy-to-store proteins like beans, chickpeas, halloumi cheese, tinned tuna, houmous, saucisson and anchovies.

Ingredients for sauces, etc.

My camp kitchen also includes tinned tomatoes and coconut milk, onions, carrots, garlic, chillies and fresh tomatoes, together with prepared spices, flavourings and dressings such as salsa romesco, mustard, French dressing, garlic and ginger paste, garam masala and chermoula. I also stuff fresh herbs into one of my Lock & Lock containers.

Snacks

Take something that is highly calorific and won't melt in the sun.

Booze

Ice is hard to come by at campsites, so you want a tipple that doesn't require it, such as whisky or red wine. My friend swears by mead. Remember the trip to the toilet is further than the short hop across the landing, so don't go overboard. The warming effect of alcohol quickly wears off, and leaves you colder afterwards.

Hot chocolate

The effort involved in making hot chocolate at night ensures it will be the finest experience you and chocolate will ever share. Don't skimp on the cocoa and melt real chocolate drops in the milk for added pleasure.

Frozen milk

Put milk cartons in the freezer for a few days before you go. Pop them in your cool bag and not only will they chill the rest of the bag's contents, they will also slowly thaw in time for you to drink.

Food for babies

Breast milk is the most convenient food for a baby when camping. Cleaning bottles and keeping enough milk is troublesome, particularly at festivals. I have nagged café stallholders for hot water to wash baby bottles with, and Matthew has bought a glass of milk from them when required. Give toddlers something to munch on while you pitch. They have no patience when it comes to their bellies, and will not wait while you struggle with the tent, so it's up to you to have foresight.

Water carrier

A collapsible one with a tap. You want water to hand for drinking, cooking and light washing.

Water flasks

Bottled water is over. Refillable flasks are where it's at, and you'll need them as being outdoors all the time will make you much thirstier than usual. Make sure the kids have their own flasks to minimize transmission of germs.

Toilet paper

Three rolls. One for out and about, one for the tent, one for luck.

Bin bags

For rubbish and for quarantining wet or dirty clothes.

Toiletries

Unless space is no problem, stick to the bare minimum. I have taken a single bottle of special wash that is suitable for clothes, dishes, skin and hair. Makes you wonder if this whole washing-up liquid, body gel, shampoo divide is entirely arbitrary. You can buy camping towels that take up far less space than the bulky ones in your bathroom. They come in pink or blue. Some anti-bacterial hand gel is particularly useful at festivals. Some of you will want contraceptives, others will be packing nappies. For small children, I pack six nappies a day for each child. Sites vary and some will expect you to take your rubbish home with you, which is particularly unpleasant when it comes to nappies; come prepared with nappy sacks and bin liners. If you are taking re-usable nappies camping, then you are far in advance of any advice that I have to offer.

First-aid kit

For bumps and scrapes. You want plasters, bandages and something to disinfect wounds. It's also worth investing in a burns kit, which my husband has required on a number of occasions. Also, a few precautionary sachets of paracetamol and ibuprofen in solution for children and adults.

Insect repellent

Citronella candles are deliciously evil. There is something satisfying about the sizzle of a fat moth in a naked flame. Take something to repel the insects, and a cream or antihistamine to treat the bites or stings. An antihistamine is a miracle cure when the toddler goes face-first into a verge of nettles.

Sun hats and sun cream

Because it is always a scorcher when you are camping.

Washing line

For drying washing, rain-soaked clothes and tea towels. Don't forget to take some pegs as it is quite hard tying undies to a line.

Solar-powered shower

Sounds fancier that it is. Basically this is a black bag you fill with cold water, and once the sun has warmed it up, you take it into the woods, strip off, hang it from a tree and let gravity do the rest. It's not a power shower, but it is good enough to refresh you mid-festival. Festival showers struggle with water pressure and what may seem like an uninhibited playful exercise in communal cleansing quickly turns into three naked people huddled under a dripping tap.

Babies don't like showers, nor do toddlers. Little babies can be bathed in sinks; otherwise a collapsible bowl filled with warm water and a sponge is your best bet – see below. If you take your toddler into the shower, don't expect it to be a refreshing, relaxing experience for you, your child or any other campers in the shower block. A couple of days without a bath won't do them any harm.

Washing-up kit

A collapsible washing bowl, in which you can wash the dishes and any babies. Tea towels, washing-up liquid, a washing-up brush, some kitchen roll and even a surface cleaner, as you attempt a basic level of hygiene.

Bed and bedding

The minimum is a decent sleeping bag and self-inflating mattress per person. You can use a thick jumper as a pillow. For family campers, the only chance you have of a decent night's sleep is if the kids are warm and comfortable, so an extra blanket and a snuggly toy are essential for them. Each of my babies slept in a double-layered sleeping bag with zip-on sleeves. Doubling or tripling the number of children in one room also keeps them warm – like gerbils. For older children, Therm-a-Rest trail mats suffice unless it is spring or early autumn, in which case I pack the various sheepskin rugs around the house and put them on top of the mattresses to provide an extra level of insulation (babies get a sheepskin at all times). Tiny babies who can't roll over go in pop-up cots. A larger bubble cot will accommodate them until they are eighteen months old. Don't skip the familiar rituals they need to go to sleep, and pack bedtime stories. Ensuring a good night's sleep for children while camping is as important as food and water.

Augment the powers of an ordinary sleeping bag with a silk liner. When packed, a silk lining takes up about the same amount of space as a deck of cards and the warmth it retains is really worth it. Silk liners are easier to wash than sleeping bags, too, and remember that the insulating properties of a sleeping bag are diminished by each pass through the washing machine. A standard air bed is unsuitable for early spring and autumn. At night it will turn into a solid block of cold air.

Torch

A torch is necessary for adults, but a torch for each of the kids adds to the sense of night-time adventure. We used to keep a small lantern on at night, but it quickly burned through batteries. Instead, pack a handful of fluorescent glow sticks to allay any night-time fears, and a small, cheap, battery-powered lantern. The worst part of camping with small children is clambering around a tent in the middle of the night in your long johns looking for clean nappies, wipes or bottles. Try to keep the tent tidy and these essential items close to hand. Glow sticks will give you enough illumination to change toddlers without startling them.

Matthew has a hefty Maglite torch, a hangover from his days as a security guard on the Liverpool docks, and I have a pencil-thin one that fits in my purse. Avoid the large lanterns, some of which burn so brightly as to extinguish the mood. Candles in fireproof paper lanterns, weighed down with pebbles and positioned well away from the tent, make a pleasant alternative when you sit outside chatting of an evening. Naked flames and tents do not mix. The one time I saw a tent engulfed by flame, the whole structure went up in a single 'poof'.

Bibliography

Anderson, H. Allen, *The Chief: Ernest Thompson Seton and the Changing West* (College Station, Texas: Texas A&M University Press, 1986).

Baden-Powell, Robert, *Scouting for Boys: A Handbook for Instruction in Good Citizenship* (London: C. Arthur Pearson, 1908).

Baldwin, J., *Bucky Works: Buckminster Fuller's Ideas for Today* (New York: John Wiley & Sons, 1996).

——, 'The Case for Long Shots', www.Strategy-business.com, August 2006.

Baldwin, Neil, *Edison: Inventing the Century* (University of Chicago Press, 2001).

Barrus, Clara, *The Life and Letters of John Burroughs* (Boston, Mass., & New York: Houghton Mifflin, 1925).

——, *John Burroughs, Boy and Man* (Garden City, N.Y.: Doubleday, Page & Co, 1921).

Barton, Susan, *Working-class Organisations and Popular Tourism, 1840–1970* (Manchester University Press, 2005).

Bey, Hakim, *T.A.Z.: The Temporary Autonomous Zone, Ontological Anarchy, Poetic Terrorism* (1985, 1991); accessed online at http://hermetic.com/bey/taz_cont.html.

Blatchford, Robert, *Merrie England* (London: Clarion Office, 1894).

Bogoras, Waldemar, *The Chukchee: Volume 7* (New York: Stechert & Co, 1904).

Bowlby, John, 'Interview with Milton Senn, M.D.' (conducted 1977); accessed online at www.beyondthecouch.org.

Brand, N., *Early Days in the Forest School Camps* (Forest School Camps Archives and Publishing Group, 2003).

Braziers, *Research Communications 13*, Braziers Park School of Integrative Social Research (1991).

Burdette, Hillary L., and Robert C. Whitaker, 'Resurrecting Free Play in Young Children: Looking Beyond Fitness and Fatness to Attention, Affiliation and Affect' (2005); accessed online at http://www.children andnature.org/research/volumes/C16/16.

Burroughs, John, 'Camping with Theodore Roosevelt', *Atlantic* (May 1906).

——, *The Heart of Burroughs' Journals* (Boston, Mass., & New York: Houghton Mifflin, 1928).

——, *Under the Maples* (Boston, Mass., & New York: Houghton Mifflin, 1921).

Carey, John, *Intellectuals and the Masses: Pride and Prejudice among the Literary Intelligentsia, 1880–1939* (London: Faber & Faber, 1992).

Carpenter, Edward, *Civilization: Its Cause and Cure* (London: Swan Sonnenschein & Co, 1889).

Cohen, G. A., *Why Not Socialism?* (Princeton & Oxford: Princeton University Press, 2009).

Constance, Hazel, *First in the Field: A Century of the Camping and Caravanning Club* (Coventry: The Camping and Caravanning Club, 2001).

Coupland, Philip, 'H. G. Wells's Liberal Fascism', *Journal of Contemporary History* 35:4 (2000), 541–58.

Deloria, Philip Joseph, *Playing Indian* (New Haven, Conn.: Yale University Press, 1998).

Drakeford, Mark, *Social Movements and Their Supporters* (Basingstoke: Macmillan, 1997).

Edgell, Derek, *The Order of Woodcraft Chivalry 1916–1949 as a New Age Alternative to the Boy Scouts* (Lewiston, N.Y.: E. Mellen Press, 1992).

Eisner, Michael, *Camp* (New York: Warner Books, 2005).

Ellis, H. Havelock, *Essays in War-Time: Further Studies in the Task of Social Hygiene* (London: Constable & Co, 1916).

Emerson, Ralph Waldo, *Nature* (1836; Boston, Mass., & Cambridge: James Monroe & Co, 1849).

Finlay, John F., *Social Credit: The English Origins* (Montreal & London: McGill-Queen's University Press, 1972).

Firestone, Harvey, *Men and Rubber: The Story of Business* (London: William Heinemann, 1926).

Fletcher, Colin, *The Man Who Walked Through Time* (1968; New York: Vintage, 1972).

Fuller, R. Buckminster, *Guinea Pig B: The 56 Year Experiment* (Clayton, Calif.: Critical Path Publishing, 2004).

Fussell, Paul, *Abroad: British Literary Traveling Between the Wars* (Oxford: Oxford University Press, 1980).

——, *The Great War and Modern Memory* (Oxford: Oxford University Press, 1975).

Galton, Francis, *The Art of Travel; or, Shifts and Contrivances Available in Wild Countries* (1855; seventh edn, London: John Murray, 1883).

——, *Narrative of an Explorer in Tropical South Africa* (1853; second edn, London: Ward and Lock, 1889).

Gardiner, Henry Rolf, *Water Springing from the Ground: An Anthology of the Writings of Rolf Gardiner* (Shaftesbury: Trustees of the estate of the late H. Rolf Gardiner, 1972).

——, *World Without End: British Politics and the Younger Generation* (London: Cobden-Sanderson, 1932).

Garrett, Garet, *The Wild Wheel: The World of Henry Ford* (London: Cresset Press, 1952).

Gorham, Barlow Weed, *Camp Meeting Manual: A Practical Book for the Camp Ground* (Boston, Mass.: H. V. Degen, 1854).

Griffiths, Clare V. J., *Labour and the Countryside: The Politics of Rural Britain, 1918–1939* (Oxford: Oxford University Press, 2007).

Hailey, Charlie, *Camps: A Guide to 21st Century Space* (Cambridge, Mass.: The MIT Press, 2009).

——, *Campsite: Architectures of Duration and Place* (Louisiana State University Press, 2008).

Hall, G. Stanley, *Adolescence: Its Psychology and Its Relations to Physiology, Anthropology, Sociology, Sex, Crime, Religion and Education* (London: Sidney Appleton, 1904).

Hargrave, John, *The Confession of the Kibbo Kift: A Declaration and General Exposition of the Work of the Kindred* (London: Duckworth, 1927).

——, *The Great War Brings It Home: The Natural Reconstruction of an Unnatural Existence* (London: Constable, 1919).

——, *Lonecraft* (1913; London: Constable, 1922).

Hendee, John C., George H. Stankey and Robert C. Lucas, *Wilderness Management* (Forest Service, US Department of Agriculture, 1978).

Holding, Thomas Hiram, *The Camper's Handbook* (London: Simpkin, Marshall, Hamilton, Kent & Co, 1908).

——, *Cycle and Camp* (London: Ward Lock & Co, 1898).

——, *Watery Wanderings 'mid Western Lochs: A Practical Canoe Cruise* (London: Marlborough & Co, 1886).

Hooper, William Hulme, *Ten Months Among the Tents of the Tuski: With incidents of an Arctic boat expedition in search of Sir John Franklin, as far as the Mackenzie River, and Cape Bathurst* (London: John Murray, 1853).

Huxley, Aldous, *Brief Candles* (1930; London: Flamingo, 1994).

Jerome, Christine, *An Adirondack Passage* (New York: HarperCollins, 1994).

Jerome, Jerome K., *Three Men in a Boat (To say nothing of the dog)* (Bristol: J. W. Arrowsmith, 1889).

Joad, C. E. M., *The Book of Joad: A Belligerent Autobiography* (London: Faber & Faber, 1935).

——, *A Charter for Ramblers; or, the Future of the Countryside* (London: Hutchinson & Co, 1934).

——, *The Untutored Townsman's Invasion of the Country* (1945; London: Faber & Faber, 1946).

Keller, Betty, *Black Wolf: The Life of Ernest Thompson Seton* (Vancouver: Douglas & McIntyre, 1984).

Keller, Jane Eblen, *Adirondack Wilderness: A Story of Man and Nature* (Syracuse, N.Y., Syracuse University Press, 1980).

Kephart, Horace, *Camp Cookery* (New York: Outing Publishing Company, 1910).

——, *Camping and Woodcraft* (1906, 1917; University of Tennessee Press, 1988).

——, *Our Southern Highlanders* (1913, 1922; University of Tennessee Press, 1976, 1984); includes the definitive biographical essay on Kephart by George Ellison.

Kirk, Andrew G., *Counterculture Green: The Whole Earth Catalog and American Environmentalism* (University Press of Kansas, 2007).

Lamartine, Alphonse de, *Travels in the East: Including a Journey in the Holy Land, Volume 1* (Edinburgh: William & Robert Chambers, 1850).

Lanier Lewis, David, *The Public Image of Henry Ford* (Detroit, Mich.: Wayne State University Press, 1976).

——, and Laurence Goldstein, *The Automobile and American Culture* (University of Michigan, 1980).

Laqueur, Walter, *Young Germany: A History of the German Youth Movement* (London: Routledge & Kegan Paul, 1962).

Latrobe, Benjamin Henry, *The Journal of Latrobe: Being the Notes and Sketches of an Architect, Naturalist and Traveler in the United States from 1796 to 1820* (New York: D. Appleton, 1905).

Laubin, Reginald, and Gladys Laubin, *The Indian Tipi: Its History, Construction and Use* (1957; University of Oklahoma Press, 1977).

Lawrence, D. H., *The Selected Letters of D. H. Lawrence* (Cambridge: Cambridge University Press, 1997).

Lutts, Ralph H., *The Nature Fakers: Wildlife, Science & Sentiment* (University Press of Virginia, 1990).

Macmurray, John, *The Grith Fyrd Idea* (Godshill: Order of Woodcraft Chivalry, 1933).

Man, John, *Xanadu: Marco Polo and Europe's Discovery of the East* (London: Bantam, 2009).

Marsh, Jan, *Back to the Land: The Pastoral Impulse in Victorian England from 1880 to 1914* (London: Quartet Books, 1982).

Mertens, Michael John, 'Leap the Quickening Flame: Early Twentieth-Century Youth Movements, Nature and Community in Britain and Germany', thesis (PhD), University of Birmingham, 2000.

Miller, Richard C., *Bohemia: The Protoculture Now and Then* (Chicago: Nelson-Hall, 1977).

Ministry of Education, *Organised Camping* (London: Her Majesty's Stationery Office, 1951).

Moore-Colyer, R., 'Rolf Gardiner, English Patriot, and the Council for the Church and Countryside', *Agricultural History Review* 49:2 (2001).

Morris, Brian, *Ernest Thompson Seton, Founder of the Woodcraft Movement, 1860–1946: Apostle of Indian Wisdom and Pioneer Ecologist* (Lewiston, N.Y.: Edwin Mellen Press, 2006).

Mosse, George, *Nazi Culture: Intellectual, Cultural and Social Life in the Third Reich* (1966; University of Wisconsin Press, 2003).

Muir, John, *Nature Writings* (New York: Literary Classics of the United States, 1997).

——, *A Thousand Mile Walk to the Gulf* (Boston, Mass., & New York: Houghton Mifflin, 1916).

Murray, William H. H., *Adventures in the Wilderness; or, Camp-life in the Adirondacks* (Boston, Mass.: Fields, Osgood & Co, 1869).

——, 'Reminiscences of My Literary and Outdoor Life', *Independent* LVII (1904).

Nash, Roderick, *Wilderness and the American Mind* (revised edn, New Haven, Conn.: Yale University Press, 1973).

Nicholson, Virginia, *Among the Bohemians: Experiments in Living 1900–1939* (London: Penguin, 2001).

Nord, Deborah Epstein, *Gypsies and the British Imagination, 1807–1930* (New York: Columbia University Press, 2008).

Order of Woodcraft Chivalry, 'The Woodcraft Way' Series, 1918.

Orwell, George, *The Road to Wigan Pier* (1937; London: Penguin, 2001).

Paris, Leslie, *Children's Nature: The Rise of the American Summer Camp* (New York University Press, 2008).

Paul, Leslie, *Angry Young Man* (London: Faber & Faber, 1951).

——, *The Folk Trail: An Outline of the Philosophy and Activities of Woodcraft Fellowships* (London: Noel Douglas, 1929).

——, 'Hitler's Youth – the Full Circle', *The Plan* (1935).

Progressive League, *Manifesto: Being the Book of the Federation of Progressive Societies and Individuals*, ed. C. E. M. Joad (London: G. Allen & Unwin, 1934).

Redl, Fritz, *When We Deal with Children* (London: Collier-Macmillan, 1966).

Reich, Charles, 'The Greening of America', *New Yorker*, 26 September 1970.

Revel, Dorothy, *Tented Schools: Camping as a Technique of Education* (London: Williams & Norgate, 1934).

Rhodes, Godfrey, *Tents and Tent-Life from the Earliest Ages to the Present Time to which is Added the Practice of Encamping an Army in Ancient and Modern Times* (London: Smith, Elder & Co, 1858).

Rosenthal, Michael, *The Character Factory: Baden-Powell and the Origins of the Boy Scout Movement* (London: Collins, 1986).

Ross, Cathy, *Twenties London: A City in the Jazz Age* (London: Philip Wilson, 2003).

Rothman, Benny, *The 1932 Kinder Trespass: A Personal View of the Kinder Scout Mass Trespass* (Altrincham: Willow Publishing, 1982).

Rutstrum, Calvin, *Paradise Below Zero: The Classic Guide to Winter Camping* (1968; University of Minnesota Press, 2000).

——, *The Wilderness Life* (1975; University of Minnesota Press, 2004).

Sears, George W. or Nessmuk, *Canoeing the Adirondacks with Nessmuk: The Adirondack Letters of George Washington Sears* (Syracuse, N.Y.: Syracuse University Press, 1993).

——, *Forest Runes* (New York: Forest & Stream, 1887).

——, *Woodcraft* (1884; New York: Dover Publications, 1963).

Sennett, Richard, *The Corrosion of Character: The Personal Consequences of Work in the New Capitalism* (New York: W. W. Norton & Co, 1998).

Seton, Ernest Thompson, *The Birch-bark Roll of the Woodcraft Indians* (1906; New York: Doubleday, Page & Co, 1907).

——, *Two Little Savages: Being the Adventures of Two Boys Who Live as Indians, and What They Learned* (New York: Doubleday, Page & Co, 1903).

——, *Wild Animals I Have Known* (1898; London & New York: D. Nutt, 1900).

Smith, Michael B., 'The Ego Ideal of the Good Camper and the Nature of Summer Camp', *Environmental History* 11:1 (2006), 70–101.

Sorensen, C. E., *My Forty Years with Ford* (1956; New York: Collier, 1962).

Springhall, John, *Youth, Empire, and Society: British Youth Movements, 1883–1940* (London: Croom Helm, 1977).

Stephens, John Lloyd, *Incidents of Travel in Egypt, Arabia, Petraea, and the Holy Land* (New York: James C. Derby, 1854).

Stevenson, Robert Louis, *Travels with a Donkey in the Cévennes* (London: Nelson, 1879).

Stillman, William James, *The Autobiography of a Journalist* (London: Grant Richards, 1901).

——, 'The Subjective of It', *Atlantic Monthly*, 2:7 (December 1858).

Sutter, Paul S., *Driven Wild: How the Fight against Automobiles Launched the Modern Wilderness Movement* (University of Washington Press, 2002).

Taylor, Benjamin Franklin, *Mission Ridge and Lookout Mountain with Pictures of Life in Camp and Field* (New York: D. Appleton & Co, 1872).

Terrie, Philip G., *Forever Wild: A Cultural History of Wilderness in the Adirondacks* (1985; Syracuse, N.Y.: Syracuse University Press, 1994).

Thompson, Laurence, *Robert Blatchford: Portrait of an Englishman* (London: Victor Gollancz, 1951).

Thoreau, Henry David, *Walden* (1854; London: Penguin, 1986).

——, 'A Walk to Wachusett', *Boston Miscellany* 1843, available online at www.walden.org.

Thulesius, Olav, *Edison in Florida: The Green Laboratory* (University Press of Florida, 1997).

Tyldesley, Mike, 'The German Youth Movement and National Socialism: Some Views from Britain', *Journal of Contemporary History* 41:1 (January 2006), 21–34.

Valentine, Herbert and Agnes W., *Tales of a Tent: A Remarkable Diary of Camping Holidays in Lakeland in the Halcyon Days before the First World War* (1913; Beckermet: Michael J. Moon, 1977).

Wadland, John Henry, *Ernest Thompson Seton: Man in Nature and the Progressive Era, 1880–1915* (New York: Arno Press, 1978).

Ward, Colin, and Dennis Hardy, *Goodnight Campers! The History of the British Holiday Camp* (London: Mansell, 1986).

Warner, Charles Dudley, 'Camping out', from *In the Wilderness* (1878); accessed online at www.gutenberg.org

Watkins, Alfred, *Early British Trackways, Moats, Mounds, Camps, and Sites* (London: Simpkin, Marshall & Co, 1922).

Webb, James, *The Occult Establishment* (La Salle, Ill.: Open Court, 1976).

Westlake, Aubrey, *Woodcraft Chivalry: Adapted from Seton's 'Woodcraft Indians'* (Weston-super-Mare: Mendip Press, 1917).

Westlake, Jean, *70 Years A-Growing* (Stroud, Gloucestershire: Hawthorn Press, 2000).

The Whole Earth Catalog 1968–1971; accessed online at http://www.wholeearth.com/index.php.

Whymper, Edward, *Scrambles Amongst the Alps in the Years 1860–69* (1871; London: John Murray, 1900).

Winter, Gordon, *The Golden Years* (1975; London: Penguin, 1977).

Wrangham, Richard, *Catching Fire: How Cooking Made Us Human* (London: Profile Books, 2009).

Yowell, Skip, *The Hippie Guide to Climbing the Corporate Ladder & Other Mountains: How JanSport Makes It Happen* (Nashville, Tenn.: Thomas Nelson, 2006).

Acknowledgements

Thanks to the Kibbo Kift Foundation, Chris Judge Smith and Jon Grey Raven; Sandy Balls campsite, Mick Tutt, Clive and Lynden Bowen for their time showing me around the sites of the Order of Woodcraft Chivalry; Wapsbourne Farm campsite and Paul and Jean Cragg; George Ellison and Janet A. McCue at Cornell University Library for their help with Horace Kephart; Jay Baldwin for his insights into Buckminster Fuller and the early days of the dome tent. Thanks to the *Idler* for publishing an early draft of my essay on the Kibbo Kift, to the Port Eliot festival, and to Joshua Glenn and the circle at Hilobrow.com for providing me with hermeneutic support and wisdom.

My agent Sarah Such encouraged, shepherded and refined the proposal, and without her work this book would not exist. Also my gratitude and thanks to everyone at Hamish Hamilton, particularly my editors Simon Prosser and Juliette Mitchell, Caroline Pretty for attentive copy-editing, and 'Penguin John' for the cover design.

It is customary for an author to thank their family for their support and patience. In my case I owe an additional debt of gratitude to my parents for all my childhood camping trips, and most of all to Cath, for the article she contributed, for her various insights that I have swiped, and for sharing a decade of camping and a year of writing.